THE PSYCHOLOGY OF HIERARCHIES

HOW WE ARE RULED BY PSYCHOS

G. A. MOHR, PhD

WORLD HONS MULT.

G. A. Mohr
The Psychology of Hierarchies
3^{d} edition
(1st private edition 2018,
2nd private edition 2019)

<u>Cover picture</u>: free clipart, PC User magazine, Dec. 1999.

The views expressed in this book are solely those of the author, and as much as possible, real or full names have not been used to reduce public exposure of people mentioned who are still living.

TABLE OF CONTENTS

PREFACE

The Psychology of Hierarchies is one of the most important aspects of psychology. One key reason for this is the Peter Principle:

In a hierarchy every employee tends to rise to his own level of incompetence, and then stays there (L. Peter & R. Hull, 1969).

The Peter Principle is remarkably accurate as, indeed, almost all organizations are hierarchical, and the higher up in the hierarchy we look, we see older and older managers who are 'past it'. For example, they may have done OK on an IQ test when circa 20, but at circa 60 or 70 their 'real IQ" is probably far less. Indeed, many older managers begin to show early signs of developing senile dementia.

Worse still, a large proportion of those who fight their way to the top of hierarchies are psychopaths, the pathology of their psychopathy including, of course, greed, lying and bullying, this being the reason for the subtitle of this book being: *How we are ruled by psychos*, the Cambridge Dictionary defining a psycho as: *someone who is crazy and frightening*.

The first chapter of this book discusses several Mohr's Laws, in particular *Mohr's Law of Hierarchies:*

In hierarchical organizations the amount of real material-producing work people do is inversely proportional to their rank or level in the organization.
The amount of compensation they receive, however, is proportional to their level, sometimes to an exponential degree.

This laments the fact that CEOs etc. have massive salaries with massive annual bonuses, whilst the 'worker-slaves' who produce real, tangible products needed for everyday life and survival such as food, clothing and housing, are paid a comparative pittance, most of which is often needed to pay rent or a mortgage.

Following chapters discuss how hierarchies affect us throughout life, that is, from family life and school days, to our working lives, and in the socio-political world around us.

Then a few chapters discuss psychology in general, and then *The Psychology of Hierarchies.*

The final chapters then discuss how to deal with problems in hierarchies, and thereby improve one's life, concluding that *real democracy* is needed to deal with such problems as income inequality and overpopulation.

Also of considerable importance, Chapter 15 discusses the Hare Checklist for Psychopaths, and a slight variation of this, The Mohr Checklist for Psychopaths (MCLP), is discussed in Appendix A.

Geoff Mohr, 2024

CHAPTER 1

MOHR'S LAWS

> *In a hierarchy every employee tends to rise to his level of incompetence; the cream rises until it sours.*
> Laurence Peter, *The Peter Principle,* ch. 1 (1969, with R. Hull).

Introduction

In the following chapter some important principles relating to hierarchies are discussed, Dr Laurence Peter's famous *Peter Principle* being of particular relevance.

Then Mohr's Law of Hierarchies is discussed, along with its associated laws and principles concerning how levels of corruption, greed, bullying, etc. are closely related to the level or rank R of people in an organization.

Finally other factors relating to and perhaps influencing how 'hiercarchically' one behaves are discussed, for example age, in the case of age suggesting that managers of 60+ are less 'hormonally driven', aggressive etc., and thus less painful and miserable to work under. Indeed, this was the first author's experience more than once, as noted in the penultimate section of the present chapter.

Some principles and laws of hierarchies

CN Parkinson and Laurence Peter proposed, a little tongue in cheek, some of the most celebrated principles and laws of business and hierarchies. It was not long, however, before it was realized how true to life they really were. Indeed, they apply to anything ranging from domestic life to large corporations, and are well worth a little study.

Parkinson's Law (of administration) (Parkinson, 1958):

> *Work expands so as to fill the time available*
> *(for its completion).*

This was conceived with the peacetime navy in mind but may well apply even better elsewhere. As a result of this law the growth in the administration separates from the work to be done. Administration officers multiply subordinates, not rivals, thereby making work for each other.

That Francis Bacon went up to Cambridge at twelve was mentioned in *The Scientific MBA* (Mohr, 2017) and it seems that Parkinson's Law applies well to education for I cannot believe that 12 years at school, which is what I endured, is necessary for all but the slowest of minds, for example the teachers. With the proliferation of Universities and tertiary courses in recent decades it seems that the problem is growing ever worse!

Parkinson also proposed the following laws:

(a) *Time spent on any item of the agenda will be in inverse proportion to the sum involved* (Parkinson, 1958).

(b) *Men enter politics solely as a result of being unhappily married* (Parkinson, 1958).

(c) **Parkinson's Law of Triviality** (Parkinson, 1980): *Committees will pass major decisions without demur but prognosticate interminably over trivia.*

(d) **Parkinson's Law of Expenditure** (Parkinson, 1960): *Expenditure rises to meet income.*

(e) **Parkinson's 'The Law' - of the vacuum, or Hoover's Law** (Parkinson, 1980): *Action expands to fill the void created by human failure.*

The Peter Principle

Dr Laurence Peter drew on his experiences in the education sector to try and explain why we always seem to have lousy leaders (Peter & Hull, 1969). The result was his celebrated *Peter Principle*:

***In a hierarchy every employee tends to rise
to his own level of incompetence
(and then stays there).***

In other words, *the sour cream rises.*

A corollary is: *In time every post tends to be occupied by
an employee who is incompetent to carry out his duties.*

In his often tongue-in-cheek book Peter gives a few
excellent historical examples of his celebrated principle,
including:
(a) Socrates was a brilliant philosopher but a lousy
defence attorney.
(b) Hitler was a brilliant politician but a lousy general.

Pareto's Law (1967): *In most situations a relatively small
percentage of certain objects contribute a relatively high
percentage of output.*

This is the basis of *contribution-by-value analysis* (also
called ABC analysis). For instance 15-30 percent of the
population contributes 70-90 percent of the tax revenue, 20
percent of the employees in an office may do 80 percent of the
work, or 20 percent of the items in inventory may account for
80 percent of the sales.
As an example of ABC analysis, the percentage of total
dollar annual sales for each product are calculated and
tabulated in descending order. Then the cumulative
percentage contribution is added as a final column to show
how much, say, the first 20% of products contributes.
This law points out that there are exceptions to Parkinson's
Law and the Peter Principle and there are a few workers who
do not 'pad out' their day and contribute more than Peter's
incompetent managers.

Mohr's Laws

Table 1.1. The ten original Mohr's Laws.

Law #	Law name	Subject	Principle
1	Mohr's morphology	human personality	three basic personality types
2	Mohr's mentation	education etc.	brainwashing
3	Mohr's metamorphosis	home, work & pub	life in three boxes
4	Mohr's mirage	sex	myth of love
5	Mohr's malady	hierarchy & power	law of the 'rat race'
6	Mohr's mechanism	achievement	madness required
7	Mohr's motto	power	power corrupts
8	Mohr's misery	crime & war	human condition
9	Mohr's mantra	man's history	the prophet Murphy
10	Mohr's metrology	final judgment	?/9

These are the ten laws about human behaviour proposed by Mohr (2002), and Mohr & Fear (2015), and shown in Table 1.1. The first (ML1) is called *Playground Principle* and asserts that there are three basic personality types, namely assertive (A), neutral (B) and placid (C). These neatly correspond to the Greek classifications of *ectomorph*, *mesomorph* and *endomorph* and thus are nothing new.

What is new is that I claim that you'll encounter and have difficulty with opposing types around age 9 in the playground and, in every new group of people you have to deal with in life, you find that the same types remain.

Indeed, the problems may get worse as some people enter second childhood prematurely with such diseases as SDAT (senile dementia of the Alzheimer's type). So at least it is some help to be warned.

The other laws concern themselves with education and 'brainwashing' (ML2), work and play (ML3), sex (ML4), hierarchy (ML5), achievement (ML6), etc., and thus can be compared to the Ten Commandments given to Moses.

The sixth law that great philosopher Zorba himself agreed with: "A man must have a little madness - - ."

The ninth (ML9) is that God's prophet is *Murphy* (of Murphy's Law), and all history seems to prove it, clearly in agreement with Parkinson's law of the vacuum and the Peter Principle. The ten laws are summarized briefly in Table 1.1 and are discussed at greater length in Appendix D.

Mohr's Metrology

This is the tenth of Mohr's Laws (ML10) shown in Table 1.1 and requires a little elaboration. It asserts that all human traits can be measured out of ten. Madness, for example, is not a black and white thing, and we should be given a score, though this may vary a little according to such factors as the weather and countless others that hardly need mention.

This law can be used to calculate the *meaning of life*. To this end we sum all the possible scores, that is 0, 1, 2 - - - 10, to obtain 55. Dividing this result by the number of scores (11) we obtain the answer 5.5. This is not correct, however, as a score of 10 (perfection) is not possible (for example perfect sanity would surely constitute insanity).

Hence the corrected calculation of the 'MOL' is 45/11 = 4.090909 - - . This pleasing result indicates that we are all doomed to failure in the end, if not sooner.

The first author had the number recurrence above stated incorrectly with only one digit recurring and a switch girl at Cambridge corrected him, whereas he never got much sense from academics the world over. Thanks Martine!

Note too that the playground principle (ML1) can be generalized to fit onto the Mohr scale (1 to10) by subdividing the personality types A, B and C into three degrees. Then type A3 rates 9, that is maximum aggression, once again a score of 10 being disallowed (meltdown). Then type C1 rates 1 on the Mohr scale of aggression. This is maximum placidity, practically speaking, as zero corresponds to petrifaction.

The Mohr scale is also useful in the study of *ethics* where the questions of what is 'right' and what is 'good' are put, quickly followed by the question: "how good?" For this purpose the Mohr scale provides a set or ordinal numbers where, for example, 9 is the maximum goodness (10 would be too good to be true).

Whilst some of this discussion is in humour, it is, however, often well worthwhile to avoid jumping to the conclusion that 'so and so is a ratbag' and instead give him a score out of 10. This might help you see things a little more objectively.

There are countless other Mohr's laws and principles, for example *Mohr's First Law of War*: **DON'T PANIC!!**
The second is: *Double check everything (before going out on a mission)*, 10 rules for making decisions (e.g. don't take first offer), and 3 laws about money and distribution.

There are also many Mohr's Laws of the 'Murphy' or pessimistic type, for example:

(a) Mohr's Law of stubbed toes: Having stubbed your toe one day, you will probably stub it again a few times over the next few days to add insult to injury, i.e., you will probably make same sort of exclamation like: *BLOODY HELL!!* after each further stubbing.

(b) Mohr's Law of bike riding: As you struggle along, riding uphill and against the wind, when you change direction hoping for some relief, the wind will probably promptly change direction so that you are once again struggling, and perhaps swearing, against it.

(c) Mohr's Law of friends: Though the way to get on in a world full of hierarchies is to have friends 'in the right places', that is, friends in high places, most of we poorer people only have friends in low places.

The latter law is in line with the 1970s book *The Rich and the Super Rich in America*, which points out that in the USA the families of the super rich intermarry, and that this, indeed, helps keep them rich, for when divorce occurs both parties are rich, so neither has to fork out millions to the other, and they go on their merry way and marry another super rich divorcee.

Mohr's Law of Hierarchies

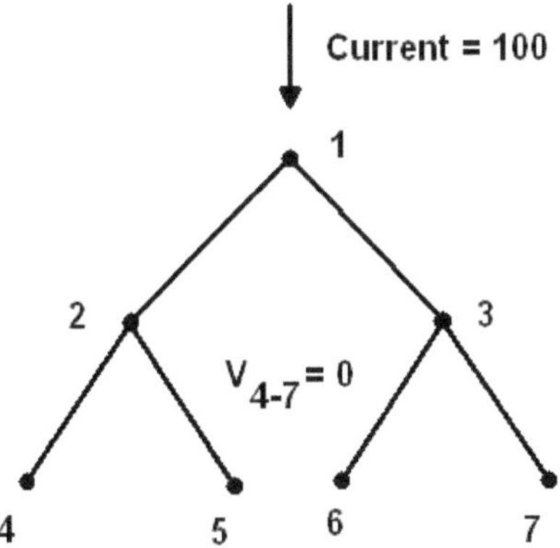

Figure 1.1. DC network model of a hierarchical network.

This derives from ML5 in Table 1.1 and can be illustrated by the small (hierarchical) network shown in Figure 1.1 which can be modelled as a DC network using the Finite Element Method procedure of adding element matrices to form a system matrix detailed in Appendix B.

At node 1 we have the pyramid building and lunatic 'boss' and a current 'load' of 100 is input with the program line: v(1) = 100 in the middle of the following BASIC program.

Then zero datum voltage is specified at nodes 4-7 and unit resistance is given to all 6 elements so that the data lines are those at the end of the program.

```
DIM NN(20, 2), R(20), C(20, 20), v(20)
a$ = "###": b$ = "######.###"
READ NP, NE, NS
FOR K = 1 TO NE
READ I, J, R: NN(K, 1) = I: NN(K, 2) = J: R(K) = R
C(I, I) = C(I, I) + 1 / R: C(I, J) = C(I, J) - 1 / R
C(J, I) = C(J, I) - 1 / R: C(J, J) = C(J, J) + 1 / R
NEXT
FOR K = 1 TO NS: READ N, S
FOR I = 1 TO NP
C(N, I) = 0: v(I) = v(I) - S * C(I, N)
C(I, N) = 0: NEXT I
v(N) = S: C(N, N) = 1: NEXT
v(1) = 100
FOR I = 1 TO NP: X = C(I, I): v(I) = v(I) / X
FOR J = I + 1 TO NP: C(I, J) = C(I, J) / X: NEXT
FOR K = 1 TO NP: IF K = I THEN GOTO NEXK
X = C(K, I): v(K) = v(K) - X * v(I)
FOR J = I + 1 TO NP
C(K, J) = C(K, J) - X * C(I, J): NEXT J
NEXK: NEXT K: NEXT I
PRINT " Node   Voltage"
FOR I = 1 TO NP
PRINT USING a$; I; : PRINT USING b$; v(I): NEXT I
PRINT " Element  Current"
FOR K = 1 TO NE: I = NN(K, 1): J = NN(K, 2)
Q = -(v(J) - v(I)) / R
PRINT USING a$; I; J; : PRINT USING b$; Q: NEXT
DATA 7,6,4
DATA 1,2,1, 1,3,1, 2,4,1, 2,5,1, 3,6,1, 3,7,1
DATA 4,0, 5,0, 6,0, 7,0
```

An almost identical program is given in Appendix B where the variable and array names are described, for example in line 3, NP = number of nodes.

The results output from the program are:

Voltage 75 at node 1.

Voltage 25 at nodes 2 and 3.

Zero voltage at nodes 4 to 7.
Currents 50 in the top two elements and 25 in the rest.

This illustrates what the 'econobabble' of economists and politicians calls 'the trickledown effect', that is, the boss of this very small hierarchy has 3 times the voltage (or power, money and status) of his subordinates (the front line managers) one rung below. The workers at the bottom have no status at all.

If we add a further bottom row of 8 nodes in Figure 15.1 then now the 'voltage hierarchy' is 87.5, 37.5, 12.5, 0 so that the boss now does 7 times as well as the 'front line managers' on the row above the bottom row.

Then if we add a further fifth row of 16 nodes the voltage hierarchy is 93.75, 43.75, 18.75, 6.25, 0 and the boss does 15 times as well as the front line managers and infinitely better than the workers at the bottom!

The latter 'voltage hierarchy' is the fundamental principle of modern management, leading to Mohr's Law of Hierarchies:

In hierarchical organizations the amount of real material-producing work people do is inversely proportional to their rank or level in the organization.
The amount of compensation they receive, however, is proportional to their level, sometimes to an exponential degree.

For such people their earnings might be expressed as an exponential function: $\$ = C \exp(kR)$

where $\$$ = salary, R = rank, and C and k are constants.

This, of course, is not fair at all.

In ancient times philosophers felt that nobody should be paid more than about 10 or 20 times as much as anybody else, and even that is a great difference, of course, but it might be justified in the case of an elected national leader who must be able to present a strong, powerful image and might have only a relatively short term in office.

In the case of big business, however, things have got out of hand and remuneration of CEOs is often tens of millions, on top of which they get huge share issues as annual bonuses, huge 'golden handshakes' when they retire, and gigantic 'golden parachutes' then the company collapses.

To add insult to the injury of poverty, the worker-slaves endure 'top-down one-way' (TDOW) communication as they did all through their long years at school, in other words, they are treated like shit.

This is grossly unjust as the poor peasants who work on farms, in factories or on building sites produce what is essential to human life, that is, food, clothing, housing etc.

So those posters often seen in the USSR decades ago which pictured the workers as heroic perhaps made some sense. Then, of course, the hammer and sickle on their flag was also symbolic of the importance of the workers.

So the bottom line is that we have to create fairer societies which have real or *direct democracy* and leaders who 'check their ego at the door'. In these, greed, hunger, famine, war and other evils will not be tolerated by the people.

Mohr's Law of Capitalism

As Figure 1.1 illustrates, the higher up you are in a hierarchy the more 'power' you have Mohr's Power Law, which might be stated symbolically as:

$$P = C R^n$$

where P = power, R = rank, and C and n are constants.

Assuming the value of n is 2 then when one is twice as high in the hierarchy one has four times as much power.

Then, as we all know, power corrupts, one of the major factors in mankind's endless history of conflict.

As noted in the previous section, salaries may increase exponentially in hierarchical organizations and this result can be related to Mohr's Law of Capitalism which is the exponential growth law of money ($) with time (T)

$$d(\$)/d(T) = c_1(\text{activity}) \quad \text{where} \quad \text{activity} = c_2 \$$$

Here, using constants c_1 and c_2, the rate at which money is made is proportional to the rate of business activity, this in turn proportional to the amount of money available to fund this activity.

Combining the two constants above as $k = c_1 c_2$ we have

$$d(\$)/d(T) = k\$ \quad \text{where } k \text{ is the } growth\ factor.$$

where $ = money made.

This is *separable* which means that it can be integrated in the form

$$\text{Integral } [\, d(\$)/\$ \,] = \text{Integral } [\, k\, d(T) \,]$$

giving, with the inclusion of the initial values, the exponential growth law $\quad \$/\$_0 = \exp[k(T - T_0)]$

If, for example, the growth factor is 10% per year, that is $k = 0.1$, then over 10 years we obtain the growth ratio $\$/\$_0 -$ 2.7, so that we have nearly *tripled* our money.

The only real beneficiaries, however, are those higher in the hierarchy. The workers at the bottom who do all the *real work* (sitting and raving at sometimes boozy board meetings is not hard work) can't usually save any money and thus are slaves to all intents and purposes.

This is an intolerable situation and the CEOs who earn 'megabucks' are, of course, corrupt, and such corruption has always sown the seeds of discontent that have always, sooner or later, ended up as revolutions.

Thus socialism tends to be ruled by a single dictator, but capitalism by a multiplicity of petty dictators:

> *Capitalism tends to produce a multiplicity of petty dictators each in command of his own little business kingdom. State Socialism tends to produce a single, centralized totalitarian dictatorship, wielding absolute authority . . . through a hierarchy of bureaucratic agents.*
> Aldous Huxley, *Ends and Means* (1937).

Politicians too are often corrupt, of course, often being found to take bribes from big business.

Monarchs and dictators, of course, have nearly always been the greediest of all. Not only do they help themselves to plenty of money and live in grand palaces, but throughout history their hunger for power and thence territorial gain has led to one war after another.

The 'maturity coefficient' of hierarchies

The rat race begins quietly in the playground but heats up on the office, though some don't notice it. Those that don't are most likely to become its victims.

In this race it is survival of the rottenest. The biggest liars and cheats will talk their way to the top while honest workers do just that, work.

These apes are not long out of the tree and want to work their way back up it.

In this way the organization's hierarchy increases the *Maturity Quotient* (MQ) usefully defined by Dr Laurence Peter:

$$MQ = 100 \times (NIC/N)$$

where NIC is the number of employees who have attained their (final) level of incompetence and N is the total number of employees in the hierarchy

As Peter states: *"Obviously, when MQ reaches 100, no useful work will be accomplished at all.*

In one book on Human Resources Management (HRM), that fascist term that I believe originated in Harvard Business School (HBS) [I still prefer the term Personnel Management], it is reported that surveys reveal the key common factor found in those who have succeeded in climbing the corporate tree is *ambition*:

> *I have no spur*
> *To prick the sides of my intent, but only*
> *Vaulting ambition, which o'er-leaps itself,*
> *And falls on th' other.*
> Macbeth (1606), Act I, Scene 7

Reflections on ambition remind one of the book *Blind Ambition* by Nixon's acolyte John Dean, the youngest ever Attorney General in the USA (Dean, 1985).

This book concentrates largely on office trivia but Nixon's book *The Real War*, in its last chapter, holds that America should never again commit troops to a major conflict on foreign soil as in Vietnam. Instead the nasty Russians, who he claimed had had ambitions to rule the world dating back to the Czars, if that makes sense at all, could be defeated by economic war.

In hindsight it seems he was proved right in the short term to some extent.

Aggression and age

It is, of course, aggression that provides the spur for blind ambition. Indeed such aggression we admire and praise, if not idolize.

So it is, therefore, that we will queue, sometimes, for miles, to watch our sporting heroes biff it out. All this usually over a ball of some sort.

What is it, this fascination with balls? And when did you last play marbles? Or have you lost them?

Come to think of it, the fashion cycle is surely due to reinvent the game of marbles, of course with a new slant.

We could have giant marbles, something like lawn bowls for example. But in this Americanized age of think big, any modern marble must be something Captain Marbles could be justifiably proud of.

Younger men supposedly running higher on hormones, particularly testosterone, are presumed to be more aggressive, whereas older men circa 60 and nearing retirement, of course, have lower hormone levels. In fact, many younger men dose up on testosterone and steroids for the purpose of body building, some of them taking part in farcical 'muscle bulging' contests.

Indeed, just like many women, some older men now have HRT (hormone replacement therapy).

The first author twice had bad luck in University lecturing jobs, being appointed by men about to retire, these being:

(a) Jack Peabody, HOD of Civil Engineering at Caulfield Institute of Technology or CIT (now part of Monash University).

(b) Cecil Segment, PhD in Maths from Cambridge, and HOD of Auckland University's very unusual Theoretical and Applied Mechanics or TAM department.

Soon after I started in these departments new, too young, too stupid, too aggressive, and new HODs appeared, both doing a great deal to ruin my career and life.

For example only, the second of these psychopathic bullies (Ian CamClod) bullied me into resigning at 38 going on 39, which I politely did (when I should have fought back and 'dumped' on him to try and get him the 'sack'). Then the thug HOD never wrote me an OK reference, instead giving confidential ones to a string of Australian Unis with words to the effect he thought me a 2nd-rate lecturer etc.

In his last year at Auckland Uni., while this thug was bullying me and softening me up for eventual surrender/resignation, I had also stupidly asked a former colleague and HOD at CIT (Bob Dilmer) for help with a book I was having trouble getting published, and which had doubled in size and scope in the process.

Dilmer was clueless, hopeless etc. but had me fly to Melbourne for 3 weeks of ignorant and mindless quizzing page by page to try and understand some of the book (torture which gave me heart pains at times), repeating this inquisition for a couple of weeks in Auckland, during which time he could swap backstabbing notes with the new bastard boss there. Having promised me 2 secretaries to type the book, he ended up giving me only half a dozen pages for me to type into the book, and these were later removed.

I therefore still somewhat regret not having dealt with these bastard bosses, perhaps with some of the measures suggested later in this book, but, of course, this book had not been written then. Now, however, I hope it will be of help to many other people working at the lower and middle levels of hierarchical organizations.

Conclusion

The Peter Principle is very relevant to hierarchical organizations of all kinds, as are Parkinson's Laws.

The simple DC network model of Figure 1.1 illustrates some aspects of hierarchies well, for example why the higher up one is, the bossier and greedier, one may become, and the notation of the simple BASIC program given for it in the foregoing chapter is explained in Appendix B.

Many of the several Mohr's Laws are very relevant to modern life, for example Mohr's Law of Hierarchies and Mohr's Law of Capitalism, and other Mohr's Laws are given later in the book, for example Mohr's Law of Bullshit in Chapter 5, and Mohr's Laws of Decisions in Chapter 18.

Finally, the ten Mohr's Laws of Table 1.1 are discussed at greater length in Appendix D in relation to the new religion Mohronism.

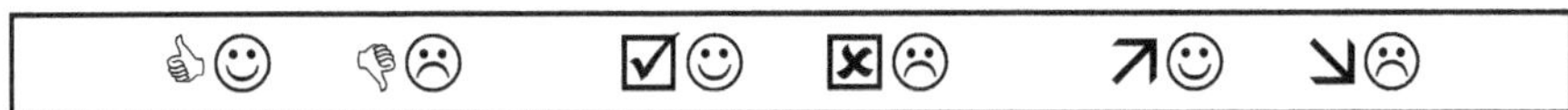

1. Mohr's Laws

Chapter 2

Family Life

Every man who is high up loves to think that he has done it all himself; and the wife smiles, and lets it go at that. It's only our joke. Every woman knows that.
Sir J.M. Barrie, *What Every Woman Knows*, act 4.
Performed 1908, published 1918.

I have been in love, and in debt, and in drink,
This and many a year.
Alexander Brome, *Songs and Other Poems*,
2nd ed., 1964, pt 1: 'The Mad Lover'

Family hierarchical structures

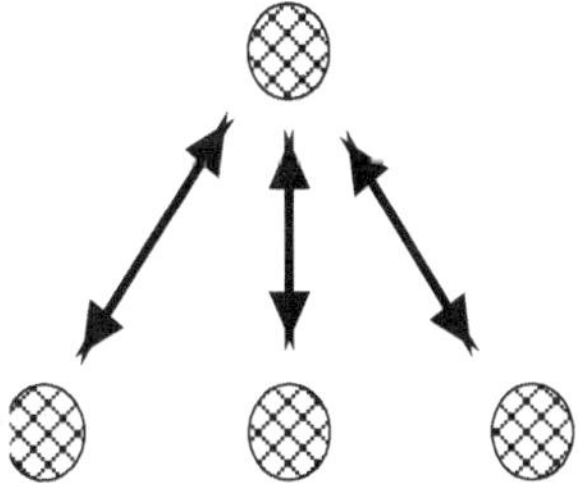
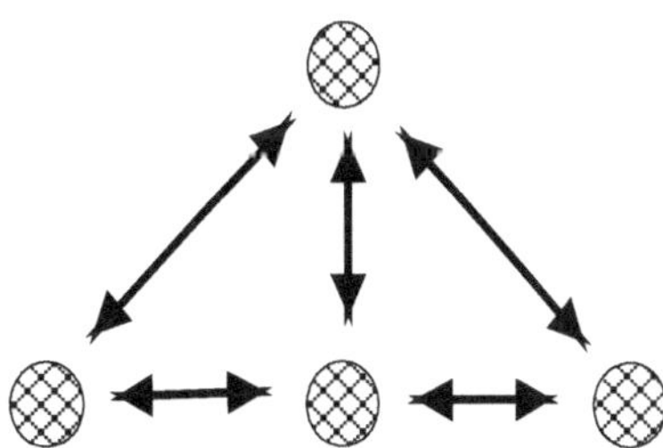

For a family with four members these may take such forms as shown above, where a hierarchical or 'one to one' structure is as shown on the left and a mixture of hierarchical and group structure is shown on the right.

In both cases one parent is at the top, with the other parent and 2 children below. In practice, of course, the second parent is higher in the hierarchy than the children, and the older children are higher than the younger ones.

Dealing with young children

Piaget borrowed from psychoanalysis to define two types of thought (Gillespie, 2017):

> ➢ *Directed or intelligent thought* is based on experience and logic and has realistic and communicable goals.
> ➢ *Undirected or autistic thought* via images, myths and symbols aimed at satisfying unconscious and unrealistic desires.

The directed mind sees objects as having certain properties and obeying certain laws, whereas for the autistic mind objects are simply there to be seen or enjoyed.

Piaget felt that children from 3 to 7 are largely egocentric and indulge in autistic thought, whereas from 7 to 11 they begin to develop the perceptual intelligence of the adult mind.

The formative years

The period from age 12 to 30 has been termed the *critical period* for formation of attitudes and it can be divided into two parts (Morgan et al., 1979):

(a) Adolescence, during which parental, educational, peer group, advertising and sociological influences are largely responsible for development of most of the attitudes a person will form through life.

(b) Young adulthood is a time when commitments such as choosing a vocation and marriage occur, and one in which attitudes tend to *crystallize* or 'freeze' for life.

In part this crystallization may involve attempts at *cognitive consistency* in which we tend to make our attitudes relatively consistent with one another and thus avoid *cognitive dissonance* or conflicting attitudes.

Heider's *balance theory* is of the cognitive consistency type and assumes that we try to maintain consistent, balanced & harmonious relationships with other people and our environment. According to this theory we wouldn't marry a person with whom we disagreed on issues about which we felt strongly, such as abortion (Morgan et al., 1979).

That attitudes do indeed crystallize or 'firm up' in young adulthood was confirmed by a US survey of women college students in the 1930s which, when followed-up 20 years later, found that for most issues on the 'conservative-liberal' dimension the women's attitudes, except for a slight "conservative drift" typical of older people, remained the same as they had been in their twenties (Newcomb, 1963).

That attitudes tend to firm up in adolescence and young adulthood has, of course, important implication for how we are likely to live the rest of our lives.

Preschool education

Children's brains develop rapidly in the first few years and it is important to take advantage of their resulting capacity for early learning to provide infants with a stimulating environment which should include a 'personal learning centre' that includes educational pictures and toys.

By the second year they should be involved in small learning groups supervised by a specialist teacher so that they can begin real learning (Packard, 1978).

In the third year they should begin kindergarten for at least a couple of days a week and these learning efforts should continue. By now they have a modest vocabulary and are capable of *cognitive learning* which processes and stores *abstract* information.

At this stage deliberate effort should be made at 'IQ building', noting that IQ tests include questions testing verbal, spatial and numerical ability. If a child has a problem with numbers, for example, early detection and correction of this will prevent far greater problems later.

Then, given a head start, they should commence school at age four, rather than the usual five in most countries.

Home schooling

In the USA home schooling has increased markedly in recent decades. The number of home-schooled children grew from just a few thousand in the early 1970s to 1.1 million in 2003, having increased 30% between 1999 and 2003 (Penn, 2007).

In 2000, only 52 percent of colleges had formal admission policies for home-schooled students, but by 2005 85% did, in that year a study showing that home-schooled students scored 81 points higher than the national average on the SAT (Penn, 2007).

Enhancing the learning process

The home learning process can be enhanced by such means as the 'Superlearning' recommended by Ostrander and Schroeder (1979). This involves encouraging physical and psychological relaxation with quite background music, slow breathing exercises, and visualizing nice scenes to achieve a reflective and receptive frame of mind.

Then the child is encouraged to affirm: *"I can do it."*

Here, developing a positive attitude is comparable to the 'teacher expectancy effect' where it is found that students who already get good marks are encouraged to do even better by a combination of the positive results, the confidence they obtain from these, and the 'expectation' and confidence the teacher shows about their ability. Here *hope* plays an important part, and students who become accustomed to getting low marks tend to lose hope, and without hope, of course, life is much less bearable.

With the scene set, the parent/teacher reads the material aloud at a careful pace while the child reads it silently. This is repeated again with quiet background music and the child is then tested on the material.

Giving children more attention and hope

Weiss and Mann (1978) refer to a project in Milwaukee that found that children given more attention by the mother or a specially trained teacher, showed markedly higher IQ. This is no doubt the reason that only children tend to have higher IQ and that, in families with more than one child, the eldest child has a slightly higher IQ on average (Vernon, 1960). The youngest child in larger families, on the other hand, does not do too badly compared to those 'sandwiched' in the middle and perhaps most deprived of attention.

Related to this, of course, is the 'teacher expectancy effect, in which students who get better marks are not only themselves encouraged by getting good results, but also by teachers often openly predicting that they will continue to do well.

As Lopez (2013) puts it:

Children also need something to hope for. They need to be excited about one thing in the future . . . then another, then another.

As Marta (2004) puts it:

Each of us has a responsibility to have a positive impact on the children we know.

Talk about the future – their dreams and aspirations – throughout their lives, not just at important milestones.

Goal setting

As with the teacher expectancy effect, goal setting and positive thinking play an important role in many other activities in life. In sports, for example, coaches do their utmost to encourage positive thinking and goal setting, and much psychological research has been done in this area, Sykes (1995) citing several examples of doctorates in education being granted for dissertations with such titles as:

"The use of goal setting and positive self-modelling to enhance self-efficiency and performance for the basketball free-throw shot" for a PhD at the University of Maryland.

Preferably, however, goals should not be 'commanded'. Rather, they should be 'suggested' and should be personal goals, not 'institutional' ones.

Bad habits

Accommodation (becoming accustomed to their surroundings, i.e., their usually small and often shared one room prison, complete with a cot with bars on all sides), and imprinting (becoming accustomed to a few 'familiar' faces), play important roles in the early learning of infants. Similarly, imitative learning (IL) and social learning (SL) play an important role in the childhood years.

Whilst parents and educators should be doing their best to inculcate good habits, including good learning/study habits, all too often they encourage the acquisition of bad habits by practicing bad habits themselves, for example parents smoking and/or drinking to excess.

Worse still, of course, criminally insane teachers and preachers prey upon children by sexually abusing them, sometimes their victims doing likewise when they grow up.

I, for example, recall smoking my mother's cigarette butts at quite a young age, then, encouraged by a couple of other friends at school, experimenting more seriously with smoking at 12-13, then at age 15 beginning to smoke cigarettes regularly and learning to 'drawback' the smoke, and thus becoming addicted.

Then, also at age circa 15, I learnt to drink booze occasionally by attending parties held by my circa 20-year-old eldest brother. At University, where some students drank regularly, I was encouraged to drink occasionally at parties etc., whilst going to the pub a couple of times with an alcoholic father in-law-to-be was one of a few other factors in my becoming a daily drinker once I had my first full-time job and thus could afford it.

'Controlling' parents

Many parents treat their children more like pet dogs than humans, for example by 'steering' them into the same career-path that they had, and encouraging them to play the same sports that they did. This is denying them real freedom of choice in life, and preferably they should be allowed to choose from a few alternative careers and pastimes.

Why women are so besotted with pets etc. amazes me, but is no doubt because of the recently postulated *maternal gene*. Whether this actually exists is doubtful, but nevertheless imitative (from mum and friends) and sociological learning (IL & SL) no doubt result in women having a real desire/need to have children, or de-facto children/pets.

Indeed, many childless women go 'nuts' later in life, the psychology term *hysteria* coming from the ancient Greek for *without a womb*.

Bullying

Unfortunately, bullying etc. is a 'fact of life' in all human hierarchies, including both 'nuclear' and extended families.

A factor in this sometimes, perhaps, is that, according to David Galton, the grandson of theory of evolution pioneer, Francis Galton, personality is 50% inherited.

More obvious, however, is that hierarchical bossiness etc. is suffered and learnt by eldest children from one or both parents, and then inflicted on their younger siblings.

This is no doubt why George Orwell's famous book *1984* uses the term "Big Brother" so much for the controlling but invisible government in the nightmarish world picture he paints in that book.

Thus I use the term *Big Brother Syndrome* (BBS), and also *Big Sister Syndrome* (BSS).

My father CBO, who had been one of Lord Rutherford's team that split the atom for the first time in Cambridge in 1931, was a bit 'up himself' at times. For example, dragging me at only about 5 along with the family on holiday hikes in the Healesville hills near Melbourne, he derided me for complaining that I was finding it hard work. At around the same age he derided me for being a little afraid of the "Big Dipper", a very fast and hilly roller coaster ride at St Kilda's Luna Park in Melbourne that was eventually removed.

One day he also bullied his wife, a chemist by training, saying that chemists were just *"glorified bottle washers"*.

Thus, perhaps, of BBS my eldest (of 2) brothers (W) became a good example, and remained something of a bully it appeared to some, at least, throughout most of his life until old age had slowed him down a good deal. Of course ML10 (see Chapter 1) must be remembered here, and on the 'bully scale' I might have only given him a score of 7 or 8/10 (he is now dead).

W bullied me a bit as a child, and pressured me to do very cheap consulting work for the company he started when he lost his job, for example, saying on the phone after I had just moved to Auckland: *If you fuck this up* - - about a job I was doing, my work on which had been slowed by the move.

Then, of course, the last straw was summarily having me committed (briefly, and with the support of my wife's backstabbing) when I refused to see a marriage guidance counsellor after I had been bullied into resigning from Auckland University. Already crucified academically, as it turned out, this was perhaps the final death blow to my career, as at that time I needed career support, and should have been able to use his company name to help get a job.

Instead, in the years following he virtually refused to speak to me, only bullying me occasionally, for example with: *I've got a photocopier*, having noticed I often needed to do photocopying but had to go out and pay for it.

My other also older brother (F) also bullied me occasionally when young, but in adult life was quite harmless.

As for BSS, I found the woman I married with little thought, and had as girlfriend or wife for some 20 years, something of a bully (verbally) sometimes, and have since those years felt that she may have 'learnt' bullying-type behaviour from her father, and also as eldest of 3 daughters.

I met this woman (Patricia) because, while my elder brother F was overseas, my mother rented his large upstairs bedroom to 2 girls studying at the nearby Kindergarten Teacher's College (KTC), typical old-fashioned pack-them in (kids, pets, renters etc. etc.) greed and stupidity that women common indulge in. Then one afternoon I sat next to her on my bed one afternoon when an old school friend of mine was visiting, the visiting friend sitting next to the other KTC student at my desk. Then somehow a relationship followed.

Later that, year, however, St Kilda won its first and only AFL Premiership by beating Collingwood by just one point. Me being a St Kilda supporter, I expressed pleasure at the result. Patricia, a Collingwood supporter, as fate would have it, then piped up:

YOU BASTARD!

A bad sign in the first year of the relationship – and there were more to follow. For example, on a couple of 'bad' occasions she provoked me with 'verbal assault' with unfortunate consequences when I responded in haste.

The first was in December 1968 (about a year before marriage), when I threw a champagne glass in her direction because she had taunted me with a jealous remark such as: *"You're weak as shit"* when I was celebrating having graduated with first class honours and being awarded a Commonwealth Postgraduate Award scholarship.

It missed by 'miles', but upset by the incident I stole a few of my mother's sleeping tablets and slept them off in hospital.

From that day on, this sometimes nasty woman bullied me by secretly telling people I was "mad", an "alcoholic", had a "communication problem" etcetera.

As this sort of disparagement sometimes reached my workplace, however, it contributed to my very promising University career, and thence my life, being ruined at less than 40.

Thus I had been foolish to marry Patricia, given the bad signs, examples of which are given above.

I was relatively young and naive at the time, still being less than half way through an engineering degree. So not only did I know relatively little about people, and next to nothing about psychology, but Patricia had been giving herself elocution lessons to make her a more convincing kindergarten teacher when she graduated. Had she not done so, I might have thought her a bit of a slob.

In addition, she must have had an at least unconscious dislike of people with Germanic names, her father having lost an eye in the Allied campaign against the "Desert Fox", Rommel, in World War 2. Indeed, a few years later I noticed some evidence of such prejudice from her mother who, noticing a German name in some context one day, was scathing, calling the person a "Hun".

A key factor in my getting 'hooked', however, had been Patricia getting pregnant during the first year of our 'association', obtaining money from her father under false pretences, along with a little from me, to pay for a 'backyard' abortion (I sold an old coin collection my late grandmother had given to contribute to the cost). Thus I mistakenly felt some obligation to continue the relationship rather than 'dump her', though I would have found it very easy then to obtain another girlfriend.

Indeed, and example of this, and the 'flukiness' of my having a relationship with Patricia for any length of time, was one day in 1966 when I had a fellow engineering student visiting my house, along with an arts student girl from the country whose flat I had visited a couple of times, on one of these getting as far as a kiss or two.

On this day I was going to drive the four of us (me, Patricia, and the engineering and arts students) somewhere, and I hesitated for a moment or two about which of the 2 girls to put in the front seat with me!

My ex-wife once having stupidly said in Auckland: *"People don't change"*, she proved that she was too stupid to change by remaining a bully. Years after our marriage breakup of 1985, she still bullied me occasionally, for example boasting that she had a better PC than me, and deriding me for often using magnifying glasses instead of my reading glasses.

I must admit, however, that we had always had something of a competitive relationship and once, for example, I got her to mow the lawns, saying she was overweight and needed the exercise.

Domestic violence

Domestic violence relates, of course, to family hierarchies and bullying, and typically the man of the house, and/or sometimes his wife, are bullies and sometimes commit acts of violence against the spouse and/or one or more children.

The first instance of domestic violence I recall is my mother threatening to whip me with a steel dog chain after I had been rude to her. Fortunately my father was nearby, however, and quickly said:

"Don't do that, you might hurt the boy".

Another instance of domestic violence I recall is my elder brother (F) pushing my head into the toilet bowl on a couple of occasions to punish me for: "Telling" on him.

An example of an unfortunate domestic incident occurred in December 1968 involving me and the woman I married (Patricia) in January 1970, is given above.

Another incident occurred in my home in Auckland near the University. In this 'the wife' stood in my way threatening me with a knife when I went to the fridge to get a bottle of beer. I pushed her aside and she fell, but was not injured.

A third and final incident between me and my wife occurred after I had been bullied by a bastard new boss at Auckland University into resigning, helped in this bullying by the backstabbing of my wife and my ex-boss back in Melbourne, with whom I had become involved over a book.

Returning home, having lost my job, house, and as it turned out career, I was confused, to say the least and, to make matters worse, had stupidly arranged for my aging parents to move in with me (in a second house they owned) so that they could be helped in what a sister-in-law then dubbed: *Ward 13.*

One afternoon I was playing a recently borrowed record on a record player I had given my father (my classic ROLLS record player had been smashed inside before it was shipped back from Auckland[1]) while having a drink, and was moved to tears by the song, as it became clear in later years an early symptom of PTSD that was often to be repeated.

My wife shouted: "YOU'RE WEAK AS PISS!"

I responded by politely asking her to leave the room.

She began to do so and then turned around, so I pushed her none too hard, and she fell, injuring her shoulder.

Soon after this she had my eldest brother visit 'out of the blue' with a psychiatrist he had used for his 2 eldest children in tow[2], and had me chased by a police van, captured, and taken by that to a mental hospital for a couple of days.

Upset by this, I took some rat poison a few days later and was committed again for a couple more miserable days.

Soon after this she had 'BB' help her move out with her 2 *children* to live with her mother, saying to me around that time: *You'll be dead in year.*

---

[1] My IBM 'golf-ball' typewriter was also damaged slightly and, strangely, my wife had it flown separately back to Australia.

[2] A couple of years later one of his sons asked me to let him sleep on the floor at my place to escape his father (BB) committing him again, suggesting the father was incapable of dealing with his children himself, and certainly I had always found him (BB) difficult.

Indeed, she had done her best to make that happen and a few suicide attempts followed, along with PTSD, mostly as a result of me having lost my 'daytime job', though in misery, poverty and isolation I continued a good deal of academic and other research and writing.

After that marriage broke down, I was 'involved' with a bossy almost 10 years older English woman, Helena, who always lied about her age to get jobs etcetera, for a couple of years.

She was an eldest child, and admitted that she had sometimes bullied her two younger sisters.

She was a bad-tempered, bossy woman and, one day when I had annoyed her by breaking one of her drinking glasses, she tried very hard to strangle me and I fell and she fell with me onto my leg, severely damaging it.

Her husband also had a bad temper. One day he visited the 'half house' flat I had let her live in free of charge, and seeing kitchen-ware set up in only one of the 2 kitchens, deduced that we were living together and he was soon sitting astride me trying to strangle me. She managed to pull him off, however, and I was saved.

Then, when she had bought a house and moved, I became involved with another older woman who also had a terrible temper.

One day she asked me the address of the English woman and I told her, so she drove rapidly to that address, rang the doorbell, and when it was answered abused her by profusely swearing at her using 'f words' etcetera, only leaving when her target threatened to call the police.

Then one day the English woman visited me and, seeing that one of two young women sharing the rented half of the house was showing off her tits a bit, became enraged and soon had her on the ground, ripping some of her hair out.

I said: *I'm calling the police. You had better leave before they get here.* She did.

An incident with the new older lady friend then occurred.

Staying one night for dinner at her Housing Commission house I was playing a tape of the Kings College Choir.

She piped up: *That's rubbish* or some such.

I inadvertently replied: *You'd fuck donkeys wouldn't you.*

She responded by repeatedly clubbing me around the head and I had to catch a taxi home covered in blood, not easy to do at circa 11 PM on a Saturday night!

As a final excellent example of domestic violence, a 'psych. case' 70-year old woman I met at a local club a few years ago once married a hard-drinking Maori who worked in a slaughterhouse. He had a bad habit of beating her up a bit and, while she was on the floor, kicking her in the head. Surprisingly, the relationship lasted "nine and a half years".

Financial cheating

In family hierarchies, as in business hierarchies, a lot of financial cheating goes on.

This ranges from children stealing a little money or cigarettes from mum's handbag, to children cheating aging parents and/or their siblings out of a great deal of money.

I do remember a good example of imitative learning at age circa 11, when one boy in the class began to appear regularly with nice new fountain pens and biros, saying he had stolen them from Coles stores. Thus me and my best friend at school at that stage copied these small acts of larceny or 'shoplifting' to pinch a few pens etcetera, soon being discouraged after being chased out of a store by a store detective.

'Grown ups', of course, cheat on a much larger scale.

My eldest brother (W), when starting his own building business had me do a lot of Structural Engineering consulting work for him very promptly indeed and for next to nothing.

BB (W) had my just retired father (CBO) sell his 'mini mansion' house for a pittance so he could build 6 home units on it, giving my father only the smallest of them in return.

Then he extorted CBO's superannuation money to build four home units, keeping two of these for himself, telling CBO giving him (BB) money would help his rapidly growing family (he had 4 children in only about 6 years). The two younger brothers, F and myself, got nothing at all, of course.

Then, when I was bullied into resigning from the University of Auckland, and returned to Melbourne with my aging parents moving in with me so they could be looked after, BB sold their house and kept about half the proceeds before buying another much cheaper house to replace it.

Around this time his wife kept all my mother's jewellery (or so I was told), and when my father died in 1986, and my mother in 1989, any money they had left as shares etc. went unaccounted for, i.e. big brother took it.

In 2000 BB and the ex-wife combined to force me to sell the house I had inherited and was living in so that I could give much of the proceeds to my two children so they could buy a house or flat. Under pressure I took $50,000 less than I should have, equivalent to circa $100,000+ today, and moved to a far cheaper house right on a railway line, a bad move necessitating another move before I reached 65.

About this greed of BB his youngest son told me he was aware of a couple of years ago over the phone a couple of times when upset by his father's refusing to help him out financially when he had hit hard times after a work accident had put him out of work.

As is well known, and read about regularly in the newspapers, disputes and cheating over family wills is commonplace, and often children are cheated by one of their siblings of any share at all of large wills when rich people die.

Conclusions

The chapter began on a positive note by discussing how encouragement that instils with hope, help, effective early learning, and home learning can improve children's lives.

On a more negative note, however, the way some controlling parents treat children 'like dogs' is discussed briefly. Indeed, recently I took a lady I know to lunch at a nearby club. At a large nearby table four women sat yakking endlessly while their children (7 or 8 in total) ran around wildly, shrieking. It was not the relaxing lunch I had planned, and my lady friend said of the 4 women: *They're treating those children like dogs.*

The sections on bullying, which seems inevitable in all kinds of hierarchies, including those of 'nuclear' and 'extended' families, and on domestic violence, are also somewhat negative but must be considered to give a balanced and realistic view of modern family life.

Apparently in agreement with this view, Liana Buchanan, in the Herald Sun newspaper of Feb. 16, 2018, wrote:

In finally recognising the experiences and needs of those affected by family violence, we still, often overlook children.

We should also be at pains to consider the affects of bullying within families, as this often has very damaging effects.

Finally, I should note that, in the examples of 'incidents' of domestic violence given in the foregoing chapter, there was usually blame on both sides (in accordance with Mohr's 10th Law), for example when 'verbal assault' or abuse was used, inciting an angry response.

CHAPTER 3

SCHOOLS

> *Twelve years of formal education is twelve years of formal ignorance.* Huey P. Nelson (1973), attributed.
>
> *Show me a man who has enjoyed his school days and I'll show you a bully and a bore.*
> Robert Morley, attributed.

The beginnings of formal education

Formal education, that is, beyond the basic training and teaching given by parents to young children in order to literally get them on their feet and functioning physically, doubtless had tribal origins in which the elders played a role.

Even before that, however, Neanderthal man adorned his caves with paintings, a practice that his children learnt by *imitative learning* (IL), and perhaps later reinforced as a habit by *social learning* (SL).

In Western Civilization our recorded history of education centres around the Greek and Roman civilizations, in which monastic education had a parallel with Buddhist training.

From those early times until today there remains for the teacher a social obligation to search for 'pure' knowledge and to impart practical knowledge and skills needed for specific roles in society.

The objectives of formal education

Dating back to Greek and Roman times the objectives of formal education were to equip the next generation for their role in society.

To do that today, preschool centres such as kindergartens begin elementary skills and social training and thus prepare the young child for more formal education at school.

With the increasing participation of women in the work force in Western society in recent decades, day care centres have combined the roles of child care with those of the kindergarten.

Primary school education, however, goes on in much the same way as it has for several decades, concentrating upon teaching the three Rs, that is reading, 'riting and 'rithmetic.

One notable difference now is that computers make an early appearance and children are exposed to computers early on in primary school.

In modern times, however, the total number of years at school has increased to, commonly, twelve years. In contrast, Francis Bacon, who wrote much about education in the sixteenth century, went to Cambridge University at age twelve and left at age fourteen without doing the final third year of his studies in Elizabethan logic and rhetoric.

In those days there was no secondary school and it was the growth of the sciences, in particular, that led to the need for as long as twelve years of schooling and thence secondary school.

In the modern secondary school much of the syllabus is as advanced as that of University courses of 100 to 200 years ago.

In Australia school is usually commenced at age five and education is compulsory until age 14, giving a total of ten years at school. In other countries there are fewer compulsory years, for example Cuba which had compulsory education from ages 6 to 11 until recently.

After this period of compulsory schooling students are deemed sufficiently educated to work in nonprofessional jobs. Many take on an apprenticeship or undertake TAFE studies in various occupations such as those in the hospitality industry.

In Australia the eleventh and twelfth years are dedicated to study for University entry but, as in other countries such as the USA, an increasingly large proportion of employers prefer, if not insist upon, employees having successfully completed matriculation studies.

School hierarchies

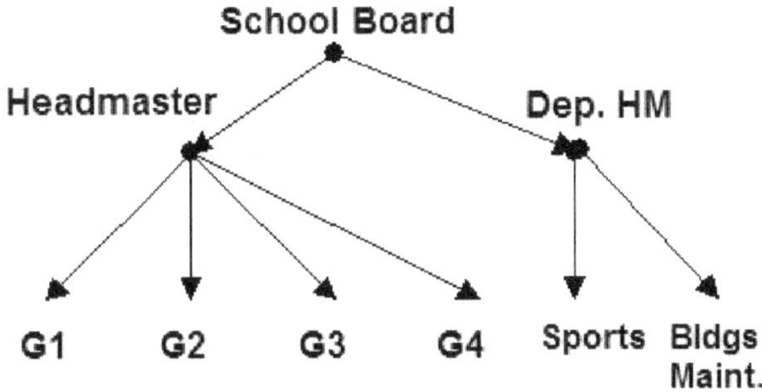

Hierarchies in schools take the form shown above with the school board governing the school, and the headmaster and deputy headmaster at level 2 in the hierarchy.

Below the headmaster in this small primary school are four grades, each of these with a teacher in charge (and, of course, a bunch of students below at the bottom of the upside down hierarchy tree), whilst the deputy headmaster is in charge of staff who supervis sports and other recreational activities, and also the contractors who carry out regular cleaning and maintenance of the school buildings and grounds.

The person with the real power, of course, is the headmaster, and he has considerable power over the teachers who, in turn have even greater power over their students who they punish and even expel in some cases.

As is always the case in hierarchies, humans simply being, as Desmond Morris put it, 'naked apes', of course, teachers often abuse their power by inflicting excessively harsh punishments upon students, sometimes bullying weaker students.

Physical abuse in schools by teachers

I went to kindergarten for a year before doing grades 1-3 at St Kilda's Brighton Road State School as it was then called.

For grade four I moved to one of two primary campuses of a private boy's only school, where I completed grades 5 – 8, before moving to the 'Senior School' campus.

At both these schools I recall the 'strap' was used quite often by teachers to hit the hands of misbehaving students.

At the private school, for more serious misbehaviour students were sent to the headmaster's office to be given 'the cane' on the back of their lower legs.

Psychological abuse by teachers

At the private school misbehaving students were often 'kept in' for an hour 'after school', which nearly all of them hated.

One nasty teacher at the private school used to 'pick on', i.e. bully, a boy who had had polio and had a wooden box under his desk to help keep his legs straight.

Sexual abuse in schools by teachers

While I was in grade 7 at the private school, our 'class master', who lived in part of the building that housed boarders, had one boy sit on his knee in front of the class a couple of times.

The next year, this boy reported him to the headmaster for sexual abuse, and the teacher left the school, no doubt having been 'given the sack', and rumour later had it that he had sexually abused some of the boarding house/resident students.

Sexual abuse in schools by students

I recall one 'bad boy' student at the private school in Grade 7 encouraging a couple of other boys to join him at lunch times to smoke cigarettes, and probably one or both of them 'got hooked' on smoking within a few years.

The same student in Grade 8 used to stand in the aisle and masturbate while the very short-sighted Latin teacher was writing on the blackboard. He also used to share a double-desk with another student and they masturbated one another, a practice they called "a mutual", and no doubt the bad boy had taught the other boy this practice.

Fortunately, this boy did not make it to 'senior school', and no doubt his misbehaviour had been discovered and he had been quietly expelled.

Student bullying

In grade 4 at the private boy's school I well remember myself and another 'new boy', who ultimately became a Rhodes Scholar, finishing the arithmetic tests much quicker than the rest of the class and the lady teacher, who had a German name, letting us out early to play on the school oval while the rest of the class finished the test.

The classroom had windows showing onto the oval, so the boys left behind could see we two roaming free there.

On a couple of occasions one somewhat fat boy sat on me at the end of lunchtimes spent on and around the oval to prevent me from getting back to the classroom, no doubt because of jealousy. He later became a lawyer working at (in my opinion) one of the world's worst Universities (in Melbourne).

In grade 7 at the private school one of a couple of 'bad mad' boys who did not make it to senior school (no doubt because they were not allowed to) stole some 2,000 pounds from his father's shop, a lot of money in those days.

He hid his 'loot' by burying it in their backyard, and used some of it to regularly pay one of the biggest boys to carry him around the school grounds on his back.

Then, after school, he and a couple of other boys (including the one he regularly used to ride on) would catch a taxi, the bad boy with the loot reportedly telling the taxi driver: *Take us on a trip around town*, and they would then spend an hour or more running up a sizable taxi fare before being, I suppose, taken to their homes one by one.

After an 'inter-house' cricket match in Grade 8 at the private school, a boy who I had caught out for a duck fielding near the wicket came up to me in the 'locker rooms' after the match and asked me:

How tall are you?

I replied: *Five foot ten*, or some such,
to which he replied:

I didn't know they piled shit that high.

He later became a lawyer and QC, and was offered the position of judge a few years ago, but declined it, and last I heard (2 to 3 years ago) was still a practicing QC, no doubt making heaps of money.

Motivation

Aristotle was first to assert that our goal was to become more nearly what we were intended to be. Psychologists refer to this is as *self-actualization* and Maslow viewed this as striving to reach our potential (Lindzey at al., 1978). He defined two kinds of needs:

(a) *Basic needs* such as hunger, thirst, sex and security.

(b) *Metaneeds* such as achievement, beauty, goodness, justice, order and unity.

Maslow defined achievement as a basic need but the present authors prefer to classify it as a 'higher' or more human metaneed.

First, we must meet our basic or 'animal' needs. That done, we can turn our attention to the higher 'human' metaneeds, and thence self-actualization as a human being.

These needs provide *primary goals* that may motivate us towards *secondary goals* such as money in order to achieve them.

Most of our basic needs are *intrinsic motivations*. Of these, *competence motivation* is perhaps the most basic and is learnt by infants challenged by goals such as standing up in their cot or walking.

Most of our metaneeds are *learned goals.* Achievement motivation, for example, can be inculcated by parents or teachers. *Social motivations* such as justice are also acquired in this way.

Some studies have found, however, little correlation between motivation and efficiency of learning, suggesting that genetics and practice are more important factors.

What has this got to do with schools?

One's motivations will, of course, greatly influence how well one performs at school and in later life, and teachers should be at pains, of course, to motivate students, for example by encouraging and rewarding effective study and good results, a personal example being given earlier of being let out of class early for finishing tests quickly.

Such positive thinking is far more effective than the traditional negative approaches to discipline which usually involved physical punishment/abuse.

Goal setting

As with the well-known teacher expectancy effect, goal setting and positive thinking play an important role in many other activities in life. In sports, for example, coaches do their utmost to encourage positive thinking and goal setting, and much psychological research has been done in this area, Sykes (1995) citing several examples of doctorates in education being granted for dissertations with such titles as:

"The use of goal setting and positive self-modelling to enhance self-efficiency and performance for the basketball free-throw shot" for a PhD at the University of Maryland.

Preferably, however, goals should not be 'commanded, but should be 'suggested', and should be personal goals, not 'institutional' ones.

Conclusions

As I have argued in many books, including *The Education System* (Mohr, 2019b), *The Pretentious Persuaders* (Mohr, 2012a, 2014c) and *The Brainwashed* (Mohr & Fear, 2016), that 12 years at school is much too long for all but the slowest of students, and 10 years should be sufficient for average students, and perhaps 8 for the brightest students.

Where possible, children should start school at four, contingent upon their having spent a year at kindergarten and, perhaps, passing some elementary physical and verbal tests. Then those deemed not ready for grade 1 would be diverted into a 'preparatory' grade at the school.

Then there should be only ten grades, six of these primary, and four secondary.

In this the final four secondary years would remain much the same as now and the preceding curriculum would be fitted into six rather than the usual eight years.

This condensation can easily be achieved by:
(a) Making kindergarten compulsory.
(b) Making unnecessary 'frills' optional and after school hours.
(c) Ensuring more efficient teaching and learning occurs.
(d) Deferring some of the curriculum in subjects like history to optional subjects in later school, if not tertiary, years.

In fact, bearing in mind that we forget most of what we learn at school, a modest shortening of the number of years at school by only two makes good sense. Remembering that kindergarten is effectively a year of schooling, in fact, the decrease in years of schooling is but one, a very modest change bearing in mind that gifted students have often been able to complete postgraduate degrees at 12 years of age.

As for hierarchical problems in schools, I have given several examples of psychological, physical and sexual abuse by teachers that I witnessed while I was at school.

I have also given examples of bullying and sexual abuse by students witnessed while I was at school.

No doubt this is why my father, a brilliant student who won a scholarship to the same private school I was sent to, won a prize as the best student at Melbourne University, and also a prestigious 1851 scholarship to Cambridge, was given Judo lessons while at school, presumably so that he could deal with bullies by threatening them with 'the chop'.

From the discovery of the skeletons of babies dating back several hundred years under ancient monasteries, up to the plague of sexual abuse that has occurred in Catholic and other religious schools, the history of hypocrisy and corruption in religious organizations is horrible, to say the least.

Recent examples reported in the media include:

(1) Ongoing reports of Catholic priests being convicted of sexual abuse in schools.

(2) Two reports in *The Weekend Australian* of February 17-18 of: (a) Four members of a circus school who

- - *allegedly raped, detained and abused three young boys.*

(b) The arrest and trial of the female principal of a Melbourne Jewish school for girls in Israel for sexual abuse: *Her grandmotherly demeanour belies the crimes she is accused of in Melbourne, where she left in ruins the lives of more than a dozen students, all girls, after making a midnight dash for the airport and finding refuge in Israel's insular Haredi community nearly a decade ago.*

These days, of course, cyber bullying is also a major issue which may affect school-age children very badly, and all too frequently teenagers commit suicide because of it

Indeed, in February 2018 a major Australian law firm called for the government to allow cyber-bullying victims to claim damages from both their abusers and platforms like Facebook.

The bottom line here, therefore, is that hierarchical abuses, whether physical, sexual and psychological, have to this very day been all too common in schools.

3. Schools

CHAPTER 4

RELIGION

Men never do evil so completely and cheerfully
as when they do it from religious conviction.
Blaise Pascal (1623 – 1662), *Pensées* (1669), no. 894.

Religion has always been the wound, not the bandage.
Dennis Potter (1935 – 1994), British playwright,
Observer, London, April 10, 1994: 'Sayings of the Week.'

Ignorance, Fables and Lies

From the outset religions involved ignorance and superstition, understandable perhaps when primitive man was still developing language and applying it to the bewilderingly complex array of objects he found surrounding him. Thus the concept of spirits that inhabit and control us, and of a host of spirits that do likewise with other things in nature, provided a crude understanding of the world.

It was to be expected, however, that our understanding of the world would evolve, with time. Indeed, it did, but very slowly at first. After all, my grandmother was born only 11 years after Darwin published his theory of evolution. Since that time the industrial revolution, and the scientific revolution that underpinned it, have accelerated greatly.

Corruption and dishonesty began to appear in religions with the appearance of shamans claiming communication with spirits and using the same sorts of tricks that magicians use today to fool their audiences (Clark, 2012). This was, perhaps, the original example of the saying 'power corrupts' which is epitomized in the quotation that opens this chapter.

Then, of course, as communities grew, so too did the power of religious and community leaders. As monarchs appeared, they usually chose to identify with, and often assume leadership of a particular religion. Indeed, sometimes they went so far as to have themselves declared gods, as did Roman emperor Julius Caesar in 42BC.

This event, no doubt, encouraged the Jews to quickly find a new messiah to free the Holy City of Jerusalem from the Roman rule that had been established by Pompey in 63BC.

Then, Jesus having being born out of wedlock probably gave his mother and her relatives the idea of pronouncing him the son of God, which a 'voice from heaven' is supposed to have done when John the Baptist, Mary's cousin, baptized him when he was circa 30.

Then Jesus supposedly spent 40 days in the wilderness, resisting temptation by the devil three times, after which he found his first four disciples by the Sea of Galilee.

Such fables of visions and voices from God occur again and again as giving yet another 'religion starter' the status of prophet, further examples being (some dates approximate):

- 1300 BC: Moses commanded by God to lead the Hebrews, and his communications with God atop Mount Sinai.

- 620 BC: Zoroaster's vision of Ahura Mazda (creator God), the basis of Zoroastrianism or Mazdaism.

- 440 BC: Buddha's visions while sitting under a tree.

- 610: Muhammad's command from heaven "Recite!"

- 1496: Guru Nanek's (founder of Sikhism) visions.

- 1744: Swedenborg's religion-founding visions.

- 1827: Joseph Smith's (founder of Mormonism) visions.

- 1852: Baha Ullah's (founder of Baha'i) visions.

- 1930: Wallace Fard's (founder of Nation of Islam) visions.

As with Jesus, in the case of Moses there was a political motive for his visions, namely to lead the Hebrews out of captivity in Egypt.

In the case of Muhammad there may also have been a political motive (Encarta Encyclopedia 1999):

Muhammad probably heard Christians and Jews expound their religious views at commercial fairs in Mecca, and, troubled by the questions they raised, he periodically withdrew to a cave outside Mecca to meditate and pray for guidance. During one of these retreats he experienced a vision of the archangel Gabriel, who proclaimed him a prophet of God.

His motive, of course, is similar to that which Jesus had, namely to proclaim a new religion which would help conquer his 'holy city', Mecca, exactly what he and his followers did in 1630. Then, as with Christianity, the Muslim faith was spread widely, much conflict often being used to subdue other religions.

That so many people would follow religions is understandable in primitive times when there was not much else to do in one's spare time. After all, the world's first printed book only appeared in 868, this being the *Diamond Sutra,* a translation of a short Buddhist script. Before then, of course, scriveners laboured hard in monasteries to produce a few copies of religious texts such as the Bible, these being used by priests to brainwash the public. Then, just as children believe fairy tales, ancient people believed religious fables.

Circa 2000BC the Babylonians had knowledge of the Pythagorean Theorem and solved quadratic equations. Pythagoras (c.580 – 500BC) and scholars of that period, however, postulated a spherical earth moving in a circular orbit about a central fire. It was not until 1984, however, that the Vatican declared that the inquisition had been incorrect in convicting Galileo of heresy in 1632 for supporting the Copernican view of the universe.

So it is that religion still fills ignorant men's minds with superstition and prejudice, leading to results such as the two centuries of conflict between Protestants and Catholics during the Reformation, and ongoing conflict between Sunnis and Shiite Muslims in the world today.

Religious Terrorism

There has been conflict between Catholics and Protestants in Northern Ireland for centuries. The roots of the problem go back to the province of Ulster where the Roman Catholic earls of Tyrone rebelled against English rule circa 1600. They were forced to flee and most of their land was confiscated by King James I who gave it to Protestant Scotch, Welsh and English settlers. Ulster was further colonized by Cromwell in the mid-17th century and in the early 20th century its opposition to Irish Home Rule led to the formation of Northern Ireland.

Since then there has often been conflict between Catholics and Protestants, this reaching a peak in the 1960s and 1970s when the Irish Republican Army (IRA) used terror tactics against Ulster Protestants and British military forces which resulted in 3000 people being killed before the 1994 ceasefire. Sinn Fein, the political branch of the IRA, was founded in 1902 and dominated the 1918 election. Its power diminished after 1926 but it participated in the peace talks on Northern Ireland in the 1980s and 1990s.

In 1995 the religious cult Aum Shinrikyo released deadly sarin nerve gas in the Tokyo subway, killing 12 people and injuring 5,500.

This small group isolated its converts and brainwashed them for long periods, and had ambitious plans which included obtaining nuclear weapons (Lifton, 1999).

Jewish radicals such as the Stern Gang and the Irgun Zvai Leumi resorted to terrorism against Arab communities and other groups during their struggle for an independent Israel in the 1940s.

The greatest Islamic grievance, of course, is the Israel issue. That much of the British mandate of Palestine was given by the UN to the Jews in 1948 was bad enough, but the territories later occupied by Israel after the 1967 war compounded this grievance greatly.

Thus in the 1960s Israel's adversaries began to use terrorism much more systematically. In the 1970s the Black September group, so-named after the expulsion of Palestinian guerrillas from Jordan in September 1970, carried out many attacks.

The Palestine Liberation Organization (PLO) has conducted commando and terrorist operations both within Israel and in other countries right up until the present day.

In response Israel has carried out actions against PLO and other targets outside Israel which can be considered as terrorism.

Islam is a very strict religion involving dress codes, countless prayers, and jihad against infidels, encouraging the most rabid Muslims sometimes, as the ongoing history of sectarian conflict continues in the Muslim world between Sunnis and Shiites, particularly in Iraq.

In the context of terrorism, Emerick (2011) states: *"Islam is misused as much as any other faith."* At present, however, rampant Islamists have undertaken terrorism to an extent unparalleled in history.

Islamists are those who derive an uncompromising interpretation from Islamic scripture. The central aim of Islamism is creation of a pan-Islamic caliphate that transcends national boundaries, an aim requiring elimination of the non-Muslim world (the West). The origins of Islamism go back to the Muslim Brotherhood founded by Hassan al Banna in Egypt in 1928. The movement rapidly spread, having 500,000 supporters and an armed wing in the 1940s that carried out many bombings and killings. It was officially banned after failing to assassinate President Nasser but still remains active in Egyptian politics on an unofficial basis.

The capitulation of Arab troops during the six-day war in 1967 brought an Islamist reaction, and in the 1970s and 1980s Islamists took part in the battle against the Soviet Union in Afghanistan, and in the Lebanese civil war.

Islamists such as Osama Bin Laden were incensed by non-Muslim troops being based in Saudi Arabia during the First Gulf War of 1990-1991, believing it had become a puppet of the West.

With the formation of al-Qa'ida and numerous other Islamic terrorist groups there has been a spate of Islamic terrorist activity, notable examples over the last couple of decades including:

➢ In 1988 a bomb destroyed a Pan American Flight over Lockerbie, Scotland, killing all 259 people on board and 11 on the ground. Subsequently two Libyan agents were charged with the crime and one of them convicted.
➢ Fundamentalist terrorism directed against the socialist government of Algeria led to virtual civil war in the 1990s.
➢ Bombing of New York's World Trade Centre in 1993.*
➢ Bombing of US embassies in Kenya and Tanzania in 1998 with the loss of 224 lives.*
➢ Bombing of the USS Cole in 2000.*
➢ Attacks on the US by three hijacked planes on September 11, 2001 which cost almost 3,000 lives.*
➢ A car bomb attack in Bali on a bar popular with Westerners that killed almost 200 people in 2002.
➢ The November 2003 Istanbul truck bomb attacks.*
➢ Chechen rebels took 800 hostages in a Moscow theatre. Russian troops gassed the building, resulting in 200 deaths.
➢ The 2004 Khobar massacre.*
➢ Train & bus attacks in Spain & England in 2004 and 2005.*
➢ June 2008 car bombing of Danish embassy in Pakistan.*
➢ The September 2008 truck bombing of the Marriot Hotel in Pakistan.*
➢ The 2009 Khost CIA bombing killed 8 agents.*
➢ 2003-2010: many bombings in Iraq.*
➢ 2010-2018: circa 50% of Iraq and Syria overtaken by Islamic State (IS), most of that territory having now been reclaimed thanks largely to Russian and US intervention.

* = known or believed to be due to al-Qa'ida.

Besides the globally active al-Qa'ida, there are many other terrorist organizations around the world, most of them Muslim, including:

➢ Iraq and Syria: Islamic State (ISIS, originally called ISIL = Islamic State in Levant).
➢ Gaza and the West Bank: Hamas and the PLO.
➢ Israel: Kahane Chai (Kach).
➢ Lebanon: Hezbollah.
➢ Iraq: QJBR (al-Qa'ida in Iraq).
➢ Afghanistan: the Taliban
➢ Bangladesh: Harkat-ul-Jihad al-Islami (HUJI-B)
➢ Sri Lanka: Liberation Tigers of Tamil Eelam (LTTE).
➢ India: Indian Mujahideen (IM).
➢ Japan: Aum Shinrikyo.
➢ Pakistan: Harakat ul-Mujahadin (HUM).
➢ South-East Asia: al-Jama'a al-Islamiya (JI).
➢ Uzbekistan: Islamic Jihad Union (IJU).
➢ Somalia: Al-Shabaab.
➢ Uganda: Lord's Resistance Army.
➢ UK & Ireland: Continuity IRA (CIRA), Real IRA (RIRA).
➢ Greece: Revolutionary Organization 11 November.
➢ Turkey: Revolutionary People's Liberation Party/Front.
➢ Spain: Euskadi Ta Askatasuna (ETA).
➢ Colombia: FARC & the National Liberation Army (ELN).
➢ Peru: Shining Path (SL).
➢ Iraq and Syria: circa 50% taken over by Islamic State (IS) circa 2015, most of that territory having now been reclaimed thanks largely to Russian and US intervention.

Osama Bin Laden, of course, had been on the side of the Americans in helping the Taliban fight the occupying Russian forces in Afghanistan in the 1980s (Nojumi, 2002).

In the 1990s, enraged at the presence of US troops in Saudi Arabia during the Persian Gulf War, he and his associates in al-Qa'ida turned on the Americans, bombing several US embassies in the Middle East and Africa, and planning the multiple plane attacks of September 11, 2001.

An article in *The Australian* newspaper on 3 November 2004 reported that Bin Laden had vowed in one of his regularly released videotapes to send the US broke. He claimed that every dollar spent by al-Qa'ida on terrorist strikes had cost the US $1 million in economic damage. He estimated the US deficit at more than $US 1 trillion.

Al-Qa'ida's attacks often involve simultaneous suicide attacks on neighbouring targets. Its aim is removal of all foreign influences in Muslim countries and creation of a world-wide Islamic caliphate. As Salafist jihadists they oppose man-made laws yet ignore any religious scripture which might forbid the murder of civilians and bloody conflict.

Al-Qa'ida is intolerant of non-Sunnis, regards liberal Muslims as heretics, and has carried out numerous sectarian attacks, for example the Sadr City bombings and the April 2007 Baghdad bombings, and such activities continue.

Al-Qa'ida operates through unregulated banks and the 9/11 Commission report estimated that it needed $30M/year for its operations which include military training, finance, operations management, and a media division.

Another Muslim terrorist group is Al-Jama'a al-Islamiya (JI). Established circa 1969, this Islamist terrorist organization is dedicated to establishing an Islamic caliphate in Southeast Asia. JI has cells in Thailand, Singapore, Malaysia, the Philippines, Irian Jaya and Australia, and has connections with al-Qa'ida and the Moro Islamic Liberation Front.

JI was responsible for the 2000 bombing of the Jakarta Stock Exchange, the 2002 Bali bombing, the 2003 JW Marriott hotel bombing in Jakarta, the 2004 Australian embassy bombing in Jakarta, the 2005 Bali bombing, and the 2009 JW Marriott and Ritz-Carlton hotel bombings in Jakarta. JI was also responsible for dozens of bombings in the southern Philippines, usually with the help of the Abu Sayyaf Group (ASG).

Several JI leaders have been captured in the last decade.

The Taliban, a fundamentalist Islamic political movement, spread into Afghanistan where it formed government in 1996 but gained diplomatic recognition only from Pakistan, Saudi Arabia and the United Arab Emirates.

The Taliban strictly interpret sharia law, limiting the rights of women. The top leadership group is the Quetta Shura, based since circa 2001 in the city of Quetta in the Balochistan province of Pakistan.

Members of Pakistan's Inter-Services Intelligence (ISI) are believed to have attended meetings of the Quetta Shurah and supported the Taliban.

In 2009 the Pakistani government acknowledged the existence of Quetta Shurah for the first time, and since that time several of its members have been detained at various locations in Pakistan.

Nevertheless, the mayhem, sectarian conflict and terrorism so ubiquitous in the Middle East continues, sometimes spreading to India, Europe, the US, Indonesia and elsewhere.

The Muslim brotherhood is the oldest, and one of the largest and most influential Islamic movements. According to Wikipedia, it is the largest political opposition organization in many Arab states.

It was founded by Islamic scholar and schoolteacher Hassan al-Banna in Egypt in 1928 as a Pan-Islamic religious, social, and political movement. The movement has often been involved in political violence, including assassination of a number of political opponents. Indeed, Egypt's just-ousted President Morsi is a member of the brotherhood, there being much political unrest as a result of his removal from power.

The Muslim brotherhood is financed by its members who allocate a portion of their income to it, many of these members being in Saudi-Arabia and other oil-rich countries.

Finally, Islamic State or ISIS has in the last decade been the most active and growing terrorist organization, though in the last couple of years concerted efforts by combined government, Kurdish and other forces have recaptured most of the territory once held in Iraq and Syria by IS.

Religious Corruption

In ancient times 'religion starters' did so for political reasons, Moses, Christ and Muhammad being notable examples, in each case their real cause being escaping domination by another culture. More recent examples are the Maori Ratana Church, Rastafarianism, and Nation of Islam.

Religion is also, of course, big business, and as noted several times in previous chapters, many a self-proclaimed prophet starting a new religion was well aware of this.

People spruiking a religion, whether new or old, are selling a product of sorts, so why is this corrupt?

The answer is that they are selling a pack of fables and lies sold as truth. The sheer multiplicity of religions is testament to the implicit dishonesty of religion itself, the endless arguments and conflicts about sometimes minor differences between religions being convincing evidence that, in the end, all religions are telling lies for the most part.

The more contemplative religions such as Confucianism or Buddhism, which place less emphasis on dogma about some god or other and countless rules, are perhaps less dishonest, and historically they seem to have caused much less harm in the way of conflict and terrorism.

Sometimes people who start religions came from a well-to-do background from which they might have learnt the sort of dishonesty required to extract money from gullible people, examples being Confucius and Buddha.

In other cases they were poverty stricken people, for example A.C. Bhaktivedanta, the founder of the Hare Krishna movement, who arrived in New York with only $50 and began chanting on a sidewalk, the small trickle of money that brought no doubt turning into a flood as the movement grew.

Such religious founders as Joseph Smith (Mormonism) and Ron Hubbard (Scientology) were also obviously bent on making money (Mohr & Fear, 2015).

Another example was Oral Roberts, a Pentecostal preacher who in the 1950s reached wide audiences through radio and television. He founded a publishing company and Oral Roberts University in Tulsa, from which he retired as president in the early 1990s, having become known for his luxurious way of life.

A further example was the conviction in 1988 of popular television evangelist Jim Bakker for fraud.

Indeed, when all is said and done, the business of religion is to make money and religious organizations cannot survive without it. Today, many major religions are fabulously wealthy, having landholdings around the world of incalculable value and on which they are usually exempt from taxes.

Indeed, the excessive power and wealth of the Roman Catholic Church was a major factor in the discontent that sparked the Reformation in Europe.

Similarly, taxation inequalities in Muslim countries have often been a cause of conflict.

The excessive power and wealth of the Catholic Church in France, and its association with the aristocracy, were in part the cause of the French Revolution of 1789. The transformed society that followed confiscated the church's vast land holdings, and by 1790 religious orders had been dissolved, the remaining clergy being made elected state employees. Many priests who refused to take an oath of allegiance to the state were forbidden from preaching, and during the Reign of Terror in 1793/4 many priests were massacred.

Today the major corruption issue facing the Christian Church is that of child sexual abuse, the Catholic Church being the main offender, perhaps because of its greater number of religious schools and hostels for children. In Australia there has been outrage in recent years over disclosures that the activities of paedophile priests have been hidden from the public for decades, offending priests being discretely moved to new locations to continue preaching and offending.

Thus, according to Anne Roche Muggeridge (1986):

*A miracle is certainly called for if the Catholic Church
is not to disappear from places where it survived or
regrouped after the Reformation, or triumphantly established
itself anew in missionary territory. It has already disappeared
from tens of millions of hearts which only lately were
committed to it in countries where, on the surface,
it still exhibits an imposing physical presence.*

The major issue facing Muslim religion leaders is the need for them to speak out strongly against Islamist terrorism. Otherwise, it seems likely that daily sectarian Muslim conflict will continue for decades in several countries, particularly Iraq.

Conclusions

In 1650 Anglican bishop James Ussher used the Bible to calculate that the world had been created during the night preceding October 23, 4004BC (Cooke, 2011).

Despite such absurdities, some 2 billion people are said to be Christians today, though I suspect that less than 10% of that number practice the faith to any real extent. Then, however, simply praying regularly will hardly achieve anything concrete. More nearly it is a waste of time and money, as have been the massive temples erected for countless religions for millennia. Donating money to charity might be a better course, so long as a sufficient percentage of the money found its way to the needy, that being in some doubt in some charities with extensive hierarchical structures at the top of which executives may make unjustifiably large salaries, just as they do in other businesses.

Generally, therefore, religion makes no more sense than following a particular sporting team, and that can become akin to a religion in the case, for example, of the British Premier League. That too, however, is a waste of time and money, and one would be wiser and healthier if one exercised one's own body and brain sometimes.

As for the spate of terrorism around the world today, most of it Islamic in origin, the vengefulness of many passages of the Christian Bible, for example reference to *"the Book of the Wars of the LORD"* in Numbers 21:14, is, like much else, repeated in the Koran, for example (Dawood, 2006):

4.74: *Let those who would exchange the life of this world for the hereafter, fight for the cause of God; whoever fights for the cause of God, whether he dies or triumphs, on him We shall bestow a rich recompense.*

47.4+: *When you meet the unbelievers in the battlefield strike off their heads and, when you have laid them low, bind your captives firmly. Then grant them their freedom or take a ransom from them, until War shall lay down her burdens.*

Thus shall you do. Had God willed, He would Himself have punished them; [but He has ordained it thus] that HE may test you, the one by the other.

As for those who are slain in the cause of God, He will not allow their works to perish. He will vouchsafe them guidance and ennoble their state; He will admit them to the Paradise He has made known to them.

He we see the invitation to conflict, and the promise of martyrdom, that has encouraged the countless suicide bombings that still occur in the Muslim world today, particularly in Iraq.

Much of that conflict is sectarian between the more fundamentalist Shiite minority and the Sunni majority, and is to some extent comparable to the many decades of conflict between Christian Protestant sects and the Roman Catholic Church that occurred during the Reformation.

Globally, little more than 10% of Muslims are Shiites, but nevertheless Shia Muslims are in the majority in Iran, Iraq, Bahrain, Azerbaijan, and perhaps Yemen. There are also large Shia communities in Afghanistan, India, Kuwait, Lebanon, Pakistan, Qatar, Syria, Turkey, Saudi Arabia and the UAE. In several of these countries considerable conflict between Shiites and Sunnis continues.

Perhaps a bottom line on key issues concerning religion today is found in the 2008 book *Why There Almost Certainly Is No God* by Richard Dawkins.

In this he talks of the "legendary" brutality which the Christian Brothers and the "sadistically cruel" Catholic nuns brought to education in Ireland. Myself, I once had a wife who attended a Catholic school in Australia who also recalled such brutality.

Asked after a lecture in Dublin about reported sexual abuse by Catholic priests in Ireland, Dawkins replied along the lines that "horrible as sexual abuse no doubt was, the damage was arguably less than the long-term psychological damage inflicted by bringing a child up Catholic in the first place."

He recalled that he received a round of enthusiastic applause from the audience.

A more important form of child abuse occurs in almost all homes. That is, more often than not parents try to direct children into some area of interest of theirs (the parents), for example musicians often appear to be trying to bring their children up as musicians almost from the outset. This, I would contend, is child mental abuse because the child should be taught with some breadth so that, in later life, there is more likelihood of it finding a vocation in line with its abilities, interests, and ambitions, as well as current conditions and opportunities in society.

In addition, very few parents provide the early teaching by 'group modelling' that research cited by Vance Packard found greatly increased their intelligence (Packard, 1978; Mohr et al., 2017). Even on a one-on-one basis, if a child is taught numeracy, for example, sooner rather than later, that will give them a head start in that area by the time they go to school. Such early teaching should begin by the age of two, if not much earlier. The author, for example, recalls his wife, a kindergarten teacher, assertively telling him that you can't teach a child of less than 3 to count to 3. Such a view is, of course, absurd and ignorant in the extreme.

Indeed, my guess is that just '1 + 1 + 1' hours of early teaching in counting, and then perhaps in addition, would give toddlers a head start. Here '! + 1 +1' refers to three separate hours of instruction, perhaps about a week apart, this idea relying in part on the notion of the 'Three Hit' theory of advertising, and in part on the assumption of a hyperbolic learning curve (Mohr, 2012a).

My point here, instead of turning young children into potential geniuses from the outset, we turn them into consumer zombies following a particular religion, a particular sporting team, and buying whatever advertising and social learning suggests is appropriate, trendy or 'cool'. This, I contend, is a form of child mental abuse that we should do well to avoid.

Finally, a recent example of the hierarchical conflict between religions were media reports on 26th February 2018 that the Israeli government was being criticized by the leaders of three Christian movements active in Jerusalem for excessive taxes and interference, claiming that this was occurring to encourage them to leave Israel.

In Appendix D the new religion Mohronism, which is based on the 10 laws of Table 1.1., is discussed, and it might be hoped that many people will adopt this religion and thus improve their understanding of the increasingly hierarchical modern world.

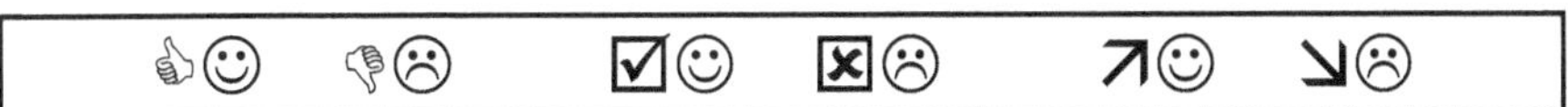

4. Religion

CHAPTER 5

ADVERTISING & PROPAGANDA

> *The professional politician can sympathize with the professional advertiser ... both must resign themselves to a low public estimation of their veracity and sincerity.*
> Enoch Powell, US General, attributed 1965.

The purpose of advertising

Nowadays there are massive and highly hierarchical media and advertising industries devoted to turning us into consumer zombies hoping that the products we buy will improve our lives. The main objectives of ads, in approximate order of priority, are to:

1. Make the brand name familiar.
2. To give the brand a distinct image.
3. Attribute at least one key attribute to the brand.
4. Associate the product with certain usages.
5. To convince us that this brand is the best (for us).
6. To persuade us that we should buy the product.

To meet these objectives ads will involve slogans, demonstrations, comparisons, testimonials, and repetition.

Comparisons, of course, are usually of price, but sometimes also some sort of semi-official rating, for example safety ratings for cars.

By way of style, ad types include basic facts, 'mood', feel-good, social setting, slice-of-life, humour, fantasy, hard-sell, and anxiety/danger/risk. An example of risk type ads are those for household insect sprays.

To make ads more appealing attractive female models, smooth talkers, or sports and movie stars are often used to promote products (Packard, 1963).

To give ads more authority statements by experts or organizations may be used to help persuade us.

To make purchase more imperative ads will scream of huge price reductions for a limited time, huge bargains for as little as two days only, and buy on the never-never deals with no interest for a year or two, if not longer.

In their efforts to get you in ads will go to ends which range from boring to extremely irritating, from dull and routine to the heights of excess and absurdity, from mere suggestion to downright pleading, and from slight desperation to screaming at us to buy the product.

More subtle are 'advertorials' of bought space in newspapers or conspicuous 'product placement' in movies.

For maximum tedium there are half-hour infomercials on afternoon or late night TV which sometimes repeat night after night, week after week, and year after year. In these and most other types of ads there are often trial offers, bonus products for quick purchase etcetera.

In monetary economic theory aggregate demand and aggregate supply are equated to obtain $MV = PQ$ where M is the amount of money in circulation, V is its velocity of circulation (in transactions per year), P is the price of goods in circulation, and Q is the quantity of goods in circulation per year. Then if, for example, we increase Q we should advertise to ensure an increase in V or turnover.

One way of maintaining higher levels of production is through planned obsolescence of which there are 3 types:
[1] Quality: the product wears out in some planned manner.
[2] Function: a new product performs the function better.
[3] Desirability: the product is 'restyled', making the old version seem obsolete.

In the context of war [1] corresponds to a failed campaign, [2] to a new alternative plan, and [3] to restructuring of the forces to be used in the new plan that politicians 'sell' to the public.

Types of advertising

The main objectives of brand advertising and the various types of ads used to achieve them are summarized in the Table 5.1 (O'Guinn et al., 2006).

Table 5.1. Types of advertisement.

Objective	Type of advertisement
Promote brand recall	Repetition Slogans & jingles
Link a key attribute to the brand name	Unique selling proposition (USP)
Convince consumers to buy a product or service through high-engagement arguments	Reason-why ads Hard-sell ads Comparison ads Testimonials. Demonstration Advertorials. Infomercials
Instil brand preference	Feel-good ads Humour ads Sexual-appeal ads.
Scare consumer into action	Fear-appeal ads
Change behaviour by inducing anxiety	Anxiety ads Social anxiety ads
Suggest a feeling or mood when product used	Transformational ads (for long term usage)
Situate the brand socially	Slice-of-life ads Light-fantasy ads Product placement (movies etc.) Short Internet films
Define the brand image	Ads relying mainly on images, not words or argument

In addition, manufacturers and retailers periodically advertise bargains and "buy now!" special deals.

Targeting advertising

Maslow defined two kinds of needs (Lindzey at al., 1978): (a) *Basic needs* such as hunger, thirst, sex and security.

(b) *Metaneeds* such as achievement, beauty, goodness, justice, order and unity, most of which are learned goals.

First, we must meet our basic or 'animal' needs.

Then we can turn our attention to the higher metaneeds which provide 'self-actualization' and meaning to life.

Both types of needs provide *primary goals* that may involve *secondary goals* such as money in order to achieve them.

Advertising usually targets the metaneeds of the *ego*. A Coke ad, for example, is not designed to remind you that you may be thirsty. If so, you might rush to the fridge and grab whatever drink you can find to satisfy that thirst. No, a Coke ad makes it look 'cool' to drink Coke with your friends and being 'cool' is a metaneed! So next day a young boy will want to be 'cool' when hanging out with his friends so they will all drink Coke and act foolishly, just like the actors in some Coke and Pepsi ads

Here again we see the downside of advertising, namely that increasingly ambitious executives will stop at nothing to sell their product, even if it has to brainwash the young into acquiring both bad behaviour and bad teeth.

In marketing to children, of course, familiar cuddly looking cartoon figures are often displayed on packaging and used to speak the lines of TV ads. Here, however, ads usually target the *Id,* the basic 'animal' personality that has basic needs like hunger.

Young children tend to eat in smaller doses and often so that almost any time they are awake is a good one to put a picture of confectionery in front of them.

One of the best examples of brainwashing, however, is the use of *consumer panels* of children in marketing research. The children are often asked what they will say and do to persuade parents to buy them the product.

Finally, the extent to which children are exposed to advertising is incredible:

- - *"it is estimated that children between two and 11 years old may see over 20,000 advertisements in a year,"* (O'Guinn et al., 2006).

Advertising, therefore, will persuade someone in your family, even if it doesn't persuade you!

In marketing to adults well-known sporting identities are often used to market such things as golf clubs, household appliances, cars and houses. Indeed, this was the basis of Mark McCormack's very successful IMG and one of his earliest clients was Greg Norman who was marketed as 'The Shark'. IMG made an awful lot of money from TV ads (McCormack, 1986).

When politicians seek to prepare us for yet another war they appeal to our *basic need* of security by instilling fear of the party against whom war is being considered, 'fear type ads' being a common form of advertising, a common example being ads for insect sprays.

Push and pull marketing

Some marketing campaigns use *push strategies* which concentrate on the availability of products. In this case the ads are 'basic' and concentrate on telling you the product name and where to get it. Examples of such ads on TV are

➢ A presenter reads a script while holding the product in question up in front of the camera.

➢ Ads with only text messages and a voice-over.

➢ Semi-humorous ads which sometimes use cartoon characters to present their message.

➢ Ads targeting children which involve cuddly characters and fantasy scenes and the like.

➢ Ads for junk food which play on having a high 'reward/effort' ratio (Govoni et al., 1988). That 50 million people a day eat McDonald's stuff is testament enough to the success of their advertising.

➤ Ads where the reader just about screams at you not to miss some bargain sale or to go to some cheap store.

Advertisements for 'basic' food, junk food, confectionery, clothing and home appliances are usually of the 'push' type.

Marketing campaigns often use *pull strategies* which promote the product in order to attract buyers. In this case the ads concentrate on 'image' to attract the audience to the product and the product name is secondary and *associated* with the imagery. Examples of this sort of ad on TV are:

➤ Sophisticated ads that show the product in 'classy' surroundings with actors dressed stylishly.
➤ "Laid back' ads were the presenter extols the virtue of the product with, for example, an island resort as a backdrop.
➤ Ads that use glamorous people such as movie stars as actors.

This type of advertising is usually used for higher priced or more 'up market' products, including fashion clothing, cosmetics, expensive furniture, luxury cars and overseas holidays.

One of the most important 'levers' in advertising, undoubtedly, is *keeping up with the Jones's*. This is exploited heavily in marketing cars and new gadgets of which the mobile phone is the supreme example at present.

Another powerful inducement is selling on the 'never-never', for example with no repayments for a year.

Ubiquitous advertising

Today advertising is literally everywhere. On TV in Australia there used to be regulations limiting the amount of advertisements per hour to something bearable. Now there seem like 20 minutes or more of ads per hour at times. Worse still, owing to the increasing cost of TV advertising time a truly bewildering string of ads appears in each ad break, sometimes up to about a dozen.

It is almost as bad on radio where there are sometimes as many as half a dozen ads at once on the higher rating commercial stations.

Junk mail from supermarkets and other retail chains has reached epidemic proportions. Other 'direct marketing' is done by phone and is increasingly irritating, often involving requests to complete lengthy market research surveys over the phone.

In addition, free local papers almost totally full of advertisements are also stuffed into millions of letterboxes in major cities.

Trams, trains and buses carry plenty of ads, as do train stations and tram and bus stops. Taxis and trucks all carry signage, as do many vehicles belonging to small businesses.

Shopping strips are becoming more and more cluttered with advertising signs above the shops, and sandwich boards and often products on the footpath.

Shopping malls are filled with advertising and more and more stalls with spruikers have appeared in them.

Sporting grounds carry more and more advertising and sporting teams now carry prominent advertising on their clothing.

Casual clothing often comes complete with the brand name writ large upon it.

The Internet is full of advertising, of course, some of it of a lurid nature.

Then there is the despicable practice of placing confectionery and soft drinks near the checkouts at supermarkets, resulting in many a tantrum as young children taken shopping throw a tantrum to get another dose of perhaps the first 'drug' of addiction, sugar.

Perhaps the most predatory advertiser of all, Coca Cola, has its vending machines just about everywhere, including pubs and clubs, office buildings, stations and heaven knows where else (they are probably there too!).

Propaganda

Politicians, of course, use increasing amounts of advertising before elections, along with a good deal of propaganda to promote the political party they represent.

Wordweb 6 dictionary's entry for propaganda is:

1. Information that is spread for the purpose of promoting some cause.

"The propaganda brainwashed many people."

As with priests coming from on high from a pulpit, politicians do likewise from prominent lecterns, all too often in history decrying some opponent in another country and ultimately urging the already brainwashed, beer drinking young men to go to war.

Using religion

In the West Christianity has been heavily exploited in marketing for example by

➢ The use of religious symbols such as stylized crosses in the jewellery business.

➢ The confectionery industry makes heavy use of Easter to sell chocolate. Bakeries join in by selling Easter buns and industries such as the entertainment and travel industries rely heavily on the Easter holiday period.

➢ Christmas, of course, is a bonanza for business and has become almost completely devoid of its original meaning. Indeed, the image of Santa is actually from a 19th century cartoon of a rich robber baron with some of *his* toys which he certainly isn't going to give away (Solomon, 1992).

➢ Not too distantly related to this are Mother's Day and Father's Day which are also exploited by, and were probably created by, big business.

Religion also makes increasing use of TV and radio programs for promotion and in the US some religious sects have also spent large sums of money to employ advertising companies to run PR campaigns to promote themselves.

New trends in marketing

Some of the many new trends of late include:
1. Healthy foods, for example low fat products.
2. Recycling.
3. Pollution free and environmentally friendly products.
4. Diets and weight watching.
5. Alternative therapies. Of these the list grows daily:
   a. Aromatherapy.
   b. Herbal remedies.
   c. Acupuncture and Chinese medicine.
   d. Group therapy.
   e. Exercise therapy, for example Yoga and Pilates.
   f. Transcendental meditation.
   g. Reflexology - and so on.

In many large cities where house prices have tended to become unaffordable to new entrants to the market there is a growing 'live for today' approach to consumer spending and this is seen in:

1. The growing fast food industry, including take-away food and packaged 'heat only' meals sold in grocery stores.
2. Increasing diversity in consumption of alcohol.
3. Increasing use of drugs which may perhaps be encouraged by the legalization of marijuana.
4. Increasing use of leisure industries such as gambling.
5. Increasing use of restaurants by young childless workers (who may remain childless).
6. Greater spending by young and independent working women on cosmetics, clothes, jewellery and other beauty and fashion products including hair dressing and magazines.
7. Greater spending on magazines, videos, books, computer games, music and other home entertainment products.
8. Greater spending on cars, holidays and other major items by young childless couples or unattached persons.

In these and many other areas there seems to be a growing market which advertisers are busy exploiting. In some communities, however, one or two of the foregoing examples may be on the wane.

Persuasion or brainwashing?

Advertising is now so effective in reducing us to consumer zombies that the results are comparable to those of classical conditioning of laboratory animals. In other words, it goes a little, if not a long way beyond just *persuasion.*

Colloquially, at least, most would agree that it would be fair to use the term *brainwashing* but, strictly speaking, this originated in connection with 'conversion' of American prisoners by the Communists during the Korean war in the early 1950s when The Three D's Method (debilitation, dread, dependency) was used in this context (Mohr, 2014a).

Sometimes referred to in psychology as *thought reform*, brainwashing is an extreme form of *social influence* aimed at changing a person's views without their consent and often against their will.

To this end brainwashing combines three approaches:

(a) The **coercive** or 'just do it' approach which is concerned only with *compliance* and not with your attitudes and beliefs.

(b) The **persuasion** or 'do it because it will make you feel good, happy, healthy or successful' approach.

(c) The group-based **education** or 'do it because it's right' approach which is much used for *propaganda* campaigns.

The 1999 Encyclopaedia Britannica describes brainwashing as **coercive persuasion**, noting its origins as a means of political indoctrination. It also notes that it is a *"colloquial term"* usually *"applied to any technique designed to manipulate human thought or action - -."*

The third edition of the American Heritage Dictionary of the English Language gives two definitions of brainwashing:

1. *Intensive, forcible indoctrination, usually political or religious, aimed at destroying a person's basic convictions and attitudes and replacing them with an alternative set of fixed beliefs.*

2. *The application of a concentrated means of persuasion, such as an advertising campaign or repeated suggestion, in order to develop a specific belief or motivation.*

Indeed, most of us now associate brainwashing with persuasive advertising, political campaigns, mass media, and perhaps education, and media brainwashing is now widespread and a search for 'media brainwashing' on the Internet gives over 2 million results.

Just three examples of 'mass brainwashing' are:

[1] Claims that after WW1 psychological warfare research at the Tavistock Centre in London resulted in *"a theory of mass brainwashing, involving group experience, that could be used to alter the values of individuals, and through that induce, over time, changes in the axiomatic assumptions that govern society"* and that this work found application in both the UK and the US media (Wolfe, 1997).

US journalist Walter Lippmann was involved in Britain's WW1 'psywar' effort and was first to translate Sigmund Freud's work into English. In his 1922 book *Public Opinion* he wrote of the brainwashed masses:

". . . the mass of absolutely illiterate, of feeble minded grossly neurotic, undernourished and frustrated individuals is very considerable, much more considerable, there is reason to think, than we generally suppose. Thus a wide popular appeal is circulated among persons who are mentally children or barbarians, whose lives are a morass of entanglements, people whose vitality is exhausted, shut-in people, and people whose experience has comprehended no factor in the problem under discussion."

[2] Hitler had a well-oiled propaganda machine led by Joseph Goebbels, head of the Ministry of Public Enlightenment and Propaganda. Goebbels banned four Berlin newspapers in 1935.

[3] Claims that, because it supposedly misled the public over the 2001 WTC attacks, the American news media *"is the largest, most expensive, mass-brainwashing machine ever assembled in human history. It is a machine that so completely brainwashes the nearly 300 million Americans, that the Nazis' infamous Propaganda Minister Josef Goebbels would be envious"* (Wolfe, 2001).

Some of this is a bit 'over the top' but, if we consider that advertising has reduced most of us to brainwashed zombies wearing uncomfortable if not ridiculous jeans and carrying a mobile phone in one hand and a drink bottle or cigarette in the other, then 'brainwashing' is a serious issue.

And make no mistake, it must certainly be fair to call today's high pressure TV and radio advertising brainwashing. After all, in line with the original brainwashing of POWs, the victims are seated in a room and screamed at for hours each day with up to 10 ads blaring at them in each of all too frequent ad breaks (make that up to 50 ads per ad break in Brazil, according to Cateora (1996)).

After all, 50+ years ago advertising made about half the adult population take up smoking, a downright unpleasant practice in reality. If advertising can do that then it can make us do just about anything short of eating shit.

For this reason the term *brainwashing* is used frequently in connection with the increasingly ubiquitous, repetitive and persuasive advertising used today. It applies equally well, if not more so, to the propaganda put out by governments to justify their every action, including those involving war.

Mohr's Law of Bullshit

To summarize how advertising and propaganda work, it is timely to mention *Mohr's Law of Bullshit*, which is simply:

$$E = BS^2$$

where E = the efficiency of promulgation of the bullshit

B = the amount of bullshit in a particular message

S = the 'speed' at which the bullshit is released, this being number of repetitions of the message/unit time, for example 5 times weekly might suffice for a political message.

This important law does much to summarize how advertising works, that is, with frequent repetition being used to reach a wide audience, and to try and wear them into 'submission' via the 'CAB' mechanism discussed at the start of Chapter 13.

Mohr's Universal Law

Junk fills the time and space available.

This law is a generalization of Parkinson's Law, where the junk is work, and the Peter Principle, where the junk is the workers. Mohr's Law of Bullshit, of course, is closely related to this law.

Consider, for just a moment, the myriad of examples that immediately come to mind, just for example:

- Advertising.
- Cars.
- Clothes: irrational jeans, shoes, ties etc.
- Chemicals (cleaning compounds, cosmetics).
- Education: new courses are invented constantly and MBAs sold on everywhere (Kaufman, 2012; Mohr, 2017).
- Drugs, including cigarettes, booze and tranquilizers.
- Fads and gadgets.
- Food fads: from exotic to health diets.
- New games and sports.
- Graffiti.
- Health fads: exercise machines, plastic surgery etc.
- Junk food (burgers and Coke etc.).
- Music: endless reiteration of the old and the new.
- Movies: ditto.
- Magazines and newspapers.
- Plastic supermarket bags are filling parts of the world.
- Pornography.
- PCs & video games.
- Phones: mobile phones need no further comment.
- Radio: it wasn't always 24 hours of music, news or talk.
- Radios/CD players: they weren't always next to the bed, in the car or carried around with you.
- Roads and road furniture (signs, speed humps etc.).
- Shares (with everything being privatized etc.).
- Toys: from cradle to grave we have rattles, skateboards, roller blades and yachts for executives.
- TV: endless new 'soaps' and lots of cable channels to show all the old junk too.

Econobabble

Extending the equations for the LMS (liquid money supply) and ISE (interest sensitive expenditure) curves slightly, I showed that *increasing interest rates increases inflation,* as intuition suggests, but economists think the opposite, one reason why in recent books this proof is included in a chapter called *Econobabble* (Mohr, 2012a/2014a; Mohr & Fear, 2016; Mohr, 2019a). I also suggest a new law of supply and demand for manufactured goods (as distinct from commodities).

Conclusion

The extent to which man has been persuaded, one way or another, to adopt countless religions, periodically fight wars over them, and in modern times become mindless consumer zombies is regrettable.

We should all hope that we will never be subjected to *coercive persuasion* or *brainwashing* in its 'original' form but few of us would disagree that we are perhaps now subjected en masse to something far more subtle, far more effective and sometimes, at least, far more sinister and detrimental to both ourselves and, in turn, the horribly hierarchical world we live in.

A good example, perhaps, of propaganda on TV is that, as my youngest son told me circa 1995, some people in Australia call the TV channel SBS1 "The Hitler Channel", because it somewhat regularly broadcasts programs with, of course much justification, negative bias against Hitler, the most recent example I noticed being the program *Hitler's Secrets* at 5.30 PM on Sunday Feb. 18 and Feb. 25, 2018.

It would restore some balance, however, to the history of World War 2 if we were reminded that American companies played key roles in the Holocaust, for example IBM via its German subsidiary Demohag collecting the data on all the Jews living in Germany and Poland, and Du Pont making the Zyklon B gas used to kill millions of Jews in 'concentration camps'.

Indeed, Australia has for several years run what most people would agree are 'offshore' concentration camps to hold thousands of refugees, some of them for several years.

Regardless of the politics of a country, however, politicians will always mislead the brainwashed public, and good examples of some of the tactics used to cover-up failures in policy include:

[1] *Eye-wash:* deliberately selecting for evaluation only those aspects that 'look good' on the surface.

[2] *White-wash:* avoid any objective evaluation.

[3] *Submarine:* 'torpedo' the program.

[4] *Posture:* use evaluation as a 'gesture' only.

[5] *Postponement:* delay needed action by pretending to seek the 'facts'.

A good example of this occurs in an episode of the TV series *Yes Prime Minister* entitled "The Smokescreen" which begins with discussion of cuts in defence spending to allow for cuts in income tax, presumably to help garner votes.

Seeing this as difficult, the alternative idea of increasing revenue with huge taxes on smoking is had, but eventually dropped, by this time the issue of cuts in defence spending seemingly forgotten by the absent minded Jim Hacker and, presumably, the public also.

One positive aspect of advertising and propaganda, perhaps, is that it tends to give us hope, albeit false hope more often than not, as noted in a 4/10/2017 article in the Herald-Sun newspaper by former Victorian Premier Jeff Kennett headlined: *In football and politics, hope keeps us going.*

In the present book, however, it is suggested that, rather than become victims of advertising and propaganda, or in other words, 'hierarchical brainwashing' and 'top-down one-way' communication, we should concentrate more on realistic personal goals that might improve our lives, and perhaps those of others.

74

CHAPTER 6

EDUCATION AND TRAINING

Nothing in education is so astounding as the amount of ignorance it accumulates in the form of inert facts.
Henry Brooks Adams, The Education of Henry Adams (1907).

The aim of education is the knowledge not of facts but of values.
William Ralphe Inge, The Training of the Reason,
in A C. Benson (ed.), Cambridge Essays on Education (1917).

A brief history of education and training

Both Greek and Roman higher education placed much emphasis on equipping young men for roles as soldier-citizens able to play a part in and protect the state. Much of our modern philosophy and science, however, we owe to the teachers of those periods.

In the last stages of the classical Roman education system the Trivium (grammar, rhetoric, logic) and Quadrivium (music, astronomy, geometry, arithmetic) evolved and these were the basis of the medieval arts course in Europe centuries later.

Elsewhere, before the medieval period academic pursuits were largely limited to clerical education in monasteries.

By the twelfth century, however, a few *cathedral schools* were well established and that these began to place more emphasis on lay education by studying law, albeit mainly clerical law.

Gradually small schools were established in most towns where basic education in reading and writing was given for a few years. Few families could afford to pay for such education, however, and much of the population was semiliterate at best.

The thirteenth century saw the development of the first Universities, in Paris and Oxford, and the fourteenth and fifteenth centuries saw many new Universities established in Europe, increasingly with a more localized emphasis.

In these training was based on the three stages of membership of the craft-guilds: apprenticeship, journeymanship and mastership.

The ancient Trivium and Quadrivium, however, were still the framework of the arts course that all had to take before moving on to the higher courses of Theology, Medicine and Law.

A preliminary examination was required for entry to the first apprenticeship stage, one of study, at the end of which the student was examined for the bachelorship. The bachelor was then still under instruction but assigned certain courses of lectures. Then finally he was examined for his mastership, a licence to teach.

Some remnant of the guild basis of University education remains today in our use of such terms as Master Plumber and Master Builder.

In the fourteenth century the Inns of Court were established in England to meet a growing demand for teaching common law

In 1368 the master-surgeons formed a guild and in 1421 they allied with the physicians to petition the king for professional recognition and a teaching centre in London. Eventually, however, the Company of Barber-Surgeons was set up in 1540 with a monopoly of practice and teaching.

In both law and medicine, therefore, professions were raised in status and competence by initiatives of their members that were more responsive to the needs of society than academic institutions.

During the renaissance, as in biblical times, apprenticeship was the method of training in many trades. Da Vinci, for example, was apprenticed as an artist at age 14, completing his apprenticeship at around 20 years of age.

The seventeenth century saw interest in mathematics and science increase in the Universities while new colleges began training in technologies such as mineralogy and glassblowing. By its end, however, most scientific work in England took place in laboratories in London, not in Cambridge and Oxford.

The eighteenth century saw many new academies established which spread higher education to a middle class of trade and industry.

By this time Universities and colleges following these models had been established in America and many adventurous academics went there.

The school curriculum had grown to place more emphasis on mathematics and science and to educate students for an increasingly technological world.

As a result the number of years at school had grown from around six to ten or more to keep up with the requirements for University entrance.

In the nineteenth century Universities and colleges were established in other European colonies around the world, such as in Australia and India. These taught arts, education, law and medicine and remain much the same today.

In Australia, as elsewhere, colleges of technology have been raised to University status, many new courses have been added, and an increasingly large proportion of school leavers go on to University.

Finally, the purpose of tertiary education is, of course to train people for vocations such as teaching and medicine.

A few decades ago there was a considerable social gulf between the white collar worker and the blue collar worker so that progressing further at school was seen as a means of crossing that gulf.

To do even better one went to University to gain a diploma or licence to practice a profession.

Gradually, however, perceptions have changed and now, certainly, Einstein's joke about wishing he had been a plumber is better understood. Now carpenters and plumbers have late model four-wheel-drives, mobile phones and power tools that take both their occupation and their income to a level well above that of the most 'sub-professionals' like secretaries and, often, above that of most professionals.

Problems in education today

There are an increasing number of problems in education today in this and like countries. These include:

Lost opportunities

Children are at their most impressionable from the outset and advantage is not taken of this to begin more rational and formal training and education as soon as possible.

Too much time in day care

Today many children only a few months in age are left in long day care while their mothers resume work.

I believe that this is, in part, the result of family financial pressures arising from increasing consumerism in society and a drop in real standards of living as house prices have escalated in major cities.

It is also the result of high divorce rates in an increasingly amoral society in which we are encouraged to consume heavily advertised 'junk' products that are generally unnecessary, if not unhealthy, such as mobile phones, antiquated soft drinks and junk food. These have a negative effect upon children, affecting their development and educational progress.

I believe that a child of less than a year or two in age is too young to be incarcerated in day care. At the outset much of a child's learning occurs by *imprinting* and in the first year or two it is natural and best for this to occur between the infant and its parents and only a few other people.

Make more use of kindergarten

In Australia many children go to kindergarten at age three, usually for only a few hours, and then at age four daily. This is to be recommended but I would like education at this stage to be a little more formal and broader, for example with more emphasis on acquisition of rudimentary numerical skills.

At this stage too more use should be made of conditioning techniques to develop both character and skills, including good study skills and habits.

Less rote learning

In primary school, and thereafter, there is too much emphasis on rote learning and tests are often too frequent and negative in manner. By this I mean that every little mistake is emphasized and this goes on, sometimes throughout a consequently miserable life.

Rote learning should be replaced, as far as possible by more modern, informed, and efficient learning techniques such as 'Superlearning' and the latter was briefly discussed in chapter 2.

As for tests, a more positive and encouraging approach should be used and students should receive positive reinforcement for simply completing a test.

By this stage too, more emphasis should have been placed on developing general ability or IQ. Weiss and Mann (1978), for example, refer to a project in Milwaukee that found that children given more attention by the mother or a specially trained teacher, showed markedly higher IQ.

This, no doubt, is the reason that Vernon (1960) reports that, in families with more than one child, the eldest child has a slightly higher IQ on average. The youngest child in larger families, on the other hand, does not do too badly compared to those 'sandwiched' in the middle and perhaps most deprived of attention.

With the world aiming at ZPG, as the dwindling of finite resources dictates that it must, this will be less of a problem in the future but the results of such studies have obvious implications in early childhood education, if not education in general.

The media environment

As early as primary school, and certainly by secondary school, the modern environment that includes media such as radio and TV may have begun to play a part in a child's development.

All this leads to stereotyping, not altogether a bad thing, but all too often this results in bad habits, for example loutish behaviour by young boys emulating the acting of 'macho' movie or other media stars, or young girls being unduly concerned with their appearance, sometimes to the detriment of their mental or physical health.

In schools the result, of course, is increasing discipline problems and greater prevalence of bullying.

Packard (1978) points out that by the age of eighteen young people in the USA have seen and heard about eighteen hundred hours of TV ads, the equivalent of a year of thirty-five hour weeks. Including radio and other ads might nearly double that. If the total time that they spend with TV and other media is considered, however, the total will be comparable to the total time spent at school.

Packard gives a quotation from *Advertising Age:*

"If you truly want big sales, you will use the child as your assistant salesman. He sells, he nags, until he breaks down the sales resistance of his mother or father."

Thus advertising companies have small theatres in which they test commercials.

Others have play-area laboratories with one-way mirrors behind which cameras and client observers view the response of a group of about a dozen children.

The children's responses are tested by pupil-dilation measurement machines, finger sensors and other modern gadgets.

After this they are interviewed by psychologists and asked how they might go about asking their parents for a product and to act out how they thought their parents would react.

This level of exploitation of the young in advertising and other media has led this author to describe today's young as *'the stolen generation.'* This phrase was originally applied to a generation of Australian aborigine children taken from their parents and reared in foster care before WWII, but it seems to apply increasingly well today as many a parent will attest.

Declining values

Despite increasing efforts by schools to introduce instruction and discussion on issues like sex, health, drugs, AIDS and life planning, there has been a considerable drop in the ethical standards of today's teenagers.

Much of this drop is doubtless owing to declining moral values in society and the increasingly ubiquitous media that encourages them to pursue self-satisfaction at all costs.

Much of it may also be because the modern approach of teaching self-esteem and confidence has led to many students believing that completing school is a 'given' no matter what they do.

The decline in values in society is perhaps emphasized by the practice of students in elementary school being warned of the dangers of physical and sexual abuse of the young.

To compound matters they may even by advised of the possibility of such problems occurring within the family and to report any family problems, however trivial, to school counsellors. This sort of practice transfers much of the responsibility for such problems from the adults to the young potential victims, also creating an atmosphere that can only be unsettling to some children.

Another problem in the US is the increasing emphasis on social rather than academic skills that came with outcome based education. The coordinated 'all at one pace' group learning that this sought to achieve discouraged students from setting their own personal standards and goals.

Social learning

Social learning plays a major part in the development of such bad habits as smoking and consumption of other drugs such as alcohol and marijuana.

Often such social learning begins by one of a group of young friends or acquaintances having observed some undesirable practice in the media or within their family circle or social group.

One answer might be to tackle the problem openly in school, admit to the madness of men, but emphasize that to gain as much as possible from the long process of education they should look to developing only good habits, otherwise much of the whole point of education itself is lost.

In part such social learning also arises from young people wishing to 'do their own thing' and one solution might be to ensure that activity options which provide more individuality are provided both at school and at home. All of us like to feel special in some way and that feeling is important to the confidence and self-belief that should be inculcated early in the education process.

Lower academic standards

Recent decades have seen a considerable decline in academic standards. Under pressure in a more pressurized society, just to be nice teachers dish out higher average marks, resulting in 'grade inflation.' Often grades have been abolished altogether.

Sykes (1995), for example, points out that between 1987 and 1994 the proportion of A grades given in US schools rose from 28% to 32%, whereas average SAT scores dropped by from 6 to 15 points in that time.

Packard (1978) attributes this decline to more permissive child-rearing practices, breakdown of the traditional family structure with high divorce rates, negative effects from TV and other media, increasing demands placed upon teachers with a need to deal with drugs and other social issues, a decrease in the quality of teaching in many cash-strapped schools in poorer suburbs, a breakdown of authority in schools, and introduction of new and gimmicky teaching fads such as the unsuccessful 'new math' in the USA.

As a consequence of this, Sykes reports that only about 40& of the school day in the US is spend on academic work, the rest being taken up by family studies (some of these asking personal and intrusive questions), consumer education, health, gym and self-esteem building.

This situation had reached the point that in four years at high school students in the US spent only about 1500 hours on maths and science whereas their counterparts in Japan spent nearly 3200 hours, those in France nearly 3300 hours and those in Germany just over 3500 hours.

To make the matter worse elementary students in Japan spent three times as long on homework, and those in Taipei up to seven times longer.

The results were demonstrated by the second international maths study. This found that the top 5% of US students were matched in ability by 50% of Japanese students and the top 1% of US students ranked bottom compared to the top 1% from other countries surveyed.

In algebra and basic calculus Japanese and Chinese students had twice the average score of US students. In geometry the US students ranked in the bottom quarter of the 143 countries surveyed.

Compared with grade eight students from 19 other countries, US students ranked only tenth in arithmetic, twelfth in algebra, and sixteenth in geometry.

Another survey of 24,000 students in twelve countries by the Educational Testing Service in Princeton found that, compared to 40% of US students scoring at the 500 level in a standard test, the results were 78% for Korea, 73% for Quebec and 69% for British Columbia.

A similar, though not as marked, decline in standards has been found in the UK and Australia.

Poor teacher training

Sykes (1995) reports widespread disillusionment with modern teacher training, much of which is a hotchpotch of psychology, sociology and history that cannot develop real expertise in any of these areas.

He cites several examples of recent doctorates in education being granted for dissertations with such titles as:

"The use of goal setting and positive self-modelling to enhance self-efficiency and performance for the basketball free-throw shot" for a PhD at the University of Maryland.

"Selected clothing characteristics and educator credibility" for a doctorate at the University of North Carolina.

Some of his other examples are almost hilarious, for example:

"An investigation into the personal meaning of golf."

After such largely useless studies, Sykes laments, 'educrats' move into educational administration and oversee a decline in standards over the whole spectrum of education comparable to that evidenced by their largely irrelevant doctoral studies.

Poor teaching practices

In the USA outcome based education (OBE) has gone a long way towards disallowing fail grades, instead allowing students to retake tests until they pass.

The idea of this is to avoid attaching negative labels to students, and much effort is also made to avoid attaching positive labels to the brightest students as well.

The purpose of this is greater equality and in pursuit of this goal tests have often been abandoned altogether.

Similarly, OBE eschews 'tracking' to permit accelerated learning for gifted students, despite conclusive evidence of its positive results, in this way ensuring that the overall standard of education is lowered further.

In the USA it is modern practice to accept 'invented spelling' that only crudely approximates correct spelling.

In addition, 'holistic grading', which assesses only the total impression given by students writing, not the accuracy of spelling, grammar and punctuation, is often used.

Phonetic teaching of reading, that is, learning to read by pronouncing the words out aloud, is gradually being abandoned in favour of "loud-say" in which far fewer words are learnt by constant repetition.

The result of these practices has been a dramatic decline in literacy in the USA.

Modern maths teaching practice allows calculators as early as kindergarten and no longer requires long multiplication or division to be learnt.

Similarly, maths rules, rote learning of maths tables and maths practice are discouraged and only approximate answers required, especially when o calculator is available.

The result has been the great decline in numeracy skills in the US evidenced by the survey results mentioned earlier.

Drugs for depressed children

The overlong school education system is naturally depressing enough. To make matters worse increasing numbers of 'unruly' children are diagnosed with such doubtful disorders as Attention Deficit Disorder (ADD) and prescribed drugs to sedate them.

In the USA and Australia in turn, increasingly large numbers of children suffer this fate. Reports of up to 15% or more children in some areas being on such drugs have not brought action to curb this disturbing trend as yet, but visions of a future society in which both parents and children have to be drugged to cope are unacceptable.

Overgrown educational bureaucracy

In the US in 1960 one third of education employees were not classroom teachers. By 1991 46.7% were non teaching staff and the teaching staff's share of the total payroll had shrunk from 54% to 41%.

Much the same has occurred in England and Australia both in school and tertiary education.

In the school sector it is the growing number of educrats who have had little else to do than dream up new and untested ideas for educational reform.

When these reforms are seen to fail and have little positive benefit a new generation of educrats appears with a new raft of reforms, often much like the old but disguised by new terminology.

The task of many of these educrats is to monitor schools extensively and many of their reforms, particularly those encouraging less stringent assessment, have helped cover up deficiencies in education in the short term but only made matters worse in the long term.

In the US in 1994 the National Education Standards and Improvement Committee (NESIC) came up with GOALS 2000, a comprehensive new set of schools curriculum standards which had inputs from 6,000 people and 35 interest groups.

One result was a 313 page document on the curriculum for world history that was a masterpiece of ethnic, racial and ideological inclusiveness that eliminated all mention of such people as Bell, Edison, Einstein or Salk.

In contrast, there were 17 references to the Klu Klux Klan and 19 to the infamous Senator Joseph McCarthy and McCarthyism.

As one expert remarked, "What got left out was traditional history."

Another idea of GOALS 2000 was that students in kindergarten through grade four be required to learn folk dances from various cultures and that in grades five through eight they should learn to describe the differences between these dances and their roles in their respective cultures.

Overall, therefore, the standards were placing so much emphasis on multiculturalism that American culture and history, except for negative aspects, was being largely ignored.

In the tertiary sector the bloated bureaucracy problem is worse and Universities have put the mighty $ above all else and invented new and often absurd courses such as sexology and puppetry willy-nilly which can only have the effect of short changing an increasingly large proportion of the population, in many cases ruining their lives.

Growing up faster

Today's young, thanks to better nutrition grow faster than in the past. Da Vinci observed that children were half their ultimate height at age three. Now that figure is about 55%.

Along with that, in part because of the ubiquitous media today, in many ways they mature faster than ever before.

Many children by their mid-teens, therefore, are becoming bored with school and drop out, particularly males these days. Robertson (1981), for example, reported that 100,000 assaults against teachers occur in US schools each year. Doubtless this is one of several factors that contribute to the increasing discipline problem in schools.

Given the advances in knowledge and technology of the last one or two centuries, however, is must be possible, if not necessary to reduce the long twelve years at school to ten on average, and this is perhaps the major proposal of this book.

In addition, if overlap between final school subjects and early University subjects is eliminated, then the overall education process could be shortened by as much as another full year.

Employment market pressures

With increasing globalization and competitiveness in the market place industries are constantly trying to improve their efficiency and thence their bottom line, often at the expense of many jobs. In many industries thousands of local jobs are lost to cheap overseas labour.

The result in some of the more advanced economies is that the jobs remaining will be more highly skilled, increasing the demand for more highly trained workers. In addition, because of a permanent pool of unemployed, employers can demand higher qualifications.

In Australia it has been the practice for two or three decades to shorten dole queues by sending people off to University.

Sometimes they do generalist courses in Arts which do not improve their employment prospects. Often they are also not far from retirement age and unlikely to be in employment for long after graduation, if at all.

From the point of view of productivity another problem is that an increasingly large proportion of the national work force is involved in the recruitment industry as human resource managers and the like.

The result is that, in part owing to mechanization of industries like farming, fewer and fewer people are doing the *real work* of producing the essentials of food, clothing, shelter and the like.

Excessive growth in tertiary courses.
There has been an astonishing increase in the diversity of University courses, some of which, like those in sexology, seem out of place to say the least.

Not surprisingly, therefore, there has also been an astonishing growth in the proportion of people in society with University degrees.

In addition, there has been a great increase in the number of postgraduate courses and the number of people taking them, to the point at which an MBA is almost worthless and doctorates likewise.

With an MBA one might now only be able to gain employment as a salesperson, if that. Then one might find that one's time studying at University would have been better spent acquiring practice and skill at selling in a job in the first place.

Need to develop inquiry and innovation
There is insufficient emphasis on developing inquiring minds capable of finding answers to their own questions, rather than zombies so used to endless rote learning and tests that they have become too tired and bored to care about anything but going through the motions of life as perpetual consumers and slaves to big businesses that produce and sell mass marketed consumer products.

More important, truly effective education should teach children both a basic collection of facts and data needed to understand a subject and then how to expand this. Given such a 'starter kit' in a subject they are then equipped for life-long learning.

Indeed, I am inclined to view that in studying for a degree in medicine, for example, students primarily learn the 'language' of the subject. Then, when they do work experience during their studies and then internship, they are able to quickly assimilate practical skills from experienced professionals.

Therefore, when students asked me what to do if they went out to work after graduation and found they didn't know how to do something, I told them to ask around the workplace and, if nobody else knew how to do it, they need not feel too bad but should sometimes ask further afield with a view to enhancing the knowledge of their workplace.

Personal experiences

In Chapter Three I mentioned how myself and another new student in Grade 4 at an expensive private school did far better at the arithmetic tests than the rest of the class, and I was bullied by a jealous student for this. I have also given other examples of bullying, both psychological and physical, dealt out by both teachers and students, and of sexual misconduct by both teachers and students.

In my secondary school days I recall well at 15 going to dancing classes held only for students of my private school and a nearby private girls school (both of them "Anglican" schools). Indeed, my first somewhat regular dancing partner at these classes was a member of a wealthy family that ran a large shop in the CBD which sold carpets, rugs, floor tiles, and other floor coverings. Indeed, she was picked up from these dances in a chauffeur-driven Rolls Royce, and I noticed when at a party at their large house with large swimming pool, in the 'rich-people' suburb of Toorak, that her brother had an expensive-looking collection of antique hand guns.

At University, of course, contact with girl classmates is inevitable, and a relatively new experience for boys from boys-only schools, as was I.

I was doing Engineering, however, and in those days girl students of this were very rare (I recall only one in my time).

Worse still, my stupid, somewhat snobbish mother had enrolled me in Melbourne University's men-only Trinity College, where I was given a bedroom which literally was like a prison cell, and forced to share a study with an Arts student from a regional Victorian boys school with many 'boarders' notorious for homosexuality amongst its students.

I was only sexually abused by this student a couple of times, and a far greater problem was that he only had about half a dozen lectures a week, whereas I had about 28 hours a week of lectures, tutorial classes, and laboratory classes.

He could therefore sleep in most days, sitting up late chatting with myself and other students who would drop in, and also playing cards, listening to the radio, drinking tea, coffee and hot chocolate drink, along with the occasional glass of sherry, the occasional student "sherry party" being held in the college as Victoria still had 'six-a-clock closing' in pubs at that time.

Therefore I found myself sleeping in and missing many classes, with the result that I only got a "compensatory pass" in first year because I had failed one of the four subjects.

The was the most boring 'Engineering Studies' subject, which being run by the Mechanical Engineering department, was largely irrelevant to me, a Civil Engineering Student.

Worse still, the other 3 subjects were Maths, Chemistry and Physics, all of them largely repeating material I had covered in my last couple of years at school.

Indeed, my father, then Dean of Science, told me that the University hierarchy deliberately did this because they felt that these subjects were not taught well enough in schools.

This belief was, indeed, arrogant BS, and really all the crooked Uni. hierarchy cared about was getting more money.

Indeed, because the Uni. council wouldn't fund lectures in a few subjects in the new M.Eng.Sci course because the M.Sc. course had no lectures, the Engineering faculty increased failure rates so the average student took 5 years to complete the 4-year UG course to gain extra funding.

In those days half the students in 'Pre-Med' or 1st year Medicine were also failed, presumably for the same reason.

Myself, after the poor result in year 1 (1964), I lived at home from then on until I got married in January 1970.

The family having moved house when I finished school, however, 2nd year Uni. found me with no friends and somewhat lonely, this perhaps a factor in my getting involved with a girl student at a college near our home in the following year (see Chapter 2 for this story).

Thus, I recall studying ancient history just before one of the 2nd-year exams, and for such reasons I failed two of the ridiculously large number of 8 subjects, getting poor marks in another couple, and was failed for 2nd year as a whole, having to repeat ALL 8 subjects the next year (1966).

The Engineering faculty did this, of course, to gain more funding, typical of how the crooks higher up in hierarchies work, whether they be big biz, other government funded organizations such as hospitals, or criminal organizations.

In that miserable, sadistically and greedily inflicted fully repeated 2nd year, however, I met the wife-to-be (see Chapter 2 for that story). I passed this time with honours in 2 or 3 subjects, doing better still in 3rd year (for example with a 'First' in Maths), and graduating in 1968 with first class honours overall, and being awarded a Commonwealth Postgraduate Award, so that I went on to do the new M.Eng.Sc. course in 1969.

Half of this was to be research, but as with my 4-th year research project topic, the topic of this was 'forced' on me because the department had got a little funding for the topic from the Brick Development Research Institute in the nearby Architecture Faculty building, which was in turn funded by that industry, of course, i.e., more hierarchical greed etc.

Cambridge nights

Having had to repeat one of the 4 years of an Engineering degree in full, I foolishly (in retrospect) used my postgraduate scholarship for only about 16 months to do the new M.Eng.Sc. coursework + research degree, whereas given the right advice I should have carried on to do a PhD as another fellow student did at that time.

Then in mid-1970 I began working as a consulting structural engineer full time for a small company, as well as doing quick and cheap work for my brother and an ex business partner of his.

Having moved on to a large structural engineering consulting firm, in mid-1971 I chanced upon an advertisement for a lecturing position at nearby Caulfield Institute of Technology (CIT).

As noted in Chapter 1, I was appointed by an HOD of Civil Engineering who retired after I had been there only about 18 months, and a new young, 'bastard boss' appeared, and he had a PhD from Imperial College, London.

This made me realize that, now that I was, though somewhat by chance, in academia, I should do a PhD.

I did not want to go back to Melbourne University, and foolishly did not consider going to nearby Monash University on a part-time basis, when I would have been able to take a year's sabbatical leave on full pay to help complete the course.

Instead, I made enquiries to Cambridge and Berkeley, and when promptly accepted by Cambridge (and 6 months later by Berkeley), I sold our house and 2 cars, and with only 25% salary from CIT spread over 2 years because I had worked there 3.5 years, not the 6 required for a full year of sabbatical leave and pay, flew with wife and then 18-month old first son to England. I also took a Finite Element Method (FEM) program I had done some work on in a steel case full of punched computer cards.

Arriving in Cambridge around the start of 1975 and moving into the "married flats" at Churchill College, I made my first trip to the Engineering Department to meet the Dean.

No doubt because I was already a lecturer, he said:

Decide what you want to do, and see if you can get anybody interested.

I then spent a few days talking to three of the lecturers, suggesting I might continue work on chemical admixture inhibition of corrosion in reinforced concrete that I had begun at CIT. Hearing that I had done some work on FEM one lecturer suggested I do work on ""shape optimization of shell structures". I mentioned this to another lecturer who had recently supervised an Australian PhD student continuing work on optimal distribution of reinforcement in suspended concrete floors, work that he had begun at Monash University for his Masters degree.

I chose this lecturer as supervisor and began work on optimization of Finite Element models of plate and shell structures, spending much of my time, however, also trying to develop new and better Finite Elements, early on running into a research student slave finishing his PhD who said: *I wish I had never heard of the Finite Element Method.*

The Computer Centre used an ICL1904A and the Houston Automatic Sequencing Program (HASP) that had been used in the moon landing projects to store, prioritize, and feed jobs to the IBM370 mainframe. Jobs were normally submitted for overnight processing, and the results collected the next day.

I found that by working all night in the Computer Centre I could get several jobs done in one night session, and was thus able to do far more computing work than normal.

This helped me complete the PhD in less than 2 years, typing up most of it after only about 15 months because I was feeling stressed about my financial situation, having limited funding (mostly my own from sale of house etc.), and finding costs in England far greater than expected, in part because of rampant inflation after the OPEC oil price hikes of 1972+.

Non-academic events in my time in Cambridge included:

(a) Regularly dropping off at the Rose and Crown pub after the Computer Centre closed at midnight on Fridays.

(b) My wife being 'screwed' by the Churchill College barman while I was at work at night in the Computer Centre.

(c) Having a quite painful heart attack, and not realizing it, after a tennis match in May 1976.

(d) Coming down with bad pneumonia for a month just after submitting my PhD in mid-December, 1976.

The 'viva' for my PhD was in January 1977, and the external examiner, a 'Cambridge man', complained that my results for a cylindrical shell element that he and a postgraduate student slave had developed at the University of Wales were not the same as theirs, which were, in fact, too good to be true.

So I had to amend my thesis by getting new results for this element, while doing so finding that the examiner's results had been fiddled by multiplying some diagonal terms in the formula for element matrix by a factor of 4, a well-known way of 'stiffening' an element and 'tweaking' the results.

I reported this verbally to my supervisor and he turned up at my flat without notice one afternoon to collect all my calculations on this issue.

Soon after this I flew back to Melbourne, receiving news that I had passed my PhD in June 1977.

In 1979, however, when I submitted a 300 pp book effort to Cambridge University Press, stupidly saying I had done it in 3 weeks to try and convince them of my expertise, it was handled by Simon Mitton, the man who advised Stephen Hawking that "adding a second equation" would "halve the sales" of his book *A Brief History of Time.*

After a few months I received 2 reviews, one OK and obviously done by the man who had been my PhD supervisor, the other I decided after years, if not decades, of thought, probably by the complaining external examiner at my viva. This was a 4-page 'rave' which concluded by exhorting that I do a much longer "treatise" of "perhaps two volumes".

Stupidly, I went along with this suggestion ASAP, when I should have sent the book to another publisher (and, of course, I should have sent to more than one publisher in the first place).

Mostly over the end of year break of 1980/81, I lengthened the book to circa 500pp and sent it back to CUP, and Mitton said he was satisfied with it but that it would have to be considered by CUP's 'syndicate'.

After a few months, and only 2 weeks after I had taken up a new lecturing position at Auckland University, Mitton wrote saying the syndicate had rejected the book, suggesting I send it to MacMillan.

This I did without success, after rapidly condensing the book to about 330 pp again, receiving from MacMillan a single review from somebody who had applied for the HOD position in the department I went to in Auckland, but failed to get it, thus perhaps having a grudge.

I continued work on what I came to call 'the tome', and greatly expanded it in scope, and it was finally published by OUP in 1992 (Mohr, 1992), but not before I had been bullied by a new 'bastard boss' in Auckland to resign at the end of 1984, got another shorter book published (Mohr & Milner, 1986, 1987), and spent several years on the 'dole' with many more to come. So, indeed, the fiasco of my first book effort, including receiving a suspicious 'rave review' and going along with it, did much to ruin my career.

Had my first book effort of 1979 been accepted by another publisher, which with a better title and OK supportive comment from somebody who had also done a book in the area, it should have been, then I would not have gone too low in the hierarchy to Auckland University, where I was too new, foreign, and low in the 'tree' to prevent myself from being bullied out of it, never to get another job again.

TAFE

TAFE, of course, is the major educational alternative to the University system, and, of course, there are now countless other small private providers of educational courses.

Indeed, many University graduates of such courses as Arts cannot get a job and go to TAFE for more practical training.

Indeed, myself, having become long-term unemployed, I paid circa $300 for the only two-week full time real estate agent representatives course in mid-2002. Too old to get a job in that area by then, I changed my mind and got a refund, spending most of it to buy a quite large whiteboard to put in my house so that, in the unlikely event that somebody I had applied to for a job came by to check me out, I could tell them it was to help deal with any questions that students of a 'scientific MBA' course I had written a few years earlier might come and ask me. In fact, I had never run that course, and had only given away a few copies of it, but I did later publish a final edition of it (Mohr, 2017).

Conclusions

Our education system of today has roots extending, as might be expected, back towards the first recorded history.

In education much positive has happened in the last hundred years.

Advances in psychology help us understand ourselves and others and can make major contributions to the learning process itself, whilst computer and information technology have already had a major impact

On the negative side, twelve years at school is clearly too long and simply a supreme example of Parkinson's Law, that is: *Work expands so as to fill the time available for its completion.*

To compound the problem, much of the early content of tertiary courses overlaps that of the last school years, making some courses up to a year longer than necessary.

The problem is further exacerbated by the proliferation of new courses, many of them postgraduate ones in such ridiculous subjects as "sexology" and "puppetry".

Furthermore, some Universities implore students to do double degrees and then masters degrees, thereby greatly increasing the head count and hence funding.

No doubt such problems arise as a result of the devastating accuracy of the Peter Principle: *In a hierarchy every employee tends to rise to his own level of incompetence*, which Dr Laurence Peter discovered in the context of educational administration.

I believe that a more streamlined and efficient education system is an urgent priority in a society so hell bent on such contradictory aims as personal freedom and workplace efficiency that it is beginning to crack at the seams.

Other hierarchical issues include:

(a) The great need for less 'top down one-way' communication in education, and friendlier group based class discussion learning. That is, less of the 'brainwashing' deplored by Mohr's Second Law (ML2 in Table 1.1).

(b) Bullying and sexual harassment, for example media reports in late February, 2018, of initiation rituals for new students involving "hazing", bullying and sexual abuse, at University colleges in Sydney, such initiation rituals also being known to occur in colleges throughout Australia, and having become a "national issue".

(c) In both schools and Universities, teachers lecture from textbooks written overseas that they often barely understand, and increasingly, many children are getting better results with far less expense and hassle with home based education.

(d) The increasing proliferation of tertiary courses, including ridiculous ones such as "sexology" and "puppetry", and many unnecessary ones such as hairdressing and bar tendering, which could be learnt in a few hours on the job.

(e) With too many degrees being 'sold for profit', more and more graduates are forced to do a postgraduate degree to increase their job prospects, often with poor results.

(f) PhD degrees involving being a slave researcher for a lazy academic higher in the academic hierarchy should be unnecessary, and historically even a Mastership was gained by only work experience in the trades, the term being adopted by academia.

CHAPTER 7

THE WORKPLACE

> *I believe in benevolent dictatorship provided I am the dictator.*
> Richard Branson, remark (1984).

Mohr's Law of Hierarchies

This is: *In hierarchical organizations the amount of real material-producing work people do is inversely proportional to their rank or level in the organization.*
The amount of compensation they receive, however, is proportional to their level, sometimes to an exponential degree.

In Chapter 1 a simple DC network model of a corporate hierarchy was given and Finite Element Method analysis used to demonstrate how the power at the top becomes greater and greater as corporate structures grow in size.

It was also shown how the amount of money people earn increases exponentially with their rank in the organization.

Then Mohr's Law of Capitalism was also used to demonstrate how the rich can invest money to increase its value exponentially with time.

Examples of corporate structure

Corporate structure is the hierarchical structure and communication channels giving rise to the chain of command and response in a company or organization. Some of the basic types of corporate structure are as follows:

[1] Functional structure. This is the usual structure for small companies and corresponds to one division of the type shown in Figure 7.1.

99

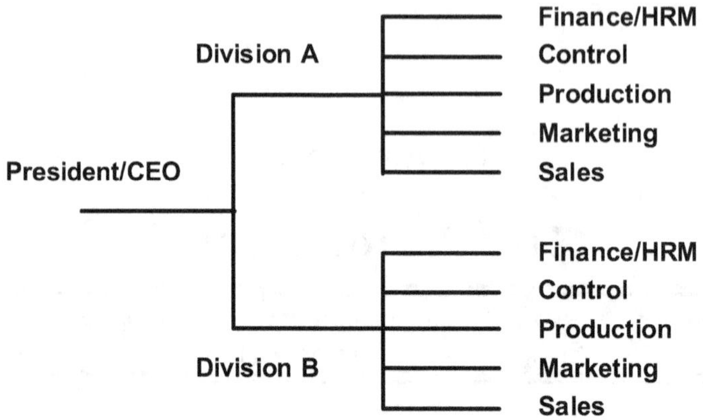

Figure 7.1. Divisional corporate structure.

[2] Divisional structure. For a corporation with just two divisions this of the form shown in Figure 7.1.

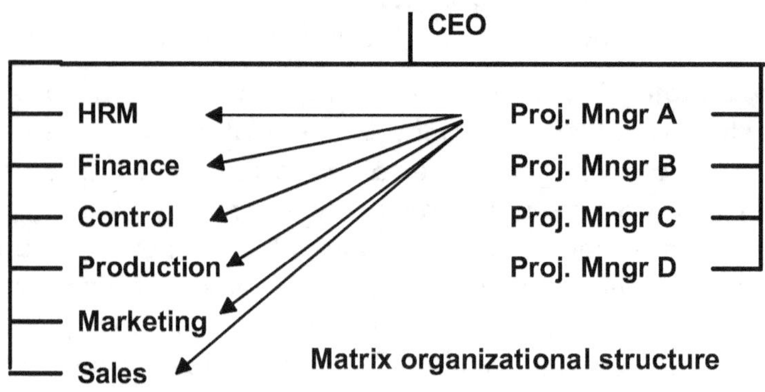

Figure 7.2. Matrix organizational structure.

[3] Matrix Structure

Note that in Fig. 7.1 Finance and HRM are combined into one group, but not in Fig. 7.2. Similarly, marketing and sales might often be one group, for example.

In a small business, of course, the boss or owner is HRM/control/marketing, finance is the bank a few doors away, and the few employees may be production and sales, including the boss.

[4] Ring structure.
This is typical of political parties, voluntary organizations etc. Such structures can be described approximately as follows:
Centre = president/CEO
Inner ring = secretary/treasurer/vice presidents etc.
   + presidents of committees for finance/membership/PR etc.
   + chairmen of branches
Outer ring 1 = clusters of members of each committee
Outer ring 2 = clusters of members of each branch
In the outer rings the 'clusters' are like satellites (at the same radius) and each is another group of members which in turn holds meetings etc., the committee presidents and branch chairpersons reporting back to the inner ring or *board* or *central committee.*

Thus committee chairpersons and branch presidents have to attend two lots of meetings, as will many members when these are delegates from the branches, as is often the case.

In the case of political parties the central committee is the elected members of the party in parliament. These 'politicians' often have to attend committee and branch meetings, as well as those of parliament, and are therefore often busier than we sometimes imagine.

The Peter Principle

The Peter Principle, of course, applies very well indeed in most hierarchies, and is thus worth further mention:

In a hierarchy every employee tends to rise to his own level of incompetence.

Parkinson's Law that

Work expands so as to complete the time available (for its completion).

is also important in hierarchies where it applies best to those higher up in them, and they, of course, are responsible for trying to make those below them work harder and faster.

Early personal experiences

My first work experiences were at the ends of my last two years at school and between my years at university in Melbourne, these being compulsory professional work experience required by the Institution of Engineers, Australia, as part of the 4-year Bachelors degree in Engineering.

For the first of the latter, I worked in one of two adjoining flats that made up the Melbourne branch of an Adelaide-based consulting civil engineering company, where I remember working on a housing subdivision plan and several other projects.

The second time I worked for a branch of the premix concrete company Pioneer Concrete in the Melbourne suburb of Collingwood, which was near my home. There I helped test the cylindrical concrete test samples regularly taken from many concrete pours around inner Melbourne, sometimes visiting sites to help collect these samples.

The other times I worked for government organizations, and this is discussed in the next chapter.

Towards the end of my undergraduate studies, and while doing a Master's degree, I did a little consulting work in structural engineering for my elder brother's then new business, working from home to do this.

I continued this work, also consulting for a former business partner of my elder brother for a few years.

My first full-time jobs

My first full-time job came straight after I had completed my M.Eng.Sci. degree, by which time I had been married about 6 months and had moved to live in St Kilda.

This was for a small consulting engineering company which worked from two adjoining flats in Queen's Road, which was only a short drive from home. The work was mostly on houses, mostly built on concrete slabs, then a quite new practice in Australia, but there were a few small factory and blocks of flats jobs as well.

One day a bright young engineer from Queensland appeared to grow our numbers to just 7, comprising the boss, now 3 other civil engineers, a couple of draughtsmen, and a secretary. This engineer had done a lot of work on multistorey buildings, and from him I learnt the simple but useful 'portal method' of structural design for multistorey buildings that originated decades earlier.

Soon after this new arrival, the boss told me he was losing money and had had to mortgage his house, and that I should look for another job. In retrospect I thought that the new engineer had somehow knocked on doors to get a job in the small business by impressing with his good experience, and this was the real reason for me having to leave.

I quickly found another job, however, this with a large consulting engineering company that specialized in the structural design of multistorey buildings. It occupied the large second floor of a four storey building, only the most senior employees having half-way private workspaces, the rest slaving away in the open plan office environment that the Japanese had pioneered to allow greater supervision of employees at all times.

This job was excellent experience and I worked on a range of jobs from small factories and home unit developments, to multistorey buildings.

One unusual job was to inspect the 3-storey Denys Lascelles wool stores building in Geelong, which had an impressive reinforced concrete bow truss roof structure built circa 1930, and the largest single span concrete structure in the Southern Hemisphere.

I found much corrosion of the reinforcement, no doubt because of the proximity of the roof to the ocean, and thence 'salt rains'. I estimated that the roof's safety factor was only about 1.2, and that in not very many years it would be in danger of collapse, so steel columns were run up through the building to support the concrete bow truss roof at the third points of its span.

This job initiated an interest in corrosion in reinforced concrete, which I studied at my own expense at home and in my next job at Caulfield Institute of Technology (CIT).

As for hierarchies, one day the boss came out of his private and sound insulated office to abuse an older engineer working at a nearby draughtsman's desk because he resented the fact that this employee did consulting work 'on the side'.

That very day I had the letter of application for the position CIT in my briefcase, uncertain about actually posting it. After seeing the boss losing his temper and raving at an employee, I posted that letter at lunchtime and got the job.

This was one of few lucky breaks in my life, as moving into academia was really the right move for me, as it allowed me a relatively private office, a limited number of hours of 'must do now' work per week, leaving most of the week for coffee, tea and lunch breaks, and then research of my own choosing, far better than being a slave 40 or more hours per week. Furthermore, in those days, at least, University-type lecturing jobs were normally jobs for life, whereas my first full-time job had only lasted about 8 months through no fault of my own. Had I been more nearly 40 in that situation, I might have had trouble getting a job in line with my qualifications. As it turned out, unfortunately, that situation did arise, as described in the following chapter.

Conclusion

Mohr's Law of Hierarchies becomes a more serious issue every year as the rich grow richer and workers get paid less in relation to the rising cost of living, and are expected to change jobs and occupations ever more frequently.

Small business has some advantages for workers over big business. It is often easier to get a job without so much 'red tape' involved, but it is also easier for a boss to 'sack' workers with little or no reason.

Government organizations are usually much more secure, however, and these are discussed in the next chapter.

CHAPTER 8

GOVERNMENT ORGANIZATIONS

Men in high places, from having less personal interest in the characters of others – being safe from them – are commonly less acute observers, and with their progressive elevation in life become, as more and more indifferent to what other men are, so more and more ignorant of them.
Henry Taylor, British writer and civil servant, *The* Statesman (1836).

Introduction

In theory, at least, in socialist countries the government runs everything and there are no private businesses.

A notable example, of course, was the USSR, or Union of Soviet Socialist Republics, which Western propaganda often criticized with pictures of long queues in Moscow shops.

Now, of course, with the Soviet Union disbanded circa 1990, Russia is hybrid economy, with private businesses making up a substantial proportion of the economy, but the government maintaining higher levels control than in the USA and like Western countries with 'democratic' governments.

In such countries, however, most people believe that government organizations such as hospitals and government schools provide more secure employment. In government schools in Australia, for example, teaching jobs were virtually guaranteed for life, unless a teacher committed grave offences, and relatively speaking at least, that remains the case.

In private industry, on the other hand, whenever there are economic downturns, or a company restructures or is bought out by another, there are often large scale layoffs of staff, whereas this very rarely happens in government organizations.

105

Health and education

The health and education sectors are two of the largest in the economy of most countries, and these constantly push for greater funding, often obtaining it to the point that they become somewhat bloated.

In hospitals, for example, patient to nurse ratios have been kept as low as about 6 or 7 in Australia, far lower than in most other countries, whilst in many 3rd world countries they run as high as 20 to 40.

On night shifts between midnight and dawn, when most patients are asleep, such ratios are perhaps too low.

With new treatments and medications being produced constantly, of course, the public cost of healthcare continues to rise.

With the 'invention' of new psychiatric ailments over the last 50 years such as PTSD and ADHD, and the production and prescription of more and more medications for them, healthcare costs continue to grow excessively.

With the incredible growth of the childcare industry in the last two or three decades, much of it partially subsidized by local government, a further burden is placed on taxpayers.

Similarly, with populations aging, thanks to improvements in healthcare and diet etc., the aged care industry has also grown considerably in recent decades, much of this also being funded by government.

Employment in the latter two areas, therefore, is growing and relatively secure, particularly in government funded organizations.

Infrastructure

In Australia, not surprisingly, roads and bridges etc. are one of the largest sectors of the economy.

With the major cities such as Sydney and Melbourne growing excessively, when 'decentralization' would be more environmentally friendly and economical, infrastructure costs have grown massively.

This area, therefore, also offers prospects of secure employment, a good example being local government jobs involving road and footpath repairs, and maintenance of parks and gardens.

Police

In the last couple of decades police numbers as a proportion of total population have grown considerably in Australia. As a result, small cream brick local police stations, with only a couple of officers on duty at any one time, have been replaced by massive police complexes.

In addition, as Australia, already the most 'Americanized' country in the world other than the USA, becomes more and more Americanized, nearly all police carry guns and wear bullet-proof jackets, so that increasingly Australia is becoming a 'police state'.

This, of course, increases the hierarchical feel of life in Australia's major cities where one can see police patrols, hear police sirens, and hear police helicopters flying around much of the time, contributing to an environment that is, to a small extent at least, like that of war-torn parts of the world.

Defence

The global arms and illegal drugs trades industries are, unfortunately, the world's two largest.

The USA, of course, spends far more than any other country on defence, and its massive arms industry is probably its largest exporter.

Russia, China, Britain and France also have large arms industries which export globally.

Around the world today conflicts and wars continue, particularly terrorism in much of the Middle East, and large scale military interventions by the USA, Russia and others to combat such organizations as Islamic State.

Sadly, substantial areas of some countries, a few of these being in Africa, remain littered with landmines that continue to kill.

More concerning, of course, is the growing threat of nuclear war now that the "rogue nation" North Korea has greatly increased its nuclear arms capability.

During the Cold War, the USA and USSR built up massive stockpiles of nuclear weapons, as discussed in Chapter 11, and this was perhaps the best example of the hierarchical nature of the 'posturing for power' that both tribes and nations have indulged in throughout human history.

So it is, therefore, that for several decades the USA and USSR were regarded as the world's two "superpowers", whilst now China has become #2 in the superpower hierarchy, the USA having been regarded until recently as the only superpower since the 'fall' of the Soviet Union.

Now, however, Russia has for several years been growing in global influence with its military efforts in Chechnya, the Ukraine, and Syria where, according to an issue of the *The Economist*, Vladimir Putin's "troops had saved the regime of Bashar al-Assad", whilst Russia's invasion of Ukraine which began in 2014, continues in 2024.

Australia's ABC and SBS networks

Australia's national ABC and SBS radio and TV networks are a very good example of a government organization that has become 'bloated' thanks to excessively generous funding.

A major part of that growth occurred when the Special Broadcasting Service (SBS) was proposed by the Member of Parliament for the NSW regional electorate of Griffith, Al Grassby, and funding secured to establish it as a network that had a multicultural bias.

Now, however, SBS has grown to three TV and three radio channels broadcasting nationally, while the ABC has four national TV channels, five national radio channels (two of them on the TV network system), and countless local regional radio stations around the country.

This has been an excessive and unnecessary growth when only the original SBS TV station is, perhaps, worthwhile, whilst only a couple of ABC TV stations are worthwhile, namely the ABC NEWS channel, and the original ABC2 channel, which could show children's programs for much of the day, making the current ABC children's TV channel unnecessary, whilst the current ABC comedy TV channel is, of course, ridiculous and unnecessary.

Personally, I find the BBC's world news program far better than the ABC's new programs, the interviews for which all too often have both interviewer and interviewee using the redundant phrase: *you know.*

Indeed, a recently retired radio host of the Monday to Thursday 10 PM to 2 AM program on ABC's 774 radio station said *you know* once or twice in dealing with almost every phone caller during this radio 'talkback' program.

For this reason, therefore, I have recently begun calling the ABC the *'we don't know network'.*

My first work experiences

My first work experience was at the ends my last two years at school and working at night sorting the Christmas mail at the St Kilda post office.

This was a well paid job for a teenager, and there being no supervisor around at night, the group of about 10, whose ages ranged from about 17 to 25, worked hard to get the sorting done in 3 or 4 hours so that we could play cards for the remaining 5 or 4 hours of our night shift.

My next work experiences were the compulsory professional work experience required by the Institution of Engineers, Australia, as part of the 4-year Bachelors degree in Engineering, and the first two of these work stints during end of year breaks were for private companies and are described in Chapter 7.

The 3rd and 4th times I worked for a government organization, the Australian Road Research Board, whose head office was close to my home. On much of these two occasions I was one of a group of four work experience students sent to work in Griffith, just across the border in the Riverina district of New South Wales.

There we ran Benkelman Beam tests of how much a loaded truck depressed the surface of roads where the water table was high because of adjacent irrigation canals of which there are many in the Griffith area.

Because it was very hot work in the middle of almost invariably sunny summer days, we started work early at circa 7 or 8 AM and stopped at circa 1 PM and went to the Returned Serviceman's League club in Griffith for lunch and a few beers. At night we were camped in tents at a nearby CSIRO (Commonwealth Scientific & Industrial Research Organization) site, and played cards for much of the evening while drinking a few bottles of beer.

Every weekend, however, we drove back to Melbourne to visit family, taking with us flagons of wine purchased cheaply from the few wineries around Griffith, particularly De Bortoli.

For a couple of weeks we did the same road tests at a private track used by General Motors Holden to test new cars. This was near Werribee, and again it was hot work in the midday sun, so we used to stop work early and go to an outdoor swimming pool in Werribee for a couple of hours to cool off before going home. On one of these afternoons one of our supervisors based at head office came to check on us and, his not being able to find us, the leader of our small workgroup of four, a slightly older student who had had two repeat years, was blamed for the situation.

As with the post office job a few years earlier, we student long-holiday period workers were able to take lots and lots of time off work for recreation, something we would not have been able to do in private industry.

A college lecturer

As noted in the last chapter, one day after seeing the boss of a private company 'raving' at another engineer, I posted an application for a lecturing job at Caulfield Institute of Technology (CIT).

I got the job, in part because I had a Master's degree and only one other person in the department had a higher degree, and in part because I had been to Melbourne Grammar School, whilst the HOD who appointed me had been a teacher at nearby Wesley College for several years.

I started at CIT in mid-1971, and only six months later the Principal Lecturer, who had a PhD from the USA, left to take up a Deanship at NSWIT. He was replaced by a young (little over 30) Queenslander with a PhD from Imperial College, London.

At the end of 1972 the HOD hit 65 and retired, and the Queenslander replaced him, probably having heard that I had applied for the HOD job also, though being much too young for it.

Before long he appointed a new lecturer, an Indian with a PhD from Sydney University, and now seeing 2 PhDs in the department, I began to regret not using the postgraduate scholarship I had won at Melbourne University to do a PhD.

This led to my going to Cambridge with limited funding to do my PhD in 1975-76, details of this having been given in Chapter 6.

When I returned to Melbourne and work at CIT in early February 1977, I was upset to find that subjects I had become accustomed to lecturing had been taken over by other people, and in one subject the new Queenslander HOD did the two lectures, making me do the two tutorials and a couple of lab classes for that subject.

His only teaching work was those two lectures, plus a 2-hour lab. session which he usually walked out of very early saying to the students, as I saw once, something like: *"You should be able to work out what to do for yourselves".*

I spent as much time as I could continuing the Finite Element Method (FEM) research I had been doing in Cambridge, now with an increased emphasis in developing new and better Finite Element formulations.

In 1978 I jointed a short course on FEM which was well attended by practicing engineers, jointing it with the new HOD and colleague from the Maths department who was doing at PhD part-time at nearby Monash University.

Soon after this I began planning to do a book on FEM, foolishly suggesting to the HOD that I might joint it with him.

Then, upset when the HOD, with the help of a Chilean senior lecturer in the Electrical Engineering Department in providing contacts, ran the 1978 short course I had written most of in Chile, I rudely said I would not joint my book with him the day before Christmas day, 1978. This proved unwise, as the HOD got revenge on me after I moved to Auckland.

Over the very short Easter break of 1979 I began typing a book on FEM, having drawn most of the diagrams for it in the preceding couple of weekends.

In mid-1979 I took a copy of the book to a small Cambridge University Press (CUP) office in a small house on the beach road in Albert Park, and near my home. This was sent to Cambridge and, as described in Chapter 6, the hassle with a suspicious 'rave review' and the subsequent hassle of lengthening the book, then condensing it again, then growing it again in both size and scope over several years did much to ruin my career and life.

Had I sent the second copy I made of the first draft of the book to another publisher, rather than to a couple of senior academics in Australia for positive comment (which I failed to get), and given the book a better title, for example by including the work 'Introduction' to increase sales, then I might well have got the book accepted for publication by 1980, and would not have taken a job too low in the hierarchy (and pay scales) at Auckland University.

A University lecturer

Two weeks after I arrived at Auckland University in mid-1980, I received news that the 'syndicate' of CUP had rejected my much longer FEM book, despite senior editor Simon Mitton having approved it.

This was a bad start and worse was to follow, for example:

(1) I was in the Theoretical and Applied Mechanics (TAM) department which, although part of the Engineering Faculty, was really only a Maths department mainly responsible for teaching the maths subjects for all branches of Engineering, and also running an "Engineering Science" degree for only about a dozen students/year, and which was mostly maths with little worthwhile engineering content, so that graduates had difficulty getting jobs.

(2) I was given very little opportunity to lecture my main areas of experience and expertise, namely Structural Mechanics and the Finite Element Method.

(3) Simon Mitton at CUP told me to send my book to MacMillan, which I did after foolishly shortening it by almost 200 pages, feeling too depressed to bother with a longer book. Towards the end of 1980 they rejected it because of another 'rave review', this one from a New Zealander in London who had applied for the HOD job in my new department, but had been rejected.

(4) In mid-December 1980 my ex-PhD supervisor in Cambridge, a New Zealander, took up a personal chair in the Civil Engineering Department which he had been offered after applying unsuccessfully for the HOD position. While still in Melbourne I had applied for a position in that department but been knocked back, and I suspected that my application had aroused the interest of my ex-PhD supervisor in returning to New Zealand, and lack of support by him was the reason for my not getting the lowly position I had applied for.

(5) The day before Christmas day 1980 a colleague who had a PhD from ANU barged into my office and said: *What did you come to New Zealand for, to get away from your family and take drugs?* This upset me greatly because I realized it was in retaliation for my day before Christmas day 'rave' to the HOD at CIT two years earlier, and no doubt the CIT HOD, seeing somebody with PhD(ANU) after their name on the staff list, had somehow evoked this act of revenge. Indeed, there had been a precursor to this not long before I

left CIT when the secretary (who I remember seeing hugging the HOD one day) said to me something like: "They smoke a lot of marijuana" in New Zealand.

(6) Upset in early 1981 at having to give my first lecture in the second year Maths subject all Engineering students did, I had a mild stroke without realizing it, and stood somewhat dazed in my office for a couple of hours before a colleague drove me home.

(7) A month or two later I had another mild stroke which left me with numbness in my upper left lip and my left foot for several months. This I did suspect as a stroke, but told no one, getting my wife to buy me a pair of black sports-type shoes to make my walking easier.

(8) After I had been in Auckland only 6 months the HOD retired, having reached 65, and was replaced. I had been involved in a farcical selection process by which he was appointed, convincing the only four department members asked by the Dean to make a choice (two were applicants themselves and thus disqualified from the selection process, and one was in the USA on sabbatical leave). With the field quickly narrowed from four to two, I foolishly pushed for a senior lecturer at UMIST because he had a Cambridge PhD, rather than a much older New Zealander who was a Professor at Oxford.

(9) Later that year (1981), upset by my book problems and having to mostly teach subjects outside my real expertise, and by the 'revenge rave' of (5), I complained about the latter to the new HOD, stupidly saying something like: "They know I tried to commit suicide once." He said tersely: "I don't want to see you for three weeks." I took just 2 days off work, during which my wife had the GP and a psychiatrist visit the house in the late afternoon. Fortunately, I was sitting in an armchair in the lounge room drinking a pot of tea, a habit that I have always indulged while working at home at my desk or a computer stand. Had I been having a beer, I'm sure that might have been used as grounds to have me committed, or at least forced into psychiatric treatment.

In fact, my backstabbing and bullying wife (as described in Chapter 2) did succeeded in having me committed briefly with the help of my eldest brother a few months after I had been bullied by the new HOD into resigning in Auckland in late 1984, details of this being given in Chapter 2.

In following years I was interviewed for a couple of jobs at Senior Lecturer Level, a couple of Research Fellow positions, several jobs at HOD level, a couple of jobs at Dean level, and a couple of jobs as CEO of large TAFE colleges with circa 1000 staff and students.

I was also interviewed for a few jobs in private industry, being told more than once that I was "overqualified", didn't have quite the right qualifications, experience, etcetera.

So it was that I never got another job, but continued my work on FEM and Computational Mechanics (of which FEM is a subset), publishing a short course on FEM and microcomputers with Pitman in Melbourne and Heinemann in London (Mohr & Milner, 1986, 1987) that I had run in Auckland with very good attendance of more than 60 people from all over New Zealand. This, to 'do the right thing', I did despite having resigned. The next day I flew back to Australia to run the course at CIT but they cancelled it, being too incompetent etc. to get just a few people to attend.

Indeed, the success of this course would have been a very good reason not to quit in New Zealand, but with Murphy's Law type bad luck I put in my letter of resignation before I had heard of the growing number of people signing on to attend the course.

A another major factor in my demise, however, was asking my ex-HOD at CIT to help with my growing again 'tome', and he flying me to Melbourne for 3 weeks painful (to me – I often had chest pains) quizzing trying to understand some of it, and then repeating this farce for 2 weeks in Auckland, during which this bastard ex-boss had used 'hierarchical communication lines' to discuss my future with the new bastard boss in Auckland.

This no doubt led to Auckland HOD bullying my into resigning, and the ex-HOD in Melbourne offering me a temporary position as his research slave when I returned to Melbourne, and which I declined, having had more than enough of his ignorance and bossiness by then.

Perhaps a bottom line on this farce was the Auckland HOD saying: *Another lousy lecturer* about my ex-HOD in Melbourne, then not knowing anything at all about him other than I had him involved in trying to get a book published.

Another is that I had never received a complaint from a student, but only the occasional compliment, whereas the Auckland HOD had put in writing that ALL the students said they had "trouble getting their questions answered' by me. In fact, I did hear the occasional complaint about the Auckland HOD who had simply got himself a nice 'pre-retirement' job and made it more secure, perhaps, by getting rid of me because I had done far more research, writing, short course presentation for practicing engineers, publishing of papers, and writing of books etc., than he could ever do, being a typical bludging Cambridge clod lecturing badly out of other people's textbooks and using graduate students as slaves.

Conclusion

Hierarchies in Government health, education etc. organizations are just as difficult to bear for those lower in them as they are in private industry, if not more so, for in Government organizations higher positions are effectively jobs for life which also offer prospects of moving to other organizations at a high level, politics and local government being just a couple of examples.

My personal experience of two almost successive new and bastard bosses who were too young, inexperienced, bossy, lazy, etc. was disastrous. Two other 'villains', my eldest brother, and my bossy, backstabbing 'big sister' wife, also contributed to my downfall, just an example of being yet another victim of the machinations of hierarchies.

CHAPTER 9

TRIBALISM AND SOCIAL HIERARCHY

*The society which scorns excellence in plumbing as a humble activity
and tolerates shoddiness in philosophy because it is an exalted
activity will have neither good plumbing nor good philosophy:
neither its pipes nor its theories will hold water.*
John W. Gardner, Former President of the Carnegie Foundation.

*The vast majority of the sons of rich men are unable
to resist the temptations which wealth subjects them to,
and sink to unworthy lives.*
Andrew Carnegie, Speech, Curry Commercial College,
Pittsburgh, June 23, 1985: "The Road to Business Success."

Evolution of tribal man

Scientific evidence continues to accumulate about the evolution of modern humans from chimpanzees, with whom we share circa 98% of our DNA. A key step in this evolution was the appearance of hominids with bipedal locomotion between 5 and 6 million years ago in Africa, remains of the first Ramapithecus species of Hominidae having been found in Kenya dating back to the Miocene epoch, 10 to 15 million years ago (Weiss & Mann, 1978).

About 5 million years ago the first Australopithecines appeared in Africa, there being two types, the Robust and the Gracile Australopithecines. These species were from 1.2 to 1.4 metres tall and weighed from 30 to 45 kg.

The Robusts, as their name suggests, were more solidly built but became extinct about a million years ago.

The more fleet-footed Gracile's survived, however, evolving from the Australopithecus afarensis form to the species Australopithecus africanas by about 2.5 million years ago (Smith & Davies, 2008).

About 2 million years ago this species evolved into the first Homo species, Homo habilis, the forerunner of modern man. Homo habilis evolved into Homo ergaster about 1.5 million years ago in Africa and spread into Asia, where it evolved into Homo erectus, a species which survived until about 250 thousand years ago.

Homo ergaster then spread from Africa into Europe, evolving into Homo Heidelbergensis, so named because the first remains of this species were discovered in Heidelberg, Germany, in 1903. This species appeared between 0.6 and 1.3 million years ago and survived until 200 to 250 thousand years ago.

It seems likely that Homo Heidelbergensis then evolved into Homo sapiens Neanderthalis between 200,000 and 300,000 years ago. The Neanderthals had similar DNA to modern man and lived only in family groups, the men being hunter-gatherers to feed the family.

Meanwhile, in Africa, Homo ergaster evolved into Homo sapiens sapiens at around the same time, spreading to Europe and interbreeding with the Neanderthals so that circa 4% of the DNA of non-African modern humans comes from them.

The Neanderthals had slightly larger brain size than Homo sapiens sapiens, but disappeared about 30,000 years ago, in part as a result of interbreeding.

Fragments of another subspecies of Homo sapiens, the Denisovans dating back 40,000 years, were recently discovered in Siberia, along with Neanderthal remains. Study of the nuclear genome of this species suggested that it came from the same origins as the Neanderthals. The Denisovans ranged from Siberia to Southeast Asia and up to 6% of their DNA is found in Melanesians, Australian Aborigines and the Mananwa, a Negrito people of the Philippines.

Comparison of the Denisovan and Neanderthal genomes showed that there was considerable interbreeding between the two species, the Denisovan DNA being 17% Neanderthal.

Some scientists believe in the 'replacement model', which holds that Neanderthals were replaced by migrating Homo sapiens sapiens. As noted above, however, the evidence now supports the 'assimilation model' in which there was a significant amount of interbreeding.

The 'assimilation' or 'multiregional evolution model' proposes that modern humans evolved more or less simultaneously in the major regions of the world, for example modern Chinese are thought to be evolved from archaic Chinese humans.

The present author believes this is true in this instance at least, and that modern Chinese people evolved from the Homo erectus species that evolved from the spread of the Homo ergaster species from Africa to Asia.

Like chimpanzees, homo sapiens sapiens formed tribes and there is evidence of religion, recorded events and art dating from 30,000 to 40,000 years ago implying the advanced language and ethics required for the ordering of social groups.

Clanning

Humans tend to form distinct groups, a process called *clanning*. In a classic psychology experiment 22 twelve-year-old boys with similar IQs, families and backgrounds were split into two groups and camped at opposite ends of the Robbers Cave State Park in Oklahoma.

The groups accidentally discovered each other, and hostilities commenced, each group rallying together in preparation and defence, one group calling themselves "the Eagles", and the other calling themselves "the Rattlers".

Minor provocations then grew into campsite raids and dining hall fights, and the psychologists tried to resolve the conflict by introducing challenges and goals that required both groups to work together, for example solving a water shortage, and pushing a broken-down truck back to camp.

When the two groups had become accustomed to working together, however, the conflicts subsided (Kaufman, 2012).

Tribalism in the modern world

Modern man still behaves in a highly tribal fashion, people of difference race, from different parts of the world, or of different social class tending to 'stick together'.

So it is that we still fight over:

(a) Racial and ethnic issues.

(b) Different religious beliefs (Mohr & Fear, 2015, 2016; Mohr, Fear & Sinclair, 2015).

(c) Sexuality, for example the feminist movement that 'took off' circa 1970.

(d) Sexual preference or practice, for example the gay rights movement.

(e) Different football and other sporting teams representing different countries, states, cities, and suburbs.

(f) Different political parties.

Religious terrorism was discussed in Chapter 4, (c), (d) and (e) are discussed in following sections, whilst (f) is discussed in Chapter 11.

The War of the Sexes

Oh yes, there is a vast difference between the savage and the
civilized man, but it is never apparent
to their wives until after breakfast.
Helen Rowland (1875–1950), U.S. journalist.
A Guide to Men, "Cymbals and Kettle-drums" (1922).

Some feminists claim that women's oppression was the first, most widespread and deepest social wrong in mankind's sorry history, one involving unpaid domestic slavery in marriage or lowly paid domestic slavery to the rich, the latter often having a racial basis.

The war of the sexes is taking a great toll and at present 40 per cent of first marriages and 60 per cent of second marriages end in divorce in the decadent West (Mohr, 2013b).

I would argue that much of this is the result of competitive, even confrontational, attitudes encouraged by the Feb Lib movement. Indeed, Tong (1998) notes that: some liberal feminists are sometimes criticized "for being too eager to adopt 'male' values." Despite this, she notes that "de facto gender discrimination lingers."

The gay movement

The gay movement has in recent decades continued to gain in strength, many, if not most, gay people insisting that homosexuality is inherited genetically, whereas myself and most psychologists believe it is a learnt behaviour, as discussed in Chapter 13.

Like the feminist movement, the gay movement tends to argue that men and women are equal in virtually all respects of any importance, regardless of sex or sexual preference.

Regrettably, in my view, the gay movement is encouraged by such events as annual gay Mardi Gras in many cities around the world.

For example, Australia's ABC News TV channel reported on 25/2/2018 that leaders of Sydney's gay "community" were pushing for gay Mardi Gras to be held in regional towns in Australia, called this plan the *"Rainbow on the plain"* plan, and citing 2018 being the 40th anniversary of Sydney's Gay Pride march as some sort of justification for this plan.

An offshoot of the gay rights movement is the LGTB movement, that is, the Lesbian, Gay, Transvestite and Bisexual movement, and the battle for equal rights for transgender people has resulted in the first transgender person being admitted to the US armed forces early in 2018.

Monkey business

Much of our so-called education of young children could be called monkey business because they are encouraged to act like monkeys on climbing frames and in often senseless ball games, some of which, like football, are positively dangerous and reduce some players to paraplegics.

Then there are the ludicrous crazes we fall for. When I was a child there was a mindless yo-yo craze. More recent were skateboard and roller blades crazes.

As for dangerous activities, roller blades and skate boards are bad enough but those concrete slopes built for kids to do bike tricks on are highly insane.

The list of insane human activities here is endless, including sky diving, climbing up vertical rock faces, skiing, and so on.

As for racing, it seems that we will race just about anything that can be made to move ranging from dogs to frogs.

Most of these activities have become spectator sports, some of them viewed by massive audiences brainwashed by hype and heavy media publicity into taking childish games played by overpaid adults seriously.

The complete insanity of this is that worrying oneself greatly over who wins a silly ball game is supposed to be recreational, that is, entertaining and relaxing. That riots often occur both off and on the field, notably in the English Premier League for example, is the last thing I would call relaxing.

Worrying too are the increasingly animalistic celebrations that accompany goals in football games and victory in most sports.

In addition, that many people enjoy watching brutal sports such as boxing and kick boxing doesn't say much good about the human race and only suggests that it is somewhat sick.

When you think about it, in fact, most of our ridiculous sport and recreational activities make us look far sillier than Krech's 'environment enriched' rats on their running wheels and slides (Packard, 1978).

The bottom line is that, as they used to say, *small things amuse small minds*, in other words we sure as hell are not getting any smarter.

The rich are getting richer

One of the major divisions in modern society, of course, is the gap between the rich and the poor. In fact, there are several levels of the hierarchy of wealth, these being:

(1) The mega rich with personal wealth in the billions.

(2) The very rich with personal wealth in the many millions.

(3) The middle class with 'good' incomes, most of whom eventually own their own house.

(4) The lower class on low incomes who never own their own house, or at best are paying a mortgage on a very cheap one.

(5) The poor, including the unemployed and disabled, who rely on government pensions for survival.

(6) The homeless who live on the streets, in parks etc.

The growing divide between the rich and the poor in many Western countries is often summed up as:

The rich get rich, and the poor get poorer.

In Chapter 1, Mohr's Law of Capitalism showed how one's power increases exponentially, the higher one is in the hierarchy, and how money invested by the rich can increase in value exponentially with time.

The rich of course, tend to stick together, for example, the book *The Rich and The Super Rich in America* pointed out that rich families intermarry to help safeguard their wealth in case of divorce, when both parties are already wealthy and need not pay any divorce settlement monies to the other.

Rich people, of course, have a far better quality of life, living in mansions, often with domestic servants to satisfy their every whim. They go on expensive holidays to the best holiday resorts in the world, to the best restaurants with waiter service of the best wines, and to exclusive clubs and casinos, the latter having special facilities for "high rollers".

The middle class, on the other hand, can barely afford to go to major sporting events, and use fast food restaurants rather than restaurants with waiter service.

The lower classes and the poor, of course, can barely afford to feed themselves and pay rent or other housing costs, whilst the homeless have to beg on the streets to provide money for food and cheap booze.

Conclusion

As was primitive man, modern man is still very tribal, and we divide ourselves in almost every possible way, that is, according to nationality, race, ethnicity, religion, sexuality, sexual preference, the football and other teams we follow, the political party we vote for, and, of course, our wealth.

Then, like primitives or animals, we fight over most of these divisions, the scale of conflict tending to grow according to the size the of groups involved, so that wars between nations, for example, are usually on a large scale, whilst the two so-called World Wars to date were, of course, on a massive scale.

Divisions in society according to wealth can give rise to the so-called "class system" in which there is often conflict between social or economic classes, especially between the capitalist and proletariat classes.

Indeed, the Westminster system of government so widely used in so-called democratic countries around the world is based on this class division, traditionally having a 'conservative' party representing the richer upper classes, and a 'labour' party representing the poorer working classes, and the early history of the Westminster 2-party system of government is discussed in Chapter 11.

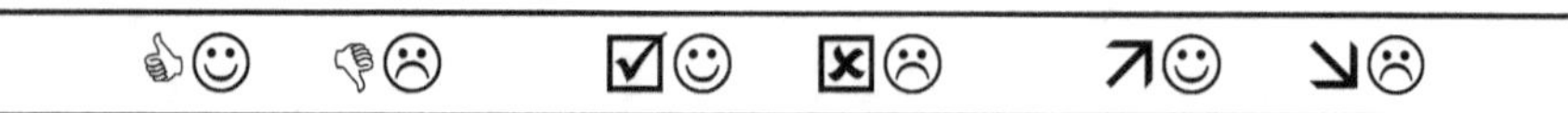

CHAPTER 10

THE CRIMINAL WORLD

Crime, like virtue, has its degrees.
Jean Racine, *Phèdre,* Act 4, Scene 2 (1677).

Crime which is prosperous and lucky is called virtue.
Seneca the Younger, *Hercules Furens*, 1. 251 (1st century).

I think crime pays. The hours are good, you travel a lot.
Woody Allen, *Take the Money and Run* (1969).

Sociological devolution

Not only is our environment in polluted and unsightly megacities unpleasant, but our societies are becoming meaner, nastier and more violent at an alarming rate.

Violence is on the increase everywhere to the point that many older people and women don't feel safe on the streets at night and, of course, there is no shortage of street crime during the day as well.

Experiments with rats show that when they are housed beyond a certain population density they begin to fight each other. Evidently humans do the same and we are now accustomed to associating crime and violence with big cities like Chicago and New York.

Increasing numbers of us are addicted to booze, illegal so-called 'party drugs,' as well as prescription drugs like Valium for anxiety, Ritalin for ADHD, and lithium for bipolar disorder (formerly called manic depression).

The bottom line is that you can see the writing on the walls, that is, the graffiti that covers much of our miserable megacities, a sure sign that we are regressing back to grunting cave men once again (Mohr, 2012c).

Criminal gangs

The Mafia has been one of the most powerful criminal networks in the world for over a century and, of course, it has a highly hierarchical structure, as epitomized by the highly successful movie *The Godfather* starring Marlon Brando, a later 'remake' starring Al Pacino.

There are, of course, several other major crime 'rings' around the world, for example in Columbia where they are heavily involved in trading drugs.

In Australia "bikie gangs" have been a major concern for many years, often being involved in "gang warfare".

More recently, some outer suburbs of Melbourne have been "terrorized" by home invasions, robberies in shops, and vandalism of public buildings, carried out by small groups of about four young men of Sudanese descent.

Australia-wide, however, the high levels of incarceration of Aboriginal and part-Aboriginal males have been a concern for many years, much of this problem having been attributed to high unemployment levels in this segment of the population.

The USA

For a decade or two mass shootings, most of them in schools, have been a major concern in the USA, whilst the annual death toll from the use of guns runs into the tens of thousands.

After the most recent school mass shooting of February 2018, there have once again been calls for stricter gun laws, and banning of sales of automatic assault rifles.

As a result, President Trump has proposed banning "bump stocks", which can be used to make an ordinary rifle fire with rapid repetition, and increasing the age at which some types of guns can be bought from 18 to 21.

The general public is calling for much tougher restrictions, however, but the powerful National Rifle Association, which contributed millions of dollars of funding to the last US election campaign, nearly all of it to the Republican Party, is likely to prevent major reform of gun laws in the USA, as it has done for decades.

The legal system

In Australia and like countries, there is a long history of 'crooked' cops and lawyers, and to estimate that perhaps 10% of them of them do, indeed, act unlawfully is perhaps reasonable.

In the USA, from 1920 to 1933 when "prohibition" banned the sale of alcohol, police were often paid by criminal gangs to turn a blind eye to bars and nightclubs illegally selling 'booze'.

In recent decades around the world, some police have been "paid off" to turn a blind eye to illegal drug manufacturing and sales.

Lawyers, of course, are paid handsomely to drag out legal cases as long as possible with delaying tactics, lies, and excuses of client poor health etcetera, and historically some lawyers have been strongly connected over many years to criminal gangs, effectively being a key part of them.

White collar crime

White collar crime has always been rife. In recent years we have only seen the tip of a great iceberg come to light in the media.

Routinely companies:

[1] Sack workers and refuse to pay them pension and other entitlements.

[2] Lie about their profitability and trade when insolvent.

[3] Fiddle their taxes using such artifices as massive and premature asset write-offs.

[4] Pay executives increasingly inflated salaries and bonuses as well as giving them huge stock parcels and options annually and upon retirement after only a few years. In contrast, shareholders, who are often struggling retirees, make minimal return on their investment after inflation is taken into account.

On the latter point it might be noted that Plato felt that the top people in a society should be paid no more than five times as much as those earning least. Several decades ago some people felt that ratio should not exceed 20. Now ratios of about 500 or more are almost commonplace.

Everyday examples of white collar crime include bank employees embezzling money, lawyers absconding with trust accounts and doctors fiddling their books with entries for treatments never carried out, for example one doctor who would issue government 'patient service' forms to friends at parties to fill out (Hall, 1979).

Examples of jailed corporate crooks in Australia in recent times include (*The Weekend Australian,* April 16-17, 2005):

➢ The CEO of a real estate company who bribed a politician.

➢ The leader of a women's group who stole $A4 million from it (such women should be in jail, not liberated).

➢ A merchant bank CEO who obstructed investigation into its failure.

➢ The CEO of an investment company who committed fraud.

➢ The CEO of a retail chain who misappropriated company funds.

➢ The CEO of a corporate empire "stripped" it of $A1.2 billion.

➢ A leading stockbroker convicted for insider trading.

IBM, though its German subsidiary Demohag, played in recording the details of Jews in Germany, Poland and Austria who were later sent to the Nazi death camps.

In 1998 a consortium of Swiss banks settled out of court to the tune of $US1.25 billion for transferring the accounts of thousands of Holocaust survivors to the Nazis around the beginning of WWII.

The fact that DuPont supplied the Zyklon B used to gas the Jews is, perhaps, even more remarkable but, in fact, a depressing reminder that fascism and big business are often one and the same.

In recent times the Enron debacle in the USA was notable and there have been a number of similar corporate collapses involving fraud in Australia, for example those associated with Alan Bond and Christopher Skase.

A few years ago the revelations that the Australian Wheat Board paid circa $A100M in kickbacks to Sadam Hussein's regime in Iraq were yet another example of 'dirty business.'
It should be noted, however, that 'power corrupts' is the truest of truisms and applies in both capitalist and socialist countries, but probably much less so in the latter.

Conclusion

There is no doubt that capitalism is inherently unfair. Few people, for example, disagree that the enormous executive salaries and other benefits that we often see today are excessive, and often company CEOs are found guilty of embezzlement of shareholder monies.

Much lip service is given to ways in which management can be socially responsible, for example the "triple bottom line" of focusing not only on profits, but also on social justice and environmental outcomes (Elkington, 1999). This has had little or no effect on business practice with CEOs taking more and more drastic measures to improve profits and thence their own benefits.

As has been the case for hundreds of years, many people still feel that banks and other money lending organizations make excessive profits, while in recent years some banks in Australia have been accused of acting criminally.

Contrary to what governments and the media assure us, therefore, living standards in the developed countries have fallen dramatically in recent decades while in third world countries things seem to be getting worse, not better.

On a personal level, I have been the victim of crime more than once, for example:

(a) As described in Chapter 8, being bullied by a new HOD into resigning a University post, and never getting another job thanks to 'backstabbing' confidential references by him. Indeed, the faculty Dean said to my face a couple of years earlier when a promotion was delayed: *Lawyers are expensive.* The reason for delay was that I'd complained about a nasty act of bullying by a colleague, my eventual 'demise' being typical of how the large hierarchies operate.

(b) As described in Chapter 2, being cheated by my elder brother more than once of 'family money' that I should have had a greater share of.

(c) Being cheated out of thousands of dollars by a 60+ year-old Egyptian lawyer with a self-professed obsession with "the Arab World" who was praised by *"Islamist"* on Facebook. He was listed in *Australian Writers Marketplace* under Publishers - in fact he did only 'self-publishing' incompetently and at exhorbitant cost.

I was bullied into sending 4 books because of an unfair contract clause. After seeing no progress on the 4th book after 18 months, I complained, unwisely using the phrase "Islamic incompetence". He went mad and "terminated" my contract overnight, refusing to refund several thousand dollars he therefore owed me.

Though a Victorian judge said he should refund the money, he cited another unfair contract clause saying all disputes should be heard in New South Wales.

Repeated phone calls were ignored, and then I was charged and fined for harassment, so that this nasty affair cost me many thousands of dollars.

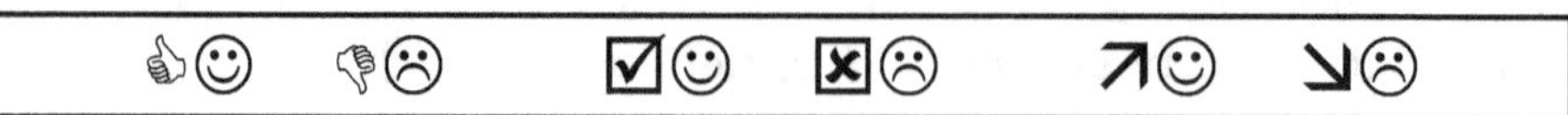

CHAPTER 11

POLITICS

> *A democracy exits whenever those who are free and are not well-off, being in the majority, are in sovereign control of government, an oligarchy when control lies with the rich and better born.*
> Aristotle, *The Politics* (343 BC)
>
> *Just as Darwin discovered the law of evolution of organic matter, so Marx discovered the law of evolution of human history.*
> Friedrich Engels, said at the funeral of Karl Marx (1883).

Mohr's law of politics

In this context Barth's Distinction is relevant:

There are two types of people: those who divide people into two types and those who do not.

This relates to Mohr's Law of Politics, that is:

When we build a political 'fence' of some kind then people will generally divide fairly equally on both sides of it.

In the farcical and outdated Westminster system, for example, the 2 main parties are relatively similar in policies, incompetence etcetera, so many a voter makes up their mind on which side of the political fence to place their vote only at the last minute.

Then for the next 3 – 5 years the government and opposition rant and rave at each other from opposite sides of the 'chamber', often in a truly farcical and, indeed somewhat insane fashion such that, were such ranting to occur outside parliament the police might be called to stop it, and the 'ravers' would quite likely be referred for psychiatric treatment, if not interment.

Democracy

Aristotle's remark about oligarchy which opens this chapter is an important reminder that, as then, we do not have *real* democracy today.

The populations of the Greek city-states of his time rarely exceeded 10,000 people, all the 'citizens' of which voted with black and white stones on the questions of the day in open forum.

Aristotle's complaint was that it was only the men and not women or slaves who were allowed this privilege and slavery, of course, can hardly be equated with democracy.

In most of the world today we do not have anything like real democracy. We have, in fact, Westminster type *parliamentary democracy,* a very brief history of which is (Mackenzie, 1950):

Pre 1066 (Saxon times). The barons and King met each year at Easter, Whitsun and Christmas.

1258 (in the reign of Henry III). A meeting of the barons of England at Oxford was the origin of the *House of Lords.*

1264. Simon de Montfort, on the King's behalf, organized a meeting of two knights from each county.

1265. Two citizens from each county were included in the latter meeting, constituting the origin of the *House of Commons.*

In the reign of Elizabeth I the puritans became the first party and were the opposition to the crown.

In the reign of James I the cavaliers and roundheads emerged as two opposing political forces.

1681. The origin of the names *Whig* and *Tory.*

This system has evolved in England, Australia and New Zealand into the two main parties being a conservative party, which supports the capitalist ruling class, and a Labour Party which traditionally supported the workers or modern-day slaves.

The Conservative Party is said to be *right wing* and the Labour Party *left wing*, a fine example of the power of emotive language.

Now, however, big business has considerable influence on both parties and the policies of the Labour Party are often more conservative than those the conservative party.

The result is a revolving door parody of democracy in which stooges become our leaders for relatively brief periods but their policies are greatly influenced by the business sector and the economic imperialism of traditional allies in war, in Australia these being the US and UK.

In this parody the 'fat cats' of the public service wield more influence in policy-making than do average members of parliament (Self, 1977).

Capitalism

> *Government of the busy by the bossy for the bully.*
> Arthur Seldon, *Capitalism,* p. 111 (1990).

While so-called democracy prevails in most of the world, the reality is that, with the world's markets becoming increasingly global, transnational companies and thence unrestrained capitalism provides the power and influence that runs the politics of most countries.

In the 1930s John Maynard Keynes proposed that a multiplier effect existed such that small increases in government spending in the community have a much greater effect upon the productivity of the nation. This is the *fiscal* approach and was widely adopted by many countries in the West for about 50 years.

Milton Friedman and other economists favour the free market or *monetarist* economic philosophy. This stems from the 17th century and is based on the equation (Wonnacott & Wonnacott, 1979):

$$MV \text{ (aggregate demand)} = PQ \text{ (aggregate supply)}$$

where
M = the amount of money in circulation (per year)
V is its velocity of circulation (in transactions per year)
P = the price of goods in circulation
Q = the quantity of goods in circulation (per year)

Here *V* is the only relatively stable quantity and is based on the fact that, when you buy a product, the money you pay for it might be passed on quite soon as wages for somebody in the company you bought the product from. Then that person spends their wages on food and other necessities, and so on. Typically *V* takes a value of around 4 in modern economies.

This little or no government monetarist approach has led to more rampant capitalism than ever before. As a result an 'establishment' that effectively rules capitalist countries is formed (Blondel, 1963).

This establishment deplores the mildest hint of socialism and thence government ownership of industry, or even influence over industry. *They* tell government to reduce company taxes further and to cut back on government spending to do it and governments continue to heed them.

Effectively running military-industrial countries like the UK and US as they do, the barons of capitalism have ensured that their governments fight the evil threat of socialism, for example leading to the British secret service providing considerable covert support to the White Russian army resisting the 1917 revolution. When that failed they began counter terrorist activities against the new Russia such as Lieutenant Agar's sinking of the Red Fleet cruiser Oleg in Kronstadt harbour in 1919 (Brook-Shepherd, 1998).

Some evidence of such policies was given by the first president of the National Civic Federation in the USA when he wrote in 1909: "Our enemies are the socialists and other labor people and the anarchists among the capitalists."

In the 1970s David Rockefeller funded the Trilateral Commission which in 1975 funded a meeting of multinational corporate executives to consider the "excess of democracy" afflicting advanced capitalist countries and to "rationalize the US economy through capitalist dominated planning and in conjunction with other leading capitalist nations to reassert US authority on a world scale" (Crough et al., 1980).

Socialism

To the ordinary working man,
the sort you would meet in any pub on Saturday night,
Socialism does not mean much more than better wages
and shorter hours and nobody bossing you about.
George Orwell, *The Road to Wigan Pier,* ch. 11 (1937).

It is important at the outset to note that *socialism* refers to the 'means of production' being owned by the state whereas *communism* refers to the means of production being owned by the people. The two terms are often confused but in a complex and highly technological modern society it is doubtful that communism is practical. It is doubtful, for example, that the very large companies required in some industries, many of these now transnational ones, can be owned and run by the 'people', taking people to mean those in a particular community.

What is clear, however, is that the 1848 Marx-Engels manifesto was anti-capitalist and this was the real spirit of the 1917 Russian revolution, a spirit which many believed would eventually spread globally. This revolution created a socialist state with a long term view towards forming a communist society.

Marxists argue that the capitalist *class* accumulates increasingly more capital or a 'surplus value' in fact created by the workers. The working class, therefore, are left to accumulate misery or, as Marx put it:

In proportion as capital accumulates, the lot of the labourer be his payment high or low, must grow worse.

Critics of this view will point out that in practice state ownership leads to totalitarian government which makes the people worse off, rather than better.

Marxists will also argue that in capitalism monopolies or oligopolies must eventually develop, in turn influencing the political system so that something akin to totalitarianism can result.

In defence against this view critics of Marxism will argue that it is better to reform the capitalist system, not replace it, for example by introducing antimonopoly laws.

Theoretical arguments aside, revolutions have always occurred when there are high levels of unemployment and poverty.

Capitalism, however, relies upon a substantial pool of unemployed to keep the price of labour down (Sweezy, 1946). As a result, some studies found little reduction in poverty in the USA in the years 1947 - 1960 (Townsend, 1970) whereas socialism has reduced poverty and famine in China dramatically (Maxwell et al., 1977).

What of the future?

Not long ago some economics texts asked the question about socialism and capitalism: "Are the systems converging?"

About the USSR, at least, it is now safe to say that its system has changed and some aspects of socialism, such as centralization of power, have been much reduced. Before the USSR was dismantled, however, there had long been changes such as a greater tendency to pay highly skilled workers more, less interventionist government and slow opening up to outside (and hence not state) capital.

About the future in the USSR, or China, for example, it therefore seems safe to say that there has been a move in the direction of capitalism (and democracy, but this is not necessarily synonymous with any particular economic system).

What can we say about the USA and like countries? Clearly there is some disenchantment with the two party system that may begin to crystallize somewhere. In Australia circa 2011, for example, three independents and the Greens party held the balance of power in both the legislative lower house of representatives, and the upper house or senate which is required to approve legislation from the lower house.

Some mention should now be made of the Arab and other Muslim countries that have attracted much attention of late. These, taken collectively, may have an increasing voice and influence in world affairs.

Finally, what can we say about China?

After the fall of the USSR the USA was deemed the only "superpower", but now China is also called a superpower, is a major player in the global economy, and thanks to its many aid programs, has increasing influence in many countries throughout Asia and Africa.

Proposals for change

Some authors suggest that inequality in capitalist societies should be reduced by reducing the inheritability of wealth, in other words by increasing death duties (Broom et al., 1980).

This is an unpopular proposal to both the rich and the middle class. As a result the Australian state of Queensland abolished death duties many years ago and other states only apply them to large fortunes.

Others have suggested a policy of equalizing outcomes, an approach that might penalize effort as well as inheritance (Jencks et al., 1975).

A more original and interesting proposal was made by Peter Jay (1981), a former economics editor of *The Times*:

- - that the enterprises which create the wealth, the firms, the corporations, should belong to, be owned by, should have their directors exclusively appointed by and their net assets and their residual earnings should belong to, and exclusively to, the people who work at them.

Jay suggested that it is an accident of history, not a law of economics, that the entrepreneur has tended to be the person who supplied the risk capital. He proposed that in modern economies worker-owned companies should be able to raise debt finance from banks and equity finance from shareholders in the usual way.

Capitalists are happy to have their workers become shareholders, of course, because shareholders do not have to be paid dividends in bad times whereas banks always require interest to be paid on loans.

Jay's proposal goes a lot further and might eliminate the absurd salaries, share and rights bonuses, and retirement packages we see today. Indeed, it would only seem fair that *all* workers for a corporation should receive share issues as a non-taxable part of their income.

War and big business

> *War is an essential part of capitalism and can only be*
> *abolished by changing the present social system.*
> *This is the task which history has assigned*
> *to all those who suffer most by war.*
> George Padmore, *Africa and World Peace* (1937).

War and big business go hand in hand. The arms trade is the world's largest (Sampson, 1977; Pringle and Spigelman, 1981) and, as a result, large tracts of land in several parts of the world remain littered with land mines which continue to maim innocent people.

The arms race of the cold war was certainly one of the best examples of Keynes' view that war was like digging a hole and pouring money into it. The staggering number of nuclear missiles (see Table 11.1) accumulated by the USSR and USA, along with of large stockpiles of biological weapons, was one of the greatest acts of insanity in history.

Had that money been spent helping educate and thence control population growth in the poorest parts of the world the outlook for the human race would not be as bleak as it is.

That humans devote so much time to accumulating weapons of war is great insanity and those responsible should be brought to justice and, of course, we need to make nuclear and biochemical weapons illegal.

Table 11.1. US & Soviet Nuclear Armaments (Bethe, 1991).

	US	USSR
Delivery vehicles		
ICBMs (intercontinental ballistic missiles)	1,050	1,400
SLBMs (submarine launched missiles)	630	950
Bombers	350	140
Total	2,030	2,490
Warheads		
ICBMS	2,150-2,250	5,500-6,400
SLBMs	4,750	1,750-1,900
Bombers	2,500-3,500	280-550
Total	9,400-10,500	7,530-8,850
Equivalent megatons		
ICBMs	1,300	5,900
SLBMs	800	1,200
Bombers	3,500	900
Total	5,600	8,000

Note that 2 megatons = 1.59 equivalent megatons. The latter is the best measure of the area that can be destroyed, whereas megatons are the best measure of fallout.

For the companies that manufacture arms war is good for business, including modern cold war or 'rocket rattling'.

Recently North Korea has done a great deal of that, having developed increasingly great nuclear strike capability, and causing great concern in the USA.

The punched card system of recording data was invented in Germany by Herman Hollerith in the late 19th century. By the 1930s, however, IBM controlled about 90% of the world's market in punch cards and sorters.

At that time the CEO of IBM was the unscrupulous Thomas Watson who happily agreed to take on the task of accumulating data on all the Jews in Germany (Black, 2001). For the purpose he gathered together a number of IBM subsidiaries in Germany under the name Dehomag and in 1933 one-half million census takers went door to door gathering information to fill out questionnaires on each household in the country. The information included the religion of the head of the household and whether the person was in a mixed marriage.

IBM continued to work for Hitler throughout WWII, as did a few other US companies such as Du Pont who provided chemicals used to gas Jews.

The purposes of terrorism

Today in numerous places around the world such as Afghanistan, Chechnya, Columbia, Iraq, Palestine, Spain and some countries in northern Africa, small groups of people are using terrorist tactics in trying to overthrow governments, seek independence for a region of their country, or evict foreign troops and bases.

In WWII the polite term 'resistance' was used by Dutch and French groups that engaged in acts of terrorism against the occupying German forces.

Often groups seeking to overthrow governments have ideological motives, of which socialism (state ownership of industry) is the most common, this usually being incorrectly referred to as 'communism' which, in reality, might not involve industry at all.

The French revolution disposed of the monarchy and had a socialist basis. So too the 1917 Russian revolution. The revolutions in China in 1947 and Cuba in 1959 also had a socialist aim.

As Fidel Castro put it:
> *Revolution is not a bed of roses,*
> *it is a struggle to death between the future and the past.*

The purpose of terrorism with a religious pretext is not always clear. The grievance of Palestinians, having lost most of the land that was the "British Protectorate" of Palestine in the 1930s when the UN implemented the Balfour Declaration to create the state of Israel in 1948, is readily understandable.

The six-day war of June 1967, when Israel took over a great deal more Palestinian territory, increased tensions and conflict, with talk of a "two-state solution" having now continued without result for decades.

Throughout the Middle East, and in much of Africa and Asia, Islamic terrorism continues, as briefly discussed in Chapter 4, and without any end in sight, whilst Israel's war against the Hamas terrorist organization in the Gaza strip has continued for 8 months (as at 9/6/24), circa 37,000 Palestinians having been killed, many of these women and children.

Psycho politicians

A major problem in world politics that now seems worse than ever is that of psycho politicians. As noted in the Preface, the Cambridge Dictionary defines 'psycho' as: *someone who is crazy and frightening.*

This is certainly true of the most obviously psychopathic politician in the world today, namely ex-KGB Vladimir Putin who, trying to restore the USSR in some form and thus recapture Ukraine, has had after two years war in the south and east of Ukraine, according to a Ukrainian estimate, 500,000 Russian troops killed in a war that has united the USA and several other countries in support of Ukraine.

The disgusting and lunatic 'dickhead' Putin had, via a corrupt electoral system, himself elected to the Russian leadership for a fourth 5-year term, so no doubt he will continue his Ukrainian war for the foreseeable future, 'rattling' the nuclear threat in most of his press conferences.

The 'dickhead' USA president, Joe Biden, on the other hand, has shown early signs of senile dementia for a few years, leading to widespread media comment about his fitness for office.

Ludicrously, his likely opponent in forthcoming US elections, Donald Trump, is an obvious psychopath, with a history of crooked business deals, lying, and power grabs.

Both he, at almost 80, and Biden at over 80, are clearly too old to be President of any country, let alone the USA with the world's largest economy. But this is simply one example amongst many of a country that does do not now have democracy, but oligarchy, as Aristotle complained about Greece thousands of years ago.

Conclusions

World politics has changed with Russia having regaining lost influence, and China having become the world's second superpower.

With Western governments continuing to decrease company taxes, the rich are getting richer, and the lower classes poorer, increasing the prospects of societal conflict.

More serious, Islamic conflict and terrorism continues in much of the world, whilst the threat of nuclear war grows as countries such as North Korea and Iran increase their nuclear capability.

In many Western nations the antiquated Westminster 2-party system is falling out of favour, and minor parties and independent candidates have increasing influence, and coalition governments involving two or three parties are becoming increasingly common. In my recent book *The Doomsday Calculation*, therefore, I make proposals regarding *real democracy* which include allowing only independent members of parliament (Mohr, 2012c).

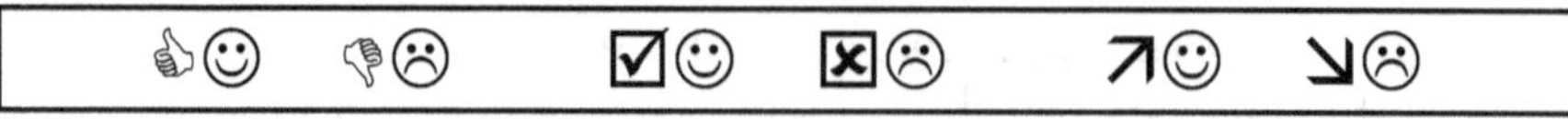

CHAPTER 12

PSYCHOLOGY AND PSYCHIATRY

Psychiatry

Sigmund Freud (1865 - 1939) developed what he called "the talking cure" or psychoanalysis which some regard as the first method of examining the human mind. He also proposed the division of the psyche into ego (our outer self), super-ego (our conscience), and id (our inner self).

Modern psychiatry now assesses a wide range of mental disorders, several of which are discussed in following sections.

The field of psychiatry, however, has a disgraceful history. As late as 1815 the Bethlehem madhouse in England exhibited lunatics every Sunday and made a considerable amount of money in the process (Youngson & Schott, 1996).[3]

---

[3]The word Bedlam is a corruption of "Bethlehem."

At the Bicêtre hospital in France attendants used whips to make the mad dance to provide traditional entertainment. At the Charenton asylum the infamous Marquis de Sade presided over theatrical performances by the inmates.

In the USSR dissidents were often confided to asylums for the insane, a policy no doubt practiced elsewhere.

The practice of lobotomy was particularly scandalous.

It can be traced back to Dr Gottlieb Burckhardt, the superintendent of a psychiatric hospital in Switzerland, who in 1890 drilled holes in the head of six severely agitated patients, thereby altering their behaviour.

Then in 1935 John Fulton at Yale University removed the frontal lobes from two chimpanzees, changing their behaviour greatly. Dr Walter Freeman, an American neurologist, was recovering from a nervous breakdown when in July 1935 he attended a seminar given by Fulton.

Egas Moniz, a celebrated Portuguese neurosurgeon also attended the seminar and two months later in Portugal he performed the first *leucotomy* by drilling a small hole in the skull and injecting alcohol into it to destroy the fibres in the frontal lobes of the patient. The operation succeeded in making the patient less agitated and overtly paranoid but made her more apathetic and dull than Moniz had hoped. Nevertheless, further operations were performed and the procedure was refined by drilling six holes in the skull.

When he published he gave no hint of the downside of his procedure and Freeman was bursting with enthusiasm to try it and he enlisted the aid of neurosurgeon James Watts to carry out his first leucotomy on 14 September 1936.

A week later the patient became incoherent and could not even recite the days of the week and when asked to write could only scribble nonsense. Her speech improved in following days and they operated on another five patients.

In November 1936 Freeman and Watts published a report in which they wrote: *In all our patients there was a ... common denominator of worry, apprehension, anxiety, insomnia and nervous tension, and in all of them these symptoms have been relieved to a greater or lesser extent.*

Freeman and Watts renamed the procedure *lobotomy* and made it more drastic by drilling only two holes in the side of the head and using a canula, the tubing from a six inch heavy-gauge hypodermic needle, to pave the way for a cutting tool to destroy targeted brain tissue.

Watts became so proficient that he could thread the canula through the brain from the small hole on one side of the head to that on the other. Though not qualified to do so, Freeman began to perform lobotomies on his own and became a celebrity in the process. He also simplified the procedure by using electroshock to subdue the patient and then plunging an ice pick into their head, usually producing a zombie-like person.

Often the procedure was repeated a second and third time and Freeman, a neurotic with severe depressive symptoms who needed 3 Nembutal to sleep at night, enthusiastically continued his crude procedure years after it had been discredited.

Such surgery had been performed on more than 40,000 people in the USA alone by 1955. Fortunately, lobotomy has fallen out of favour though it is probably still practiced occasionally.

The misinformation that allowed this brutal procedure to be performed for some 30 years, however, is all too typical of a world in which we are fed misinformation and brainwashed into accepting any new procedure or product no matter how dangerous.

Little better, however, is widely used electroconvulsive shock therapy (ECT) in which electrodes are placed on either side of the head and short bursts of high-frequency and high intensity electrical current passed through the brain. ECT can produce a strong amnesic effect, but it is not clear by what means this occurs (Atrens & Curthoys, 1982).

Psychopaths

This is the largest category of abnormal psychological types, involving the following behaviours such as (Davies, 1971):

[1] Assertiveness, aggression and bullying.
[2] Dishonesty and lying.
[3] Alcohol and drug addiction.
[4] Excessive sexual behaviours.

Psychopaths usually have two or more of the above traits, but are not normally classified as mentally ill, in part perhaps because they are so common.

Through their assertiveness, dishonesty etc. psychopaths often rise high in the hierarchies of business. Gillespie (2017), having had "many good managers" in his "various careers", cites a personal example of a psychopathic boss:

He was constantly meddling - - micromanaging the workplace - -. He trusted nobody and his impact on the workplace was devastating.

This boss made a habit of giving select people subtle but excruciating public punishment. - - The longer I knew him the more convinced I became that everything he said was a lie.

He cites a few examples of famous people from the past and present who might be described as psychopaths, including Caligula, Lance Armstrong, and Donald Trump, quoting Tony Schwartz, the co-author of Trump's autobiography, as telling the *"New Yorker* that if he were writing *The Art of the Deal* today, he'd call it 'The Sociopath'.

Bullying may be learnt by an eldest brother or sister, and the first author knew examples of both cases both within his own 'nuclear family', his extended (by his own marriage) family, and people with whom he was friendly for a while.

Evidently the eldest is able to boss younger siblings around from an early age, and often stays bossy with both these siblings, and perhaps others, if not most, people throughout most of the rest of their life until too old and feeble to be bossy anymore.

Bullying usually involves a boss, or somebody with psychopathic aggressive tendencies based on feelings of superiority, 'bad mouthing' the victim to their face with brief but hurtful and disturbing insults. These insults are repeated regularly to both the victims, often a 'loners' in an isolated situation, and to the bully's small group of friends and supporters who then repeat the same insults to the victims, increasing their feelings of isolation and helplessness.

In the schoolyard, for example, the bully is often bigger and stronger than the victim, who may be of the 'nerd' type. Indeed, the bully is often better at sport, but jealous of the victim getting better marks in class and perhaps occasional praise from teachers and others.

In the workplace the reasons for bullying by bosses or 'superiors' in the workplace hierarchy are often less clear, but often, for example, involve male bosses abusing women with 'sexual insults' that they are ugly, or that women in general are in some way inferior.

Mania

Typical manic behaviour involves a period in which an expansive, elevated, or irritable mood, along with enhanced activity and reactivity persists abnormally. During this episode symptoms such as increased talkativeness and grandiosity, distractibility, decreased need for sleep, inflated self-esteem, and excessive involvement in pleasurable yet risky activities may be present.

Such symptoms occur during normal mood changes, but it is their magnitude and frequent recurrence that may indicate a psychiatric problem. The frenetic and driven behaviour of mania results in a non-functional individual who cannot work effectively (Atrens & Curthoys, 1982).

It is well established that drugs effective in the treatment of mania are those that antagonize dopamine and serotonin. The mechanism responsible for the therapeutic efficacy of lithium for the treatment of mania is not yet clear. Although mood disorders tend to have a familial background, the evidence for a genetic component is not convincing.

Depression

Depression is very common, and it is normal to feel depressed from time to time. Severe depression, however, is characterized by despondency, diminished interest in most or all activities, weight fluctuation not due to dieting, disruption in sleep patterns, psychomotor agitation or retardation, feelings of worthlessness, excessive quiet, and recurrent thoughts of death or suicide.

A professional diagnosis of depression is made, however, when a person suffers frequent and/or prolonged bouts of depression of more than usual severity, perhaps associated with thoughts of self-harm or suicide.

Major depression is associated with decreased brain levels of the neurotransmitters norepinephrine and serotonin, and the most effective therapy consists of drugs that inhibit the breakdown of these compounds.

Much less common, manic depression, or bipolar disorder, involves both manic 'highs' of greater energy and activity, alternating with bouts of depression or 'lows'. Manic depression is often treated with lithium salts.

Anxiety

It is normal to feel anxious about things ranging from minor issues such as getting behind with one's work or household chores, to worrying when a child is late coming home from a party. Many people have abnormal levels of anxiety, including phobias and fears, and tranquillizers such as Valium, which enhances the inhibitory actions of the neurotransmitter GABA, are used to relieve anxiety and relax muscles.

Obsessive Compulsive Disorder

Obsessive Compulsive Disorder (OCD) is a form of anxiety which makes people worry about certain things and 'overreact' to their concerns, the two most common behaviours being washing and checking, for example some people wearing away skin on their hands by frequently washing them, others repeatedly checking such things as whether the door is locked when they leave home.

One OCD sufferer, for example, feels compelled to do many things four times, another to count to seven between each mouthful of food (Carter, 2007).

Hypochondria

Hypochondria is an anxiety disorder in which people worry excessively about their health, for example just hearing someone mention a certain illness triggering fears that they might have that illness.

Tourette's syndrome

Tourette's syndrome is also an anxiety disorder, and certainly sufferers do appear anxious and disturbed when they have a bout of Tourette's and stressfully utter a nonsensical word while some part of their body, usually the face, has a 'tic' or twitches.

Asperger's syndrome

This is a psychiatric disorder usually noted during early school years and characterized by impaired social relations and by repetitive patterns of behaviour.

Autism

This an abnormal absorption with the self marked by communication disorders, short attention span, and inability to deal with other people.

In 2016 a Finish study of 258 people found that religious people could be compared with those with autism because they didn't view the world realistically, many believing in such supernatural phenomena as demons, gods and inanimate objects being alive in some way.

ADHD

Attention Deficit Hyperactivity Disorder (ADHD) is normally associated with school children who have difficulty sitting through classes without feeling distracted and wishing to be elsewhere doing something else. They thus have trouble concentrating and their learning is affected adversely.

There is much current controversy about this condition, many feeling that it is diagnosed too freely with children needlessly being put on long-term medication that may do more harm than good.

Dyslexia

This is an impaired ability to comprehend written words usually associated with a neurological disorder. The cause of dyslexia is believed to involve both genetic environmental factors and it often occurs in people with ADHD and is associated with similar difficulties with numbers. It may begin in adulthood as the result of a traumatic brain injury, stoke or dementia. The underlying mechanisms of dyslexia are problems within the brain's language processing.

Dyslexia is diagnosed through a series of tests of memory, spelling, vision, and reading skills and should not be confused with reading difficulties caused by hearing or vision problems, or insufficient teaching.

Treatment involves adjusting teaching methods to meet the person's needs which, while not curing the underlying problem, may decrease the symptoms. Treatments targeting vision are ineffective.

Dyslexia is the most common learning disability and occurs all around the world. It affects 3–7% of the population but up to 20% may have some degree of symptoms. While dyslexia is more often diagnosed in men, it has been suggested that it affects men and women equally.

Dyslexia should not be confused with 'mirror writing', for which Leonardo da Vinci was famous, some believing that he wrote in this fashion deliberately as a sort of coding.

Schizophrenia

Schizophrenia is a chronic neurological disease of distorted thoughts and perceptions which usually begins during adolescence or early adulthood (Sweeney, 2009) It has a strong genetic component, one which research shows may be largely physiological, and not a result of a "disturbed environment" (Atrens & Curthoys, 1982).

Schizoid people worry obsessively about being watched by others and being talked about, fearing that people know too much about them and have invaded their 'space'. When walking in the street, for example, they will worry that other people are watching them, in this way 'distorting' reality.

Schizophrenia is relatively common, occurring in about 1 percent of the general population worldwide. Because the incidence of schizophrenia among parents, children, and siblings of patients with the disease is increased to 15 percent, it is believed that heredity plays an important role in the genesis of the disease (Atrens & Curthoys, 1982). However, other studies suggest that non-genetic factors such as a "disturbed environment" are also influential.

In the last decade or two, for example, a correlation between excessive and prolonged marijuana use and the development of schizophrenia has been observed.

The biochemical basis of the disease may be an excess of the neurotransmitter substance dopamine, as high levels of dopamine and its metabolites, as well as increased dopamine receptors, are found in the brains of persons with schizophrenia. Further evidence for this hypothesis is that the drugs most effective in treating the disease are those that have a high capacity to block dopamine receptors.

Psychosis

Psychosis is any severe mental disorder in which contact with reality is lost or highly distorted, including severe schizophrenia. The drug chlorpromazine was developed and widely used to treat psychosis, by 1964 ten thousand peer-reviewed articles having been published on it. According to Lieberman (2015),

Like a bolt from the blue, here was a medication that could relieve the madness that disabled tens of millions of men and women - - the widespread adoption of chlorpromazine marked the beginning of the end for the asylums.

The commercial success of this drug encouraged pharmaceutical companies to search for new antipsychotic drugs, leading to the massive pharmaceutical industry of today.

Hysteria

This is a neurotic disorder characterized by violent emotional outbreaks and disturbances of sensory and motor functions. The term hysteria comes from the Greek word *hustericos* meaning 'of the womb' because ancient Greeks associated such highly emotional and neurotic behaviour with childless women. This indicates that man has long had an interest in trying to understand human psychology and behaviour.

Dementia

Dementia is simply mental deterioration usually associated with old age. Senile dementia of the Alzheimer type (SDAT) is a result of advanced Alzheimer's disease, a progressive form of pre-senile dementia that is similar to senile dementia except that it usually starts in the 40s or 50s, the first symptoms being impaired memory which is followed by impaired thought and speech, and finally complete helplessness.

Homosexuality

Homosexuality is on the increase. Once a trait one had to keep secret it is now rampantly displayed at gay Mardi Gras festivals, at gay bars in major cities, and in late night TV ads for homosexual dating services.

Some claim that homosexuality is inherited and a study of 113 people in 33 families in which at least two brothers were homosexual found a genetic marker on the X-chromosome (Xq28) that had a very high correlation with sexual orientation (Galton, 2001).

Genes may play a minor 'predispositionary' role but, largely, homosexuality is a learnt behaviour. Typically, for example, the normal heterosexual male has one or two homosexual experiences in adolescence (Robertson, 1981), and no doubt the same applies to women.

Those who become homosexuals, therefore, presumably do so as a result of imitative learning at an early age. There are, no doubt, also psychological factors involved, for example a lack of confidence in approaching the opposite sex coupled with the fact that there are earlier homosexual experiences to draw upon as an alternative behaviour model.

If alcoholism is to be regarded as a psychiatric illness, as it often is (Davies, 1971), then homosexuality is even more obviously a treatable psychiatric condition as well.

That said, most of our heterosexual behaviours are also learnt ones, many of them hardly natural or healthy, an example being 'tongue kissing', a truly revolting and very unhealthy practice like many other modern sexual practices.

Post-traumatic Stress Disorder (PTSD)

PTSD is caused by events of great stress and trauma in a person's life, a well-known example being Vietnam war veterans, whose symptoms of PTSD such as depression and suicidal thoughts were increased by feelings of isolation as a result of having fought in a war which many thought to be mistake in the first place, and which the West ultimately lost.

Losing one's job, or the death of a spouse or young child are also common causes of PTSD.

According to Cozolino (2002):

Someone suffering from PTSD is, in essence, in a continual loop of unconscious self-traumatization, coping and exhaustion. When these symptoms are experienced on a chronic basis, they can devastate every aspect of the victim's life, from physical well-being to the quality of relationships to the victim's experience of the world.

Madness, bullying and genius

A somewhat simplistic way of categorizing 'mad people' is to divide them into just three categories in order of how commonly they occur these being:

1. **Sad mad.**

2. **Bad mad.**

3. **Good mad.**

The pathology of type 1 includes depression, anxiety, and OCD. That of type 2, the psychopaths, includes aggression, lying, bullying, cheating, 'backstabbing', fraud and other crimes.

A 2016 "anti-bullying conference" in Melbourne reported that "children as young as three are being identified as bullies amid concern many childcare centres and kindergartens aren't doing enough to stamp out the problem" (The Herald-Sun, 6/8/2016).

Recent research also shows that young bullies at school are likely to become anti-social adults, whilst a 2006 survey found bullying in the Victorian public sector to be "frequent", with almost 24% of staff saying they frequently thought of leaving the public sector. Similar findings have been made in Australian hospitals.

The third category refers to such people as 'mad scientists' whose discoveries are often of great benefit to mankind. Newton was an example, an accidental fire in 1692 in which he lost the records of 20 years of his work affecting him greatly (Egerton Eastwick, 1896), perhaps contributing to him being remembered as somewhat eccentric:

He lived the life of a solitary, and like all men who are
occupied with profound meditation, he acted strangely.
Sometimes in getting out of bed, an idea would come to him,
and he would sit on the edge of the bed,
half dressed, for hours at a time.
Louis Figuier, *Vies de Savants* (tr. B.H. Clark, 1897).

Newton had two nervous breakdowns before retiring from Cambridge at age 42 to go into politics, saying: *Tis best to do a little well, and leave the rest to those that follow.*

No doubt these were a result of bullying, for example cartoons of him sitting under a tree and discovering his law of gravity with an apple falling on his head. In fact, this may also relate to him spending a period on his family farm, perhaps to recover from a breakdown.

Writers and artists, many of whom work in relative solitude, have also often been associated with depression, (Thomas & Hughes, 2006), Vincent van Gogh being a notable example (Sweeney, 2009).

Conclusion

Freud has often been accused of an obsession with sexual feelings (Gillespie, 2017), whilst both he and Jung seem to have been overly obsessed with the importance of dreams, leading many people to distrust formal "talk therapy". Psychology and thence psychiatry can, however, play an important role in understanding and dealing with the psychopathic leaders that abound in hierarchical organizations of all kinds.

CHAPTER 13

THE PSYCHOLOGY OF ATTITUDES

> *The body of science described in this book could only have been developed in democratic societies, where attitudinal influence is the form of control that is most often relied upon.*
> Alice H. Eagly and Shelly Chaiken,
> *The Psychology of Attitudes* (1993).

The psychology of attitudes

Attitude can be defined as 'psychological *tendency* expressed by *evaluating* a particular entity with some degree of favour or disfavour.'

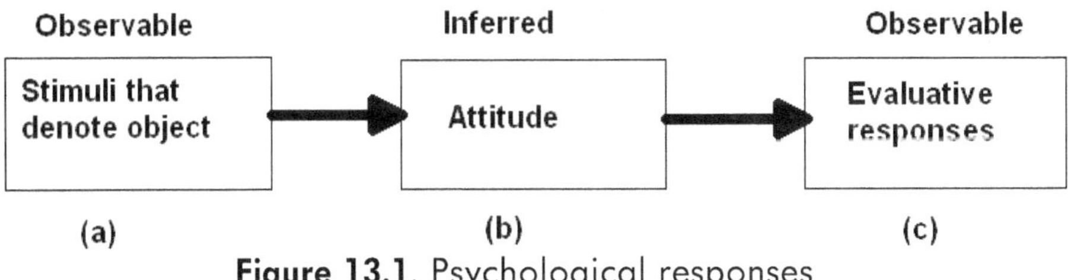

Figure 13.1. Psychological responses

Figure 13.1 illustrates the three types of response involved in attitudinal psychology. These are:

1. *Cognitive response.* This response is that of recognition of, for example, a name, a picture or other stimulus.

2. *Affective response.* This is a hypothetical construct and a latent variable. Here the sympathetic nervous system responds to (1) with feelings or emotions.

3. *Behavioural response.* This is the outward expression of (2) and may be a positive, neutral or negative response of some degree or intensity involving some observable action.

In this context conservatism, environmentalism or racism are objects. Then when we label a person a conservative, environmentalist or racist we infer an attitudinal position. Such attitudes are evidenced and also developed by the 'CAB' mechanism illustrated in Figure 13.1.

Schemas are cognitive structures that represent a person's past experience in a stimulus domain by a higher order or abstract cognitive structure. Then attitude is a subset of such a schema. Schemas have a selective effect on the remembering of information so that people have a better remembrance of stimuli that 'fit' their schemas and also for those that 'oppose.' This same selectivity applies to the 'output' of information as well as its input.

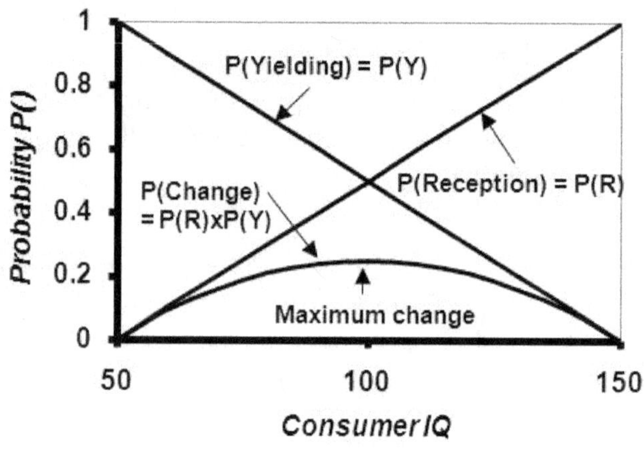

Figure 13.2.
Probability of reception, yielding and attitude change.

Figure 13.2 illustrates McGuire's reception-yielding model of attitude formation (McGuire, 1960; Eagly & Chaiken, 1993). Here 'reception' refers to comprehending a 'message', for example an advertisement. This model postulates that the probability of attitude change is given by:

$$P(C) = P(R) \times P(Y) \qquad (13.1)$$

so that a maximum change is obtained where the reception and yielding curves intersect, as shown in Figure 13.2.

One application of this idea is to 'get them young' so that advertising companies target the young and naive before they have the maturity or 'consumer intelligence' to develop resistance. Indeed, it is for this reason that the horizontal axis in Fig. 13.2 is labelled Consumer IQ.

Then, of course, ads need only persuade/brainwash some of the target audience and then imitative or 'social' learning ensures that many of the rest follow them.

Advertisements having achieved this, regular advertising reminds the audience of a product. Then in Figure 13.1 the 'C' response will be one of recognition of a brand, the 'A' response will be one of approval of it, and the 'B' response will be to make a mental note to buy it.

Learning curves

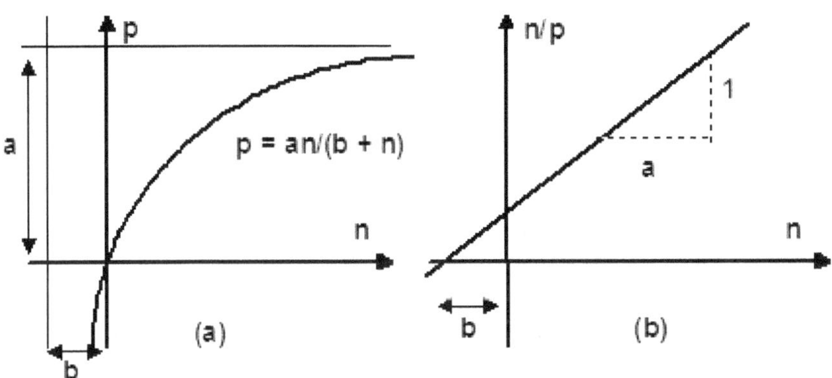

Figure 13.3. The Mohr Plot for learning.

Suppose the degree to which a person or group has learnt something or been conditioned is given by the probability p = 0 to 1, and p depends on n, the number of repetitions of the learning process.

If we assume that the learning process is hyperbolic so that the degree of learning gradually increases towards 100% or the asymptote $p = a$ with $a = 1$, then this is represented by the hyperbola of Figure 13.3(a), the equation for which is $p = an/(b + n)$.

This equation can easily be rearranged to give

$$n/p = (b + n)/a$$

so that if we plot n/p against n the straight line of Figure 13.3(b) is obtained and the magnitude of the intercept with the n axis $= -b$ whilst, of more interest, the inverse slope of the line equals the horizontal asymptote a of the hyperbola.

In experimental situations this plot is useful in testing whether results are indeed hyperbolic and, if so, estimating the 'ceiling' value towards which some variable is converging. Applied to the memory of a single person we set $a = 1$ and a typical result might be $b = 3$, $n = 3$, giving $p = 0.5$, or 50% memory retention after three repetitions. Here p is either:

(a) How well an item is learnt. People's names are a good example of this, and I often think one needs about three repetitions of such things to remember them.

(b) How much of a 'block' of information is learnt. An example might be a list of names where, because of *interference,* words at the beginning (the *primacy effect*) and end (the *recency effect*) are remembered best.

For a slower learner, on the other hand, b might double to 6 so we need $n = 6$ to get $p = 0.5$ or 50% learning.

Applied to conditioning of the populace by advertising, p is the proportion of the population affected and larger values of the asymptote b which flatten the curve might occur when there are two or more competing advertisers in the market.

In politics this highlights the advantage of dictatorship.

In education it perhaps highlights the importance of avoiding conflicting messages so that it is often best to learn one subject at a time.

Forgetting curves

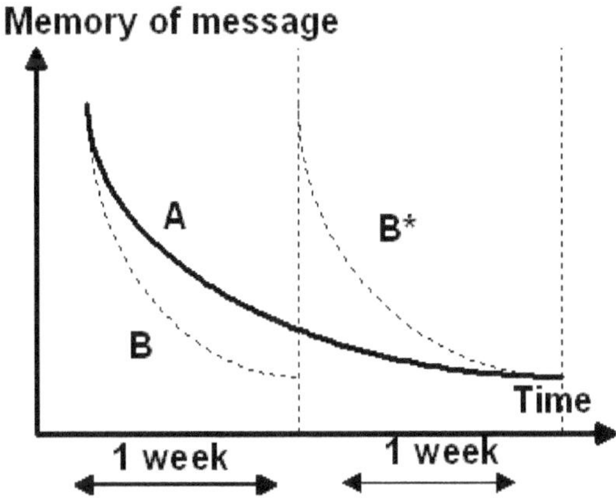

Figure 13.4. Forgetting curves.

The forgetting curves of Figure 13.4 also have important application in the psychology of attitudes. Here curves A and B are for two messages and curve B* is the result after the second message is repeated.

Then, when time has elapsed after an advertisement its 'residual' effect depends upon both the *primacy* (strength) of the ad compared to others, and its *recency*.

In Figure 13.4, after two weeks ad B* has greater recency than ad A, but less primacy so that they have nearly equal effect.

Such repetition of ads will ensure long-term potentiation of the remembered message, an important objective (Vander et al., 1994). Correlation between retention and persuasion, however, is by no means guaranteed and ads can be tailored to these two ends.

Information integration models of attitude formation

The information integration theory of attitude formation calculates the response to a series of stimuli i as

$$R = w_0\, s_0 + {}_{i=1}\Sigma^n\, w_i\, s_i \qquad (13.2)$$

where w_i and s_i are respectively the weight and scale of a person's attitude to a set of n items of information, and w_0 and s_0 are the weight and scale value of the person's initial attitude (Eagly & Chaiken, 1993).

Here the scale value of information is its location on the evaluative dimension and the weight is its *importance* or psychological impact in relation to the individual's judgment.

Simple summation models such as that of Equation 13.2 emphasize the importance of using multiple 'selling points' in advertising.

If the sum of the weights is required to be one then the model becomes an averaging model, but averaging models are more generally expressed as

$$R = (w_0\, s_0 + {}_{i=1}\Sigma^n\, w_i\, s_i)/(w_0 + {}_{i=1}\Sigma^n\, w_i) \qquad (13.3)$$

The initial attitude parameters w_0 and s_0 may in some instances, that of religion being perhaps the best example, represent 'intergenerational' attitudes acquired from a very early age from family and society at large.

Such initial attitudes, of course, may involve *prejudice*, for example ethnocentricity or racism, and, as history shows, such prejudices are often firmly rooted and perhaps could only be modelled by assigning them an exceptionally large weight.

More important in the modern consumer society, however, is social or imitative learning and in this context w_0 and s_0 represent initial attitude acquired by social learning from a peer or social group.

For example, a person believes that Christianity provides good moral codes (attribute 1) and that Christ did exist and provide a good exemplar of how we should live (attribute 2), but doubts that God really exists (attribute 3). Even if God did exist, however, in view of man's disastrous history he has a low evaluation of this last attribute, so that, using scales 0 to 10 for both w_i and s_i, he might thus rate Christianity as follows:

Attribute 0 (initial attitude): $w_0 = 5$, $s_0 = 5/10$ (i.e. 'halfway' values)

Attribute 1 (morality): $w_1 = 8/10$, $s_1 = 8/10$

Attribute 2 (good life model): $w_2 = 8/10$, $s_2 = 8/10$

Attribute 3 (God): $w_3 = 2/10$, $s_3 = 1/10$

giving a response score

$$R = [(5 \times 5 + 8 \times 8 + 8 \times 8 + 2 \times 1)/100]/[(5 + 8 + 8 + 2)/10]$$

$$= [155/100]/[25/10] = 1.55/2.3 = 0.674$$

whereas a 'middling evaluation score' with 5/10 for both the weights and scale values for attributes 0-3 would give $1/2 = 0.5$.

In contrast to simple summation models such as Equation 7.2, averaging models emphasize the need to have a limited number of effective selling points in advertising.

Set size effect can be demonstrated by assuming all weights = 1 and an initial attitude score of 50 on a scale of 0 to 100. Then if all further pieces of information have a score of 100 the resulting weighted average score for k additional attributes is

$$R = (50 + 100k)/(1 + k) \tag{13.4}$$

giving the values 50, 75, 83.3, 87.5, . . . for 0, 1, 2, 3, . . . pieces of information, resulting in the hyperbola converging towards the asymptote $R = 100$ shown in Fig. 13.5.

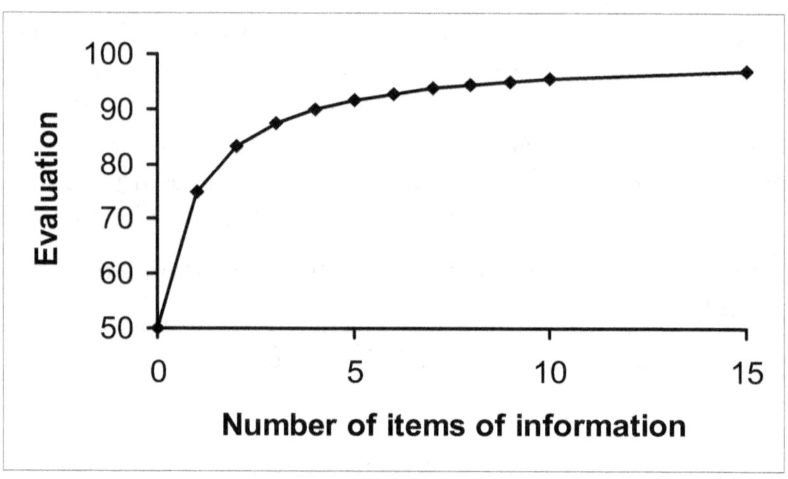

Figure 13.5. Theoretical set-size effect.

As might be expected, this hyperbolic result has the same general shape as a learning curve, emphasizing that there is a diminishing return for each additional piece of information about a given subject, albeit with the unrealistic assumption that every piece of information has the same weight (w_i).

The *three hit theory* of advertising, namely that three consecutive ads are needed to make people aware of a product, its relevance, and its benefits, would give (with $k = 3$) $R = 87.5$ (on a scale 0 to 100) in Equation 13.4, or $R = 75$ if there is no initial attitude, i.e. $s_0 = 0$ so that the number 50 in the numerator is omitted.

This is a reasonably good result and, indeed, the present authors often find that it takes three goes to remember items of information, presumably because they were not retained in the short term memory register long enough in the first instance.

Mere exposure research

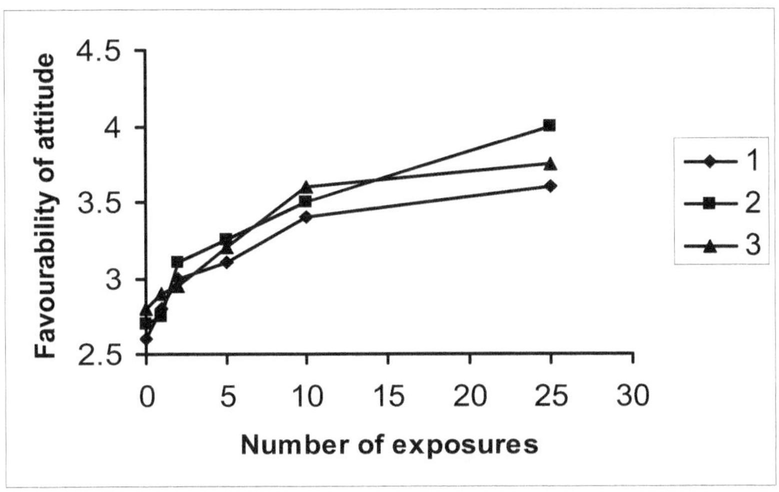

Figure 13.6. Increase in attitude favourability with increasing number of exposures to: 1. Turkish nonsense words. 2. Chinese-like characters. 3. Photographs.

Persuasion studies on message repetition usually focus on the effects of repeated exposure to *information* about attitude objects. In a classic monograph Zajonc dealt merely with the objects themselves (Eagly & Chaiken, 1993).

Figure 13.6 illustrates the increase in attitude favourability with repeated exposure to three types of stimuli, showing a somewhat asymptotic behaviour similar to that of learning curves.

This result is comparable to the size effect seen in Figure 13.5 insofar as increasing response is seen with increasing amounts of information, albeit repetition of the same information in the case of mere exposure.

It should be remembered, however, that oft repeated attempts at persuasion can also be irritating and result in negative attitudes, and some especially loud, haranguing radio and TV advertisements are good examples of this.

Implications of mere exposure in education are obvious, principally that students grow accustomed to new and perhaps difficult at first subjects, if not blasé about them, given time and repeated classroom exposure to them.

The latter observations might remind us that with repeated exposure we become accustomed to, if not hardened to, 'bad things' in life. For example, this is how children endure an excessive number of hours and years in classes and how adults endure jobs which may be, in reality, exceedingly tedious, arduous and boring.

It is also how, unfortunately, individuals become accustomed to essentially bad things such as cigarettes, alcohol, and drugs, perhaps in that order. This is, of course, good news for purveyors of such products.

Measurement of attitudes

Likert's *method of summated ratings* is one of the most widely used methods of measuring attitudes. In this approach a large pool of items which are chosen intuitively for their relevance to the attitude object is used (Likert, 1961).

These items usually consist of statements of belief but statements about behaviours or affective reactions can also be used. Typically each item is presented to respondents in a multiple-choice format such as:
1. Strongly disagree.
2. Disagree.
3. Undecided.
4. Agree.
5. Strongly agree.

Then, for example, a survey on attitudes towards women might contain questions like:

(a) Swearing is more objectionable from a woman.

(b) Intoxication in women is worse than in men.

With scores from 1 - 5 given to each of perhaps a dozen or so such questions the total score is then obtained for each respondent.

Desirably an initial pool of items should be pilot tested on a group of people to eliminate ambiguous and non-discriminating items which tend to result in neutral responses.

This can be done by examining the *item-total score correlations*, each of which correlates the respondents' scores on an item with their scores summed over all the items. Then a good item will have a positive correlation and better items have higher correlations.

Likert Scaling is widely used in market research, for example to assess the response to political advertising campaigns.

Guttman scaling

This gives stimulus-person scaling simultaneously and results in a matrix of data called the *Guttman scalogram*.

For example, suppose we have five rods of from 5 to 7 feet in length (the exact lengths are not known) and ask each respondent to place a one in the Guttman scalogram matrix shown in Table 13.1 when they are taller than a particular rod. This raw data is then reorganized to obtain Table 13.2.

Table 13.1. Guttman scalogram.

Persons	Stimuli (rods)				
	C	E	B	D	A
2	1	1	1	1	0
4	0	1	0	1	0
3	1	1	0	1	0
6	0	0	0	0	0
5	0	1	0	0	0
1	1	1	1	1	1
* e.g. person 2 is taller than C, E, B, D but not A					

Table 13.2 is obtained by placing the column with least ones at the left, the column with the most ones at the right, and so on. Then the row with the maximum number of ones is placed at the top (this is for person '1' in our example and hence this is the tallest person), and that with the least ones is placed at the bottom.

Table 13.2. Reordered Guttman scalogram.

Persons	Stimuli (rods)					Score
	A	B	C	D	E	
1	1	1	1	1	1	5
2	0	1	1	1	1	4
3	0	0	1	1	1	3
4	0	0	0	1	1	2
5	0	0	0	0	1	1
6	0	0	0	0	0	0

The result is an upper diagonal matrix, as shown in Table 13.2, resulting in a score for each person shown on the right side in Table 13.2, this giving the ordinal ranking for each person.

The preceding example of Guttman scaling was for physical stimuli, when a perfect upper triangular matrix resulted. Generally, however, this is not the case when attitudinal stimuli are considered.

An example is Bogardus' social stimulus scale, illustrated in Table 13.3, in which respondents are asked to judge how closely they would relate to people of various nationalities or races.

Table 13.3. Bogardus' social stimulus scale.

	Acceptance level					
	Would marry	As a friend	Would give a job	Allow as citizen	OK as visitor	No contact
Armenians						
Bulgarians						
Canadians						
etc.						

Such attitudinal stimuli do not yield a perfect upper triangular matrix but it has been suggested that when about 90% of the non-zero entries do appear on or above the diagonal that this *coefficient of reproducibility* value is acceptable.

The Guttman scalogram has the advantage that the degree to which the reordered response matrix is 'triangularized' gives an immediate indication of the reliability of a survey. More complex to use, it is generally only usable for relatively small surveys, such as in-house surveys of consumer groups in advertising offices where it is an ideal tool.

Conclusion

The reception-yielding and information integration models of attitude formation are indicative of how attitudes are developed.

The results of mere exposure research compellingly indicate how attitudes to new stimuli tend to improve given repeated exposure to them, the bottom line being that it is by such means that we are reduced to 'consumer zombies' by ubiquitous modern advertising.

Likert scaling can be used to quickly measure attitudes, and is widely used in market research.

More complex Guttman scaling can also be used to give an accurate ordinal measure of attitudes.

Bogardus' social stimulus scale is used to measure the attitudes of respondents to people of different ethnicities, and is therefore useful in studies of the psychology of conflict, which is discussed in Chapter 14.

CHAPTER 14

THE PSYCHOLOGY OF CONFLICT

There is no contradiction between saying (a) that contact tends to reduce the cultural differences among ethnic groups and (b) that contact also tends to stimulate efforts to preserve or increase these differences.
H. D. Forbes *Ethnic Conflict,*
Commerce, Culture, and the Contact Hypothesis (1997).

Contact hypothesis

Forbes (1977) proposed that ethnocentricity of different ethnic groups tended to be increased by cultural differences and (presumed negative) contact between them, expressing the ethnocentrism within two groups A and B as

$$E_a = a_1 \, C_T \, D_T \tag{14.1a}$$

$$E_b = b_1 \, C_T \, D_T \tag{14.1b}$$

where a_1 and b_1 are assumed to be positive, and are measures of the latent tendency of each group to respond ethnocentrically to each other, C_T is the amount of contact between the two groups at time T and D_T is the magnitude of the cultural differences between the two groups at time T.

He further proposed that the amount of contact and the cultural differences between the groups depended upon their proximity, incentives for contact such as trade, and upon the ethnocentrism of the groups, expressing this as

$$C_{T+1} = C_T \, (1 + g)/(1 + a_2 E_a + b_2 E_b) \tag{14.2}$$

$$D_{T+1} = D_T \, (1 + a_3 E_a + b_3 E_b)/(1 + h C_T) \tag{14.3}$$

171

where g is a factor that represents the factors that determine growth or decline in contact other than the repulsive ethnocentrism and cultural differences of the two groups.

In equations 14.2 and 14.3 ethnocentricity decreases contact and increases cultural differences, as might be expected.

The denominator of the last equation ensures that cultural differences are reduced by contact so long as h is positive (the normal situation).

Contact theory has obvious application in marketing, PR and other activities involving persuasion, for example:

[1] It emphasizes that attitude changes with contact or, in general, information transfer.

If contact is 'positive', however, rather than negative as has generally been the case throughout man's sorry history, then equations 14.1 could be modified to reflect this by writing them in the form

$$E_{a,T+1} = E_{a,T} - a_1 C_T + a_4 D_T$$

where a_1 and a_4 are positive. Indeed, it might be hoped that the latter situation might be more likely in today's age of electronic communication and high speed travel. Moreover, it is in this situation that such equations might be applicable to advertising with E = 'resistance.'

[2] It reminds us that ethnic or 'local' considerations are important in international marketing of a product.

[3] It reminds us of the importance of targeting advertising towards an appropriate demographic for a product, and that cultural differences exist between teenagers and their parents and, more so, their grandparents.

An attitudinal model of conflict

Mohr (2014a) proposed a simple 'first approximation' formula for assessing the potential for conflict between persons or groups. The basic formula takes the form:

$$A^* = A + xB + yC + zD \qquad\qquad (14.4)$$

where A^* = current 'overall' attitude,
A = initial or 'basic' attitude (based on 'known history'),
B = attitudes towards behaviours of the second party,
C = contact history between the two parties,
D = degree of difference between the parties considered,
and x, y, z are scaling factors that indicate the relative importance of the terms and here these will be assumed unity for simplicity.

Equation 14.4 can, of course, be used to assess the attitude of both parties involved in the assessment.

Here attitude is assessed in the same way as attitude is measured by the information integration model of Equation 13.2 but for simplicity only scale values (but not weights) will be given to a small set of items in measuring A.

Similarly, only scale values are used in assessing B, C and D. These extra terms add a great deal to the 'basic' A assessment to give a 'picture' of the 'overall' attitude.

Example application

As an example of application of the simple model of Equation 14.4 the attitude of a typical individual towards a hypothetical terrorist organization 'HTO' is considered.

To assess this only five items are assessed by simple questions for the initial attitude, behavioural, contact and difference terms in Equation 14.4. Assessment is similar to that used for the 'five-factor' model of personality (Larsen & Buss, 2002) and uses five possible scores:

+2 = strongly like/very similar etc.
+1 = like/similar etc.
0 = neutral
-1 = dislike/different etc.
-2 = strongly dislike/very different etc.

Table 14.1. Person's hypothetical attitude towards 'HTO'.

SCORE:	-2	-1	0	1	2
A, initial/basic attitude	Dislike/Like				
The people			0		
Their government(s)		-1			
How they look		-1			
What they say	-2				
What they do	-2				
B, group behaviour	Dislike/Like				
Sectarian conflict		-1			
Negative rhetoric		-1			
'Pushing' their religion	-2				
Threats	-2				
Terrorism	-2				
C, contact history	Uncomfortable/Comfortable				
See on TV			0		
See on street			0		
Close to		-1			
Talk to		-1			
Socialize	-2				
D, differences	Different/Similar				
Language		-1			
Economic				1	
Culture		-1			
Religion	-2				
History		-1			
TOTAL SCORE, *A:**	-22				

Table 14.1 gives an example assessment for a hypothetical individual. Here total scores less than -30 are 'very negative', -10 to -20 'negative', -10 to +10 are moderate, +10 to +20 'positive', and more than +20 'very positive'.

Thus the results of Table 14.1 are mostly 'negative', the total of -22 indicating a considerable degree of disapproval. It is only very negative scores of less than -30 that might be a cause for concern if they were obtained for a significant percentage of a population.

Weighting factors can be assigned to items in Table 14.1 to reflect differing importance associated with them, for example the 9th and 10th items might have weights >1.

Effect of Societal views

The effect of the views of society on individuals and groups can be included in Eqn 14.4 by adding an extra term comparable to the inclusion of 'social norms' in Eqn 13.2:

$$A^{**} = A^{*} + fS = A + xB + yC + zD + fS$$

where *f is a scaling factor* here assumed = 1 for simplicity, and the factors *x, y, z* are also assumed =1 so that:

$$A^{**} = A + B + C + D + S \qquad (14.5)$$

and *S* is the person or group's assessment of the attitude or 'position' of society, society here including the media, politicians, religious leaders, the public, friends and family.

Then measurement of *S* is done in the same way as for *A, B, C* and *D* in Table 14.1.

Table 14.2. Person's assessment of society's attitude.

SCORE:	-2	-1	0	1	2
S, perceived society view	Negative/Positive				
TV/radio/papers		-1			
Politicians			0		
Religious leaders		-1			
The public		-1			
Friends & family		-1			
TOTAL SCORE:	-4				

For the views of a typical person regarding society's attitude towards 'HTO' the result might be that shown in Table 14.2. Adding this result to that of Table 14.1 the aggregate score is -26, a 'negative' overall result.

A 'very negative' score would be less than -30, so the combined result of Tables 14.1 and 1.2 (i.e. -26) for an individual or a group is not of concern but worth taking some notice of.

Responses to conflict

When the group, attitudes towards which are sought, is in some form of dispute or conflict, whether this be economic, concerning mistreatment of a few people, or armed conflict on any scale, the attitudes concerning what measures should be taken against the group can also be measured in like fashion to Table 14.1.

Table 14.3. Attitudes towards measures against group.

SCORE:	0	1	2	3	4
	Level of support for action				
Government condemns					4
Cut diplomatic ties				3	
Trade embargo			2		
Public demonstrations				3	
UN sanctions		1			
War	0				-
TOTAL SCORE:	13				

Table 14.3 shows an example of such an assessment for a hypothetical individual concerning his or her views towards HTO's terrorism around the world. The total score is $R = 13$ out of a possible 24, perhaps a 'fail' mark by way of assessment of the group in question, but not an extremely bad score.

Total scores of close to 20, on the other hand, would indicate very strong feelings of which, perhaps, considerable notice should be taken should they be found to apply to a significant number of people.

The results of Tables 14.1 – 14.3 can be combined as:

$$A^{***} = A + B + C + D + S - (R - 12)$$

with the last term adjusted to allow for its different scale of measurement, giving $A^{***} = -27$ for the present example case.

Other factors affecting attitudes & conflict

[1] Hierarchical influences.

These include the influence of strongly hierarchical organizations that have very great influence on society and its individual people, some of these being:

(a) Governments of any type, whether they be monarchies or dictatorships have considerable influence on the populace by way of propaganda and enforceable laws, for example those of conscription.

(b) Political parties. Even when they are not in government, supporters of political parties are often considerably influenced by their views.

(c) Religions. These, of course, have had great influence throughout history but have less influence in the West now, whilst in contrast Muslim sects still have great influence on many of the world's 1.5 billion Muslims.

(d) TV, radio and print media also tend to come from 'on high' and also have considerable influence.

[2] Social norms.

Social norms have a great influence on the thinking of individuals and groups within any society, for example the wearing of scarves, veils and burkas by Muslim women is still very widely practiced.

The structure of society has also been an important factor. Fairly soon after the Agricultural Revolution and the formation of man's first permanent towns and farms the first small armies would have been formed to defend them, at first only temporarily.

Indeed, with the diversification of occupations that the Agricultural Revolution brought, permanent armies were one eventual result, notably in Rome and its empire, for example. Then, of course, given the availability of armies, there has always been a tendency to use them sooner or later, most obviously as the 'external police force' to deal with external problems, albeit a very large force all too often in history.

[3] Economic factors.

Economic considerations have often been the cause of human conflict, for example competition for resources, a good historical example being the Spanish Empire's enthusiastic search for gold in the Americas.

Man has always been inventing new tools and weapons, particularly since the Industrial Revolution. Now the arms industries have become massive and are able to considerably influence government policy in many countries whose economies have suffered a steep decline in their manufacturing industries in recent decades (Sampson, 1977; Thomas, 2006).

An example of the absurdity of it all, the CIA knew that chemical weapons were pouring into Iraq from Chile and South Africa in the 1980s. Cardoen industries in Santiago, for example, sent its chemical weapons, and the German-made artillery 'cups' or shells to contain them, to Iraq (Ben-Menashe, 1992). Then, the US later condemned Iraq for using these weapons on the Kurds and used this as an excuse for their first invasion of Iraq early in 1991.

[4] Growing populations.

Even as far back as early man's troglodyte days it is not hard to imagine an extended family group growing to the point at which a second cave was needed.

Similarly, when man had towns and then cities these too grew in size, needing ever more space and, more importantly, resources, particularly food.

This, coupled with man's habit of exploration, which no doubt dates back to his hunter-gatherer days and thence the hunt for food, has led man to engage in conflict with neighbouring populations.

Conflicts may have arisen simply out of the suspicion that the sight of strangers aroused when they suddenly appeared. Perhaps, for example, a spear might be thrown to scare them away. Then, of course, there might be retaliation and thus conflict.

As man's population continued to increase, of course, the tendency for migration and thence conflict must have increased, for example people leaving crowded and disease-ridden cities in Europe to colonize the 'New World' from the 16th to 19th centuries.

[5] Proximity.

Proximity also affects people's attitudes as does contact which, of course, is facilitated by proximity, the more 'negative' the contact the more negative the attitude formed.

Thus for tribal man, as with his chimpanzee relatives, proximity was a key factor in regular tribal conflicts.

Indeed, until only about two thousand years ago, human conflicts were only between neighbouring cities, regions, or countries. With the building of ships capable of sailing hundreds of miles, however, came the ability to explore more widely, and human conflict began to occur over greater distances and on a greater scale.

[6] Competitiveness.

In the Roman Empire, for example, there was a competitiveness in its governments, an obvious drive that made it wish to become 'bigger and grander' and go out and conquer other lands to achieve that end.

This obsession with competition runs all through the history and cultures of Homo sapiens, an example being our obsession with sport, or any kind of competition even if it is called a 'game.' It seems fundamentally related to the alpha-male behaviour of several other animal species.

Man, however, takes the alpha-male issue to absurd lengths, for example the original Olympic Games in Ancient Greece being conducted in the nude and, indeed, it seems to be returning slowly towards that situation now.

Equally, man has often indulged in war without good reason, usually because some loony leader and his acolytes want to 'beat' some other foe.

Conclusions

Very relevant to attitude also is the vexatious question of ethnic conflict and, indeed, the equations of Forbes' contact hypothesis do emphasize that, over time, attitudes change. Moreover, models like that of contact hypothesis could be applied to the behaviours in hierarchical organizations.

The simple formula of Equation 14.4 combines the measurement techniques of attitudinal psychology with the concepts of the contact hypothesis to assess the attitudes of individuals and groups of people to other groups of people. The point of this exercise is that, when the attitude of one group to another is very negative, then conflict between the groups is, of course, more likely.

The attitudes of leaders are of particular importance, as it is these that may lead to conflict and war. The attitudes of leaders will, of course, be influenced by many of the same factors and stimuli that affect the public.

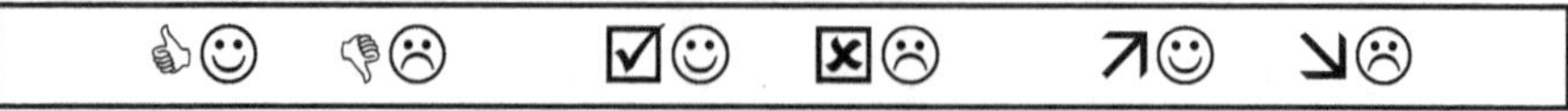

CHAPTER 15

THE PSYCHOLOGY OF HIERARCHIES

> *Detestation of the high is the involuntary homage of the low.*
> Charles Dickens, *A Tale of Two* Cities (1859).
>
> *In every one of those little stucco boxes there's some poor bastard*
> *who's never free except when he's fast asleep*
> *and dreaming that he's got the boss down the bottom*
> *of a well and is bunging lumps of coal at him.*
> George Orwell, *Coming Up For Air,* pt 1., ch. 2 (1939).

Mohr's Law of Hierarchies

The higher up a person is in a hierarchy the more 'power' they have, which Mohr's Power law expresses as:

$$P = C\,R^n$$

where P = power, R = rank, and C and n are constants.

Assuming the value of n is 2 then when one is twice as high in the hierarchy one has four times as much power.

Then, as we all know, power corrupts, one of the major factors in mankind's endless history of conflict.

Mohr's Law of Hierarchies highlights one aspect of such corruption, that is, how little *real work* bosses do, and thus how unfair it is that they are paid far more than the workers:

In hierarchical organizations the amount of real
material-producing work people do is inversely proportional
to their rank or level in the organization.
The amount of compensation they receive, however,
is proportional to their level,
sometimes to an exponential degree.

181

How hierarchies operate

Hierarchies operate through a chain of command, leaders meeting with a chosen few top-level executives responsible for overseeing the various operations of the organization. In the case of government, for example, there are ministers for defence, treasury, education, health etc.

In each of these areas there are several levels of seniority ranging from head of the organization to department heads and front-line managers.

Through the whole chain of command there is an implicit level of intimidation and fear that usually makes sure that everybody does as they are told. At the front line, however, things often get ridiculous, for example the traditional screaming of army sergeants at their miserable subordinates.

It is through such bullying and intimidation, of course, that soldiers are brainwashed into following orders without question or delay, essentially becoming expendable slaves to satisfy the whims of their leaders. Don't worry about 'executive stress,' therefore, worry about 'slave-stress.'

Indeed, our many sports with a relationship to conflict, for example absurd rugby with its 'charge at the enemy' no matter what the risk of injury, or archery and rifle shooting, all relate to our historical predilection for conflict.

Throughout hierarchies there is ambition to rise, often leading to a good deal of competitive behaviour, much of it often downright dishonest. In politics, for example, plenty of 'backstabbing' goes on day in, and day out.

This corresponds quite closely, perhaps, with the alpha-male behaviour seen in several animal species, notably our close relatives, gorillas.

The problem, of course, is that people who have proved themselves good at the 'rat race', tend to be the worst leaders, exactly in accordance with the Peter Principle.

The psychology of hierarchies

The psychology of hierarchies has been the subject of a considerable amount of research in the last decade or two, bullying being one of the main issues studied.

Clearly, being higher in hierarchical organizations, and thus being able to 'play boss' and tell people what work to do, supervise that work, and pass judgement on the results of the work, gives one considerable power over subordinates.

Unfortunately, all too often people in a position of power 'abuse' or misuse that power, for example by:

(1) Verbal bullying and threatening of subordinates.
(2) Unjustified claims that work is unsatisfactory.
(3) Financial penalties such as reducing pay rates.
(4) Physical and sexual abuse.
(5) Forcing workers to 'quit', or 'sacking' them.
(6) Corporate fraud.

Most of these bad behaviours involve bosses having negative psychological traits.

In his book *The Pyramid Climbers*, Vance Packard wrote about the amount of control and influence companies had over their employees in the early 1960s (Packard, 1962).

In the mid 1950s personality and psychological testing began to be widely used, along with regular assessments of how a well a man was doing his job, and how he was perceived by his manager and co-workers.

For executives it was deemed important what sort of wife they had, what sort of house they lived in, and what clubs they belonged to, whilst Jews, women, and recent immigrants stood little chance of reaching executive positions.

The book likens big corporations to cults where in the early 1960s companies began using 'head hunters' to lure executives away from other companies, rather than promote from within.

Thus, the outrageous 'Robber Barons' were replaced by WASPS, white Anglo-Saxon protestants, as members of Boards of Directors who commanded increasingly huge salaries, whilst demands for increased production year after year led to unethical practices in order to meet quotas.

Studies of workplace bullying

A study of "Personality traits of bullies as a contributory factor in workplace bullying" using two well-known 'personality inventories' concluded that "bullies are aggressive, hostile, and extraverted and independent", and also that they are "egocentric, selfish, and show little concern for the opinion of others."

The researchers also concluded that: "High levels of aggressiveness, assertiveness, competitiveness and independence are traits that are also associated with leadership" (Seigne et al., 2007).

A study of the extent to which both workplace bullies and victims possessed bully-typifying traits used a 22-item scale to assess traits of 224 Canadian university students aged 18-47. It concluded that bullies exhibited measures of authoritarianism, narcissism, psychoticism, aggression, and disinhibition, and that victims also exhibited some of these traits.

An important finding was that 89.7% of bullies, and 41.7% of victims were "bully/victims" who had been both bullies and targets at least once per week in the preceding 6 months (Linton & Power, 2013).

A study of workplace bullying and discrimination of African Americans, homosexuals, and the obese, amongst American University students used self-reporting questionnaires to measure "prejudice and personality traits."

The results indicated that "social dominance", being male, being white, "right wing authoritarianism", and anxiety affected discrimination, concluding that "prejudice influenced relations between personality and discrimination, but not bullying" (Parkins et al., 2006).

Sexual harassment

Sexual harassment in the workplace and elsewhere has long been a major social issue. Thanks to the Harvey Weinstein case in particular, the long-standing jokes about the "director's couch" in the movie industry became a major issue in 2017, resulting in the rapid growth of the ME TOO movement and widespread claims of sexual misconduct in the movie industry and elsewhere.

Meanwhile, claims of sexual abuse by clerics dating back decades continue to crop up, a notable example being the many complaints of sexual abuse by Catholic priests that have surfaced over the couple of decades.

Another very recent example, are many thousands of claims of sexual abuse in the Boy Scouts in England dating back several decades.

Psychopathic bosses

In 1980, Canadian clinical psychologist Dr Robert Hare, who worked in prisons, released the first version of the Hare checklist for identifying psychopaths, and several further versions followed.

As shown in Table 15.1, it divides 20 personality traits into four groups: interpersonal, affective, lifestyle, and antisocial, these measuring traits including charm, propensity to lie, lack of remorse, and need for stimulation.

After an interview each trait is scored as 0 (not present), 1 (present but not dominant), or 2 (dominant), so that the maximum possible score is 40.

Average people score from 3 to 6, non-psychopathic criminals score from 16 to 22, whilst in the UK and US respectively, scores of >25 and >30 are taken as a positive diagnosis of psychopathy (Gillespie, 2017).

Table 15.1. The Hare checklist for psychopaths.

	TRAIT	SCORE
	Facet 1: Interpersonal	
1	Glibness or superficial charm	0 – 1 - 2
2	Grandiose sense of self-worth	0 – 1 - 2
3	Pathological lying	0 – 1 - 2
4	Cunning or manipulative	0 – 1 - 2
	Facet 2: Affective	
5	Lack of remorse or guilt	0 – 1 - 2
6	Emotionally shallow	0 – 1 - 2
7	Callous or lack of empathy	0 – 1 - 2
8	Failure to accept responsibility for their own actions	0 – 1 - 2
	Facet 3: Lifestyle	
9	Need for stimulation (easily bored)	0 – 1 - 2
10	Parasitic lifestyle	0 – 1 - 2
11	Lack of realistic, long-term goals	0 – 1 - 2
12	Impulsivity	0 – 1 - 2
13	Irresponsibility	0 – 1 - 2
	Facet 4: Antisocial	
14	Poor behavioural controls	0 – 1 - 2
15	Early behavioural problems	0 – 1 - 2
16	Juvenile delinquency	0 – 1 - 2
17	History of conditional prison release being revoked	0 – 1 - 2
18	Criminal versatility	0 – 1 - 2
	Other traits:	
19	Many short-term marital relationships	0 – 1 - 2
20	Promiscuous sexual behaviour	0 – 1 - 2
TOTAL SCORE		**0 - 40**

Note, because if was developed for the prison system, several items in Table 15.1 such as those of Facet 4, are not generally applicable, and for most purposed only items 1 – 13 and 19 & 20 should be used to evaluate bad bosses.

Thus criteria for judging a bad boss should include:
- ➢ Bossiness.
- ➢ Assertiveness.
- ➢ Dishonesty and lying.
- ➢ Selfishness and greed.
- ➢ Vanity.
- ➢ Bullying.

A more comprehensive psychological evaluation can be made using The Big Five Inventory (BFI), a self-reporting questionnaire with five personality 'dimensions' and 44 items.

A shorter test is the Ten-Item Personality Inventory (TiPi) which uses self-reporting to rate the following ten pairs of adjectives (Gosling et al., 2003):

Extraverted, enthusiastic
Critical, quarrelsome
Dependable, self-disciplined
Anxious, easily upset
Open to new experiences, complex
Reserved quite
Sympathetic, warm
Disorganized, careless
Calm, emotionally stable
Conventional, uncreative

using the scale:
1=Disagree strongly, 2 = Disagree moderately
3 =Disagree a little, 4 = Neither agree nor disagree
5=Agree a little, 6 = Agree moderately

Other personality inventories include the Raymond Cattell 16PF which is similar to the TiPi, but somewhat more comprehensive (Cattell & Shuerger, 2003), and the very comprehensive Personality Inventory for DSM-5 (PID-5) which is a personality trait assessment scale for adults aged 18 or more with 220 items which are rated using scores of:

0 Very false or Often False
1 Sometimes false or Somewhat false
2 Sometimes True of Somewhat true
3 Very True or Often true

Repeated use of such tests over time which give consistently high scores for a facet or 'domain' may indicate significant traits and perhaps problem areas that might required treatment (Krueger et al., 2012).

Conclusions

Chapter 1 introduced Mohr's Laws for hierarchies, how power corrupts, and capitalism (i.e., how the rich are able to grow their wealth exponentially).

Several other laws were discussed, particularly The Peter Principle which, though made somewhat tongue-in-cheek, most people tend to agree with.

The chapter concluded by discussing aggression and age as factors in how bossy a boss is, myself twice having been appointed to University posts by HODs who were soon to retire, being replaced by new, too young, inexperienced, and incompetent HODs who ruined my career and life.

It is also clear, however, that as people rise in hierarchies, their behaviours and thence personality traits change, usually for the worse as they tend to become greedier, bossier and nastier the higher they rise.

Some understanding of the psychological traits, especially negative ones such as those in the Hare checklist, can be helpful in assessing and dealing with bad bosses, as discussed in the following chapter.

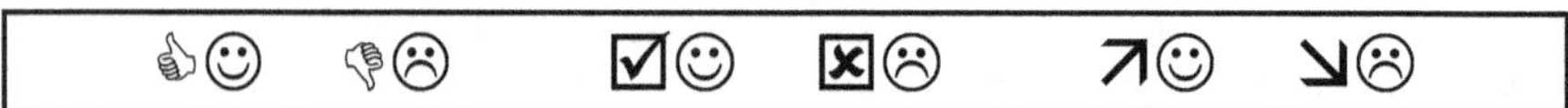

CHAPTER 16

DEALING WITH HIERARCHY PROBLEMS

> *I'm the boss. I'm allowed to yell.*
> Ivan Boesky, q. in *Den of* Thieves, James B Stewart, 1991.
>
> *At too many companies, the boss shoots the arrow*
> *of managerial performance, and then hastily paints*
> *the bullseye around the spot where it lands.*
> Warren Buffet, *Shareholder,* June 1989.

Life assessment

One can assess the quality of a particular aspect of one's life using the Information Integration method of attitude assessment discussed in Chapter 13.

To assess the quality of several key aspects of one's life such methods as those discussed in Chapter 13 can be used, the simplest and most widely used of these being Likert Scaling.

Table 16.1 shows an example assessment for an adult person, scoring being done simply by using a printed copy of this table and circling the scores/ratings given to each of the items listed in the first column.

An 'average' rating of 3 on all 20 items gives, of course, a total score of 60. More important, perhaps, ratings of 1/poor for such important items as the first two (job and pay) might motivate one to try and improve these important life factors.

Similarly, a low rating for some of the health items might spur one into taking action to improve one's health.

Table 16.1. Life quality questionnaire using Likert scaling.

Aspect of life: Circle the appropriate number	Very good	Good	Aver -age	Fair	Poor
Your work:					
1. Your job	5	4	3	2	1
2. Your pay	5	4	3	2	1
3. Relationship with boss	5	4	3	2	1
4. Workplace conditions	5	4	3	2	1
5. Relations with workmates	5	4	3	2	1
Your home life:	5	4	3	2	1
6. Your financial situation	5	4	3	2	1
7. Your home	5	4	3	2	1
8. Your parent(s) or partner	5	4	3	2	1
9. Your siblings or children	5	4	3	2	1
10. Your health	5	4	3	2	1
Recreation and social life:	5	4	3	2	1
11. Evening activities					
12. Weekend activities	5	4	3	2	1
13. Friends	5	4	3	2	1
14. Regular outings	5	4	3	2	1
15. Social, sport etc. groups	5	4	3	2	1
Your health:	5	4	3	2	1
16. General health	5	4	3	2	1
17. Fitness					
18. Diet	5	4	3	2	1
19. Weight					
20. Mental health	5	4	3	2	1
Add the numbers you circled:	Score/100:				

In the wide range of items in Table 16.1 some items are much more important than others. Generally recreation and social life, for example, are not as important as one's job, and some jobs, of course, involve long hours 6 or 7 days a week, allowing little time for social life in any case.

Thus an evaluation such as that of Table 16.1 could be extended to include weights for each factor, as in the Information Integration method of attitude assessment discussed in Chapter 13, and this is done for the 'work' items of Table 16.1 in the following section.

Assessing workplace conditions

One can assess the quality of a particular aspect of one's life using the Information Integration method of attitude assessment discussed in Chapter 13.

As an example, we shall now assess the five 'work' items of Table 16.1 for a 'typical' person using the Information Integration method, giving the following result with weights and scores 1-10.

Attribute 1 (job): $w_1 = 5$, $s_1 = 5/10$ (i.e. 'halfway' values)

Attribute 2 (pay): $w_2 = 8/10$, $s_2 = 3/10$

Attribute 3 (relationship with boss): $w_3 = 7/10$, $s_3 = 4/10$

Attribute 4 (workplace conditions): $w_4 = 5/10$, $s_4 = 5/10$

Attribute 5 (relations with workmates): $w_5 = 4/10$, $s_5 = 5/10$

giving a total score

$= 5 \times 5 + 8 \times 3 + 7 \times 4 + 5 \times 5 + 4 \times 5$

$= 25 + 24 + 28 + 25 + 20 = 122$

whereas a 'middling evaluation score' with 5/10 for both the weights and scale values for all five items would give a total score of 125, so that the situation is perhaps 'satisfactory', for the present at least, but the low score of 3/10 for 'pay' is deserving of some attention sooner rather than later.

Improving the work situation

Having made the assessment of the preceding two sections, one may decide to address any issues raised by the only 'middling' score for the five work items obtained above. Though the 'pay' issue is the main concern, it is best to deal with all five work factors as doing so is more likely to improve the pay problem.

Table 16.2. Action plan re. job.

Item		Actions	Timing
1	Job	Stay Look for another job	1-2 years Now
2	Pay	Ask for a pay rise	Now
3	Boss	Talk to boss Make complaint	Next week In 3 months
4	Conditions	Talk to union Talk to boss	Next month In 3 months
5	Workmates	Meeting to raise issues	Next month

Table 16.2 illustrates an action plan to improve the work situation with one or two actions suggested for each of the five work items, including an approximate timing for each action.

Perhaps the key item is 1, where the plan is the cautious and sensible one of staying for a couple of years, but beginning to look for another job immediately – sensible because, of course, it can take a long time to find a job, and even longer to find a better one.

Most important, however, is that a simple plan such as this is far wiser than, for example, impatiently barging into the boss's office and abusing him about being underpaid, not an entirely unheard of situation.

Furthermore, having a sensible plan gives one hope for the immediate and medium term, as well as time to come up with other ideas to improve one's work situation, and to obtain help and advice from others on it.

Dealing with psychopathic bosses

Gillespie (2017) suggests that organizations which are run using 'Management by Objectives' (MBO) are not conducive to psychopathic bosses:

"The only way for a psychopath to succeed in a structure based on MBO would be to fall in with the objectives of his team and his superiors. Anything else would mark him out for removal from the organisation."

Alternatively, Gillespie suggests that persons deemed to be psychopaths can be got rid of by getting them 'fired', but this, of course, is very difficult to bring about when the only person in the part of the organization in question able to do firing is a psychopathic boss, as is often the case.

When you do go above his or her head seeking to get them fired they counterattack, usually resulting in the person or persons complaining being disciplined or fired.

Most workers, therefore, simply have to endure bad and mad bosses and a 2016 study of Australian workplaces with "toxic leaders" concluded that the following strategies were unwise (Gillespie, 2017):

- ➢ Confronting the leader.
- ➢ Avoiding, ignoring or bypassing the boss.
- ➢ Whistleblowing.
- ➢ Worrying to excess about the boss.
- ➢ Continued anger and frustration.
- ➢ Focussing on work to try and forget about the boss.
- ➢ Taking sick leave (giving only short-term relief).

Instead, Gillespie says one should behave as a polite and compliant employee and do whatever one is told, no matter how much one dislikes it. Then to survive in this way one should also:

- ➢ Think about a future, better job.
- ➢ Make sure your fellow workers don't 'tell' on each other.
- ➢ Check the accuracy of what the boss says.
- ➢ Don't show any anger and frustration.
- ➢ Build a support network.

> Document every bad thing the boss does, noting the time, date and names of any witnesses.

In this way one can survive for the medium term, at least, and perhaps build a case against the bad boss that might result in him being disciplined, demoted or shifted sideways, or even fired.

Personal experience

As noted more than once in this book, I 'walked the plank' when bullied by a new and nasty/prejudiced/boozy etc. HOD in Auckland into resigning meekly, when, of course, I should have put my case for promotion that had been unfairly delayed in writing and gone to the Dean to talk about the problem.

Indeed, during the couple of years my long overdue promotion was delayed, the Dean said in almost involuntary fashion to me in the staff tea room one lunchtime:

Lawyers are expensive.

That is, of course, true, but legal or any other help to deal with the problem, rather than meekly quit to never get another job, was, indeed, just thoughtless.

Another mistake, was not taking careful note of any bullying, stupid statements etc. by the HOD, for example:

(1) In his letter to the Dean that held up my promotion he said that "all the students" said that they had difficulty getting their questions answered (by me). I recall only once having difficulty with a student question, and that was because it was a joke one when I was a new foreign/Australian member of staff, and I should have said so quite forcibly to the Dean, also using the questionnaire of Table 16.1 to support my case.

(2) His saying "another lousy lecturer" when I became involved with my ex-HOD in Melbourne to help get a long-running book published.

(3) His suggesting in the corridor, and not in writing, that if I resigned he would (illegally) give me a couple of months pay in advance to help me with the costs of selling my house and moving my family back to Australia. In fact the exchange rate had blown out to about 1.72 at that time, causing me to lose a great deal of money, as well as my career.

I should have put in writing complaint about these lies and bullying and sent them to the Dean and Vice-Chancellor, whereas I meekly sent them an overly polite (in the circumstances) letter of resignation.

Conclusions

There are many things one can do to help deal with hierarchy problems, including:

(1) Use the life assessment questionnaire of Table 16.1 to assess workplace conditions, home life etc.

(2) As in the second section of this chapter, use the information integration method to assess one's workplace situation more accurately.

(3) Use a job action plan like that of Table 16.2 to try and improve the workplace situation, including the possibility of finding another job.

(4) Note the strategies for dealing with bad bosses suggested by Gillespie (2017), and discussed in the fourth section of this chapter entitled 'Dealing with psychopathic bosses'.

(5) Avoid the sorts of mistakes and omissions that I made that are listed in the preceding section. Then do positive things to improve relations with the boss, and perhaps one or two workmates, by inviting them to dinner, for example. Indeed, my wife (then) and I did this a couple of times, but not with the bad boss in Auckland, and this was perhaps a costly mistake.

CHAPTER 17

HOW TO RISE IN HIERARCHIES

> *Boss your boss as soon as you can; try it on early.*
> *There is nothing he will like so well if he is the right kind of boss.*
>
> *Instead of the question "What must I do for my employer?"*
> *substitute "What can I do?"*
> Andrew Carnegie, Speech, Curry Commercial College,
> Pittsburgh, June 23, 1885: "The Road to Business Success."

Languishing too low

Languishing too low in a hierarchical workplace for too long can have many bad consequences, including:

(1) Become miserable and depressed, perhaps reducing one's effectiveness on the job, and almost certainly making one look less effective, motivated etc.

(2) Having little or nothing in the way of wage or salary increases for several years means that one's 'real income', allowing for inflation etc., may decline.

(3) Being more miserable and poorer is likely to 'rub off' onto your family, and can often lead to arguments and even divorce, thus ruining your life.

(4) While stuck at the same level, colleagues on that level may be promoted, making one feel hard done by.

(5) While stuck at the same level, a new boss may be appointed, probably reducing one's prospects of ever reaching that level in this organization, if not others as well.

It is important, therefore, to at least occasionally give thought to how one might improve one's promotion prospects, and following sections give a few ideas on this.

Evaluating job performance

Table 17.1 (on the following page) is a questionnaire which uses Likert scaling to assess the performance of a lecturer.

I wrote and used this in 1978 and students enjoyed the revenge [in advance] of giving a mark out of 100, especially as I asked them to also give marks (with different colour pen or ringed etc.) to the HOD who shared teaching of the subject with me. He scored pretty badly. Though it looks a little formidable, this survey worked well and I was pleased with the results.

I didn't inform the HOD of the results, but I dare say rumours of the test might have reached his ears.

In fact, I did not tell anyone the overall results, and perhaps should have done so to give myself some good publicity, and the HOD some bad publicity.

Worse still, in the middle of 1982 at Auckland University, I was held up on promotion to Senior Lecturer, I remain sure because I had complained a couple of months early about a nasty act by another department member. The HOD put in writing the obvious lie that *"all the students"* said they had difficulty getting their questions answered.

Subsequently he bullied me into resigning, ruining my career, and life.

In hindsight, I realized that I should have used this questionnaire again to compare student evaluation of myself and the HOD. I'm sure that I would have rated better than him, proving the lie upon which my promotion was delayed.

Worse still, however, alone and with nobody to talk to, I was stupid enough not to reply in writing to the HOD's unjustified grounds for delaying my promotion.

Table 17.1. Questionnaire for rating lecturing performance.

Circle the appropriate number:	Very good	Good	Aver -age	Fair	Poor
Rate your lecturer's:					
1. Choice of material	5	4	3	2	1
2. Performance generally	5	4	3	2	1
3. Explanations of theory	5	4	3	2	1
4. Use of practical examples	5	4	3	2	1
5. Development of theory	5	4	3	2	1
6. Stressing of important points	5	4	3	2	1
7. Choice of tutorial examples	5	4	3	2	1
8. Time given to individuals	5	4	3	2	1
9. Choice of lab. experiments	5	4	3	2	1
10. Helping understand subject	5	4	3	2	1
11. Style	5	4	3	2	1
12. Teaching report writing	5	4	3	2	1
How well does lecturer do in:					
13. Getting you interested	5	4	3	2	1
14. Knowledge of subject	5	4	3	2	1
15. Motivating you	5	4	3	2	1
16. Giving explanations	5	4	3	2	1
17. Lecturing at OK rate	5	4	3	2	1
18. Giving good lecture notes	5	4	3	2	1
Other:					
19. Are the tests useful?	5	4	3	2	1
20. Course relevant to needs?	5	4	3	2	1
Add the numbers you circled to obtain a score/100:					

Indeed, I believe that a more 'legal', sensible procedure would have been for the Dean to ask me to provide such a written reply.

Unfortunately, just as with candidate interview and selection procedures, in which 'confidential' reference statements from previous employers are obtained, the usual procedures of hierarchical organizations involve top-down, one-way communication very much like the intimidating procedures in courts.

It might help, therefore, to obtain a questionnaire evaluation of one's job performance, an example of which is shown in Table 17.1, by a few people who might be, for example, customers or a few carefully selected colleagues. Then the same questionnaire, or a slightly modified one to reflect their different job responsibilities, can be used to evaluate the performance of the boss, and if they score badly on this, the results might be circulated to the 'appropriate' people, giving careful consideration as to who they might be.

Get some help

Primarily, of course, one needs at least one or two helpers within the organization in question. A problem here is that the workers at the same level in the hierarchy are also competing for the same promotion that you are. Thus, if you are in a group of, say, 10 seeking promotion to 'Senior xyz', then one might establish a mutually supportive relationship with just one of them, hoping that you will both be the next two workers promoted.

It is important to be able to judge which fellow workers one really can get on with, one simple test being how well you communicate with them. For example, those who tend to speak to you only in 'one-liners' one can generally assume to be no better than neutral, if that, and not friendly.

One should also, of course, seek the help of family and friends, including one's partner if one is married.

Often it might also be worthwhile getting professional help with promotion problems. Some of the people who advertise in local newspapers every week as resume writers, for example, may also give career advice and, if they are any good at helping people get jobs, then they should also be of potential help in helping them get promotions.

In life it always helps, of course, to have friends in the right places, not just old school friends etc. People in 'high places', of course, tend to mix with each other, and the 'workers' at the bottom of hierarchies do likewise, and thus don't have friends in the right places.

Sometimes it is possible, however, to make friends with one or two people higher in the hierarchy, for example a HOD of another department, or the person directly above your HOD with whom you may, perhaps, have something in common, such as being a graduate of the same school or University, or living in the same suburb etc.

Propaganda

In the modern world in which we are reduced to *consumer zombies* by endless marketing, it is also worth considering using a little propaganda to improve one's position in the workplace.

A survey such as that of Table 17.1, for example, can be used to provide feedback on both yourself, and your boss, and the results can be used as propaganda to both promote your image in the workplace, and to lessen the boss's standing.

Then, of course, as discussed in Chapter 5, repetition of such messages is usually necessary before they have much effect.

Sometimes 'thought coupling' can help in this, for example, frequently comparing the bad boss to a well-known 'bad person' often mentioned in the media, for example by calling them a 'little Hitler', and often such 'labels' stick after a few repetitions.

Life improvements

Efforts at improving one's home life can help improve one's work situation. Improving one's health with better diet, more exercise, and better relaxation periods, is likely to make one look and perform better at work and elsewhere.

It should also help if one dresses better, and is polite at all times, remembering as an example the term 'stroking' that was used in the Nixon White House to describe how members of it would 'butter up' people to get them to do and/or say what they wanted (Dean, 1985).

It can also help to improve one's social life, for example by joining the local branch of a political party.

Myself, I joined the St Kilda West branch of the Liberal party in 1987, and this provided evenings out for me and my new lady friend at that time, having been divorced by then for a couple of years. In the next couple of years I ran for two pre-selections, one for the state parliament, and one for the state upper house or senate.

Clearly the best candidate on the first occasion, I was 'white anted' on a minor technicality by another contender, while the other pre-selection was for a district far from where I lived and I was an 'outsider' with no chance of winning.

Through a lady I met at one branch meeting, however, I was introduced to a rich woman whose husband had just died of a sudden heart attack. She lived in Brighton's "golden mile" in a large house with its own tennis court, and immediately adjacent to the beach, and I had dinner with her on a couple of occasions. Without a job, but Cambridge PhD, single, etcetera, I might have stood a good chance of 'hooking up' with her permanently, and thus solving my unemployment problem because she owned a large supermarket a couple of suburbs away.

At those branch meetings I also met the local member in the state's senate, who I could perhaps have as used as a referee in my job applications because he'd spent time working in London's exclusive legal district, whereas I'd done my PhD in Cambridge, our having both worked in England giving us something in common.

Getting another job

I have just given an example of someone who might have been an OK referee for my many job applications, and one or two people did advise me to change referees after I'd spent a few years making unsuccessful applications.

Stupidly, however, having for many years being interviewed for jobs around Australia at HOD level and above, I never insisted on obtaining copies of the references written by my ex-bosses etc., when on reflection of how the very first interview went, the bastard ex-HOD in Auckland was backstabbing me badly by saying that I was a poor lecturer, was 'mad' etc.

It is, of course, usually best to get another job before quitting one's present job.

Indeed, sometimes a boss, upon hearing that you are looking for another job, might decide to give you a promotion and/or pay rise to keep you in the organization.

At the very least, however, if a boss is thinking of getting rid of you, knowing that you are looking for another job may prevent them from taking drastic action and 'sacking' you or forcing you to resign somehow, giving you more time to find a job, or to somehow deal with the boss, perhaps by getting him or her disciplined, moved 'sideways', demoted, or sacked.

In Universities, for example, many Professors who are made HOD fairly young are happy to relinquish the position after 5 or 10 years, and sometimes this might, in fact, be done under 'pressure from above' after people have complained about them.

Candidate selection

Table 17.2.

Candidate selection using weighted attribute scores

Attribute	Weight	Score			Weighted score		
		Tom	Dick	Harry	Tom	Dick	Harry
Qualifications	2	8	5	3	16	10	6
Experience	3	5	7	6	15	21	18
Age	1	5	5	8	5	5	8
Interview	2	3	5	8	6	10	16
Referees	1	5	5	5	5	5	5
Total					47	51	53

It is wise to be aware of how candidates applying for a job are selected, for this may give one ideas of how to improve one's prospects of promotion, or getting another job. An example is the task of selecting the 'best' of three candidates Tom, Dick and Harry, for a job using the *decision table* of Table 17.2, each member of the selection panel filling out this table and their results being combined.

Here five attributes: qualifications, experience (relevant), age (or total experience), impression made at interview, and strength of recommendations made by referees, are used and each of these is given a weight in the second column.

Then the three candidates are given a score out of ten for each attribute by each member of the selection panel and the results averaged (to the nearest round number for simplicity here), giving the results shown in columns 3,4,5.

Finally, these scores are multiplied by the weights, giving the results of columns 6,7,8, and these figures summed to give the totals shown.

The final result indicates Harry as the best candidate, though only marginally, so that some further deliberations might be appropriate before a final decision is made.

In practice, however, it is best to include other considerations such as:

[1] Who top scored in the most important attributes?

[2] If the candidate is an existing employee (in another position) has there been any bias?

In this sort of analysis the choice of attributes is crucial, as is their weighting, so that such factors can also be reviewed before making a final decision.

Personal experiences

My lack of appropriate action in dealing with a promotion being delayed by lies was discussed a couple of times earlier in the book, including in the last chapter. The bottom line on this, however, is that I should have put my case for promotion in writing, along with my complaints about the new HOD's bullying (examples of this were given in the last chapter), and perhaps got legal or other professional help to deal with the problem, rather than resigning meekly and ruining both my career and life.

Other mistakes I made included:

(1) Not accepting a job offer from the Tasmanian Institute of Technology in 1972 that would have taken me from the bottom of the lecturer scale to half-way up it. Had I gone there for just a few years, I should have been able to get a job at Senior Lecturer by the age of about 30.

(2) Doing a rave at my HOD at CIT the day before Christmas in 1978 because I was upset that he was going to run a short course I had written most of in Chile. In fact, having that course run overseas, however, was another positive point for my CV.

(3) Not telling anyone that I'd had a mild stroke in 1981 which left me with after-effects for months (in fact I had 3 or 4 mild strokes or TIAs that year). This might have bought me a little sympathy, latitude, and tolerance.

(4) Not doing anything about a colleague at Auckland stealing a copy of my growing 'tome' that was waiting in the Secretary's office to be posted overseas for supportive comment.

(5) Not doing anything about a colleague in Melbourne hiding a new phone linked computer terminal that I had got the department to buy in 1979, also hiding a book I had lent him in a cupboard in his office, and lying that he had "left it at home." This strange behaviour from a competitor I should have resolved somehow, perhaps by asking him to contribute to my first book effort on the Finite Element Method, rather than the clueless HOD. At least this colleague had then just spent a year in the USA in the same department as one of the top names in the subject, so he must have had access to material worth putting in my book, whilst that 'top name' person might have been asked for supportive comment to help the book get published.

Conclusions

Languishing too low, for too long, in hierarchies is depressing and, indeed, can ruin one's health and life.

A questionnaire evaluation like that of Table 17.1 can be used to evaluate one's job performance, and a similar one can perhaps also be used to evaluate the bad performance of a bad boss. Then, with careful circulation of the results, one's position, or at least standing or reputation, in the organization may be improved, and the reputation of the bad boss tarnished.

It helps, of course, to have friends in the right places, and some effort should be made to find some, and then they might be of help in circulating positive propaganda about yourself, and negative propaganda about a bad boss.

In looking for another job it helps to be aware of common selection processes and criteria such as those of Table 17.2.

Finally, if just one of the examples of my personal experiences provides a valuable lesson for others of what not to do, and what to do, to deal with work-related problems, then I may be able to forgive myself for boring readers with them.

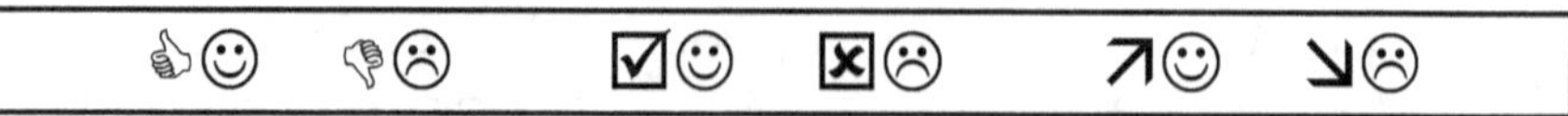

CHAPTER 18

CONCLUSIONS

He who does not hope to win has already lost.
José Juaquin Olmedo, (1780-1847), attrib.

I asked why he was a priest and he said that
if you have to work for anybody an absentee boss is best.
Jeanette Winterson, *The Passion*, ch. 1, 1987.

Mohr's Laws

Chapter 1 discussed a few well known laws, including Parkinson's Law, The Peter Principle, and Pareto's Law.

Then the original 10 Mohr's Laws I proposed in 2002 were given in Table 1.1., the 9th of these being that Murphy (of Murphy's Law) is God's prophet and, indeed, his law does sum up mankind's disastrous history very well.

The 10th is *Mohr's Metrology* - that we should not judge complex matters as merely 'black and white', or 'right or wrong', but give them a score out of 9, scores of 0 and 10 being disallowed because, in the case of health, for example, 0 would be dead, and 10 or perfection is impossible.

Other Mohr's Laws were then discussed, including Mohr's Laws of War: (1) *Don't panic,* and (2) *Double-check everything.*

Then Mohr's Law of Hierarchies (MLH) was discussed:
In hierarchical organizations the amount of real
material-producing work people do is inversely proportional
to their rank or level in the organization.
The amount of compensation they receive, however,
is proportional to their level,
sometimes to an exponential degree.

This law is modelled by a small DC (direct current) network and analysed using a simple BASIC program, the results of which demonstrate how the amount of power and money the person at the top of a hierarchy has tends to exponentiate as the hierarchy increases in size.

Then Mohr's Power Law and Mohr's Law of Capitalism are given, the latter showing how the rich can invest their money to grow it at an exponential rate over time.

Chapter 1 then concluded with discussion of how aggression and age affect the behaviour of bosses, citing two examples of my being appointed to jobs by men about to retire, being replaced by relatively young, inexperienced, and incompetent new HODs who ruined my career and life.

Hierarchical effects throughout life

Chapters 2 – 11 discussed how we suffer in hierarchies for most of our lives, beginning with families and 'big brother syndrome' (BBS) and 'big sister syndrome' (BSS), and continuing through our days in school, in religions, as 'brainwashed' consumers, in higher education and training, working in private or government organizations, in society, in the criminal world (itself hierarchical, and often with connections to big business, government etc.), and in politics.

The psychology of hierarchies

Chapter 12 discussed psychology and psychiatry, psychology, of course, playing a major role in hierarchies.

Chapter 13 discussed attitudinal psychology as this plays a major role in human behaviour, especially in hierarchical organizations.

Chapter 14 discussed the psychology of conflict, including the well-known *contact hypothesis* and my own multi-factor attitudinal model of conflict (Mohr, 2014a; Mohr & Fear, 2016; Mohr, Sinclair & Fear, 2017).

Chapter 15 discussed the psychology of hierarchies and the Hare checklist for psychopaths which can, preferably with some modifications, be used to evaluate bad bosses.

Dealing with hierarchy problems

Chapter 16 discussed how to deal with hierarchy problems, giving a questionnaire to evaluate one's quality of life, the first category evaluated being one's work conditions.

Then it is shown how to use the Information Integration method introduced in Chapter 13 to evaluate the work condition attributes of one's life more accurately by applying both weights and scores to each of five attributes.

A simple example plan is then given which gives timelines for various actions, including talking to the boss about your problems, and looking for another job.

Then lists of things one should not do, and things one should do, to help deal with "toxic leaders" suggested by Gillespie (2017) are given.

The chapter closed with a few personal examples of mistakes I made in dealing with bad bosses, these mainly being doing nothing and just 'copping it on the chin', when I should have put some complaints in writing and put them on the right desks.

How to rise in hierarchies

Chapter 17 began by discussing how miserable being too low in a hierarchy for too long can make people.

It then gave a 20-item questionnaire I once gave to a class of students so that they could score my lecturing performance, and also that of the HOD, who I shared teaching that subject with for a year or two. I scored much better than the HOD, but was too foolish and/or inhibited to use these results as positive propaganda for myself, and negative propaganda against the bad boss.

Getting help from family, friends, and perhaps colleagues to deal with bad boss etc. problems was then discussed, along with using propaganda to improve one's image in a workplace, and to damage that of a bad boss.

Finally, life improvements (i.e. health, social life etc.), and getting another job are discussed, giving an example of the sort of candidate selection table often used by selection panels.

Once again, the chapter concludes with examples of personal mistakes I made, for example not accepting a quite good job offer very early in my career, once losing my temper with the HOD (his getting revenge for this later was a factor in my career disaster and 'academic crucifixion'), and not telling people about health problems, or bad behaviour by colleagues.

The new religion Mohronism

The book has 4 appendices, the first giving checklists to diagnose psychopaths.

The second is on the 'mechanics of the brain', showing how memories are often stored in a hierarchical fashion, and using the same BASIC program for DC networks given in Chapter 1 (with minor differences), and explaining in detail the notation etc. used in this program.

The third appendix is a 'pilot episode' for a comedy TV series involving a party to which family, friends and two ex-bosses are invited. In this I try to obtain in farcical fashion some sort of revenge upon people who had treated me badly.

The fourth, and perhaps most important appendix, shows how the original 10 Mohr's Laws were used to start the new religion *Mohronism* (Mohr & Fear, 2015).

As noted in Chapter 1, the 9th of these laws is that God's prophet is Murphy, and in Appendix C the story of how Murphy's Law came into being is told.

Much of Appendix D then makes various suggestions as to how adherents to the new religion Mohronism should behave, for example a sign they should make with their fingers, how they should dress, how small sacrifices should be brought to regular Mohronic services, and how Mohrons could give public exhibitions similar to those of inmates of the Bethlehem 'madhouse' that were held until 1815.

Mohr's Laws of Decisions

Essentially, the major problem of the human race is the habit of making bad decisions.

Some of us, at least, are very good at creative thinking to produce new ideas and products, and others are good at making the things we most need such as food, clothing and shelter.

As a result of the devastatingly accurate Peter Principle, all too many of our leaders and managers are, more often than not, guilty of bad decisions, if not corruption.

If a leader commits us to an unjustified war then, just as architects do, he praises his mistake. If a worker makes a small error or two he is dismissed.

Self-evident as they may be, Mohr's Laws of Decisions (Mohr, 2014b) are some help:

1) Don't rush.

2) Don't take the first offer or 'run with' the first idea.

3) Look for alternative ideas and build an ideas/options list.

4) List the requirements or inputs for each option.

5) List the results or outputs for each option.

6) Calculate the ratio of the outputs to inputs for each option.

7) Double check the accuracy of 4 - 6.

8) Select the option with the highest output/input ratio.

9) Ask at least a second opinion.

10) Sleep on it.

The analysis of steps 4 - 6 corresponds to *cost-benefit* analysis, a simple technique widely used in economic studies of infrastructure and other plans to decide on the best program of work.

Many a housewife probably uses a somewhat similar decision making approach but the usually moronic politicians who run countries find such stuff hard going and have to employ thousands of economists and statisticians to perform these rudimentary analyses.

Needless to say they usually get it wrong, often when somebody's palm is greased, for example by a construction company seeking the contract for a major government project.

Conclusion

Lynne and Vanhanen (2002) note that in the richest nations the correlation of IQ with earnings is only 0.35. This is a low figure bearing in mind that high earnings should enhance performance. Indeed, if we do bear this in mind, then the real correlation would be a negative one showing that the fattest capitalist pigs have more animal cunning and greed and less intelligence.

The bottom line is, therefore, that our hierarchical leaders are usually greedy unethical pigs of pretty average intelligence, if that, thus being an important cog in the machinery of our *reverse evolution*.

Thanks to lousy leaders, as usual, mankind's disastrous history of conflict seems unlikely to end and we face other threats as a result of overpopulation, resource depletion, climate change etcetera that decrease our chances of avoiding the extinction forecast for many other animal species.

As noted in the present book, we should push for *real democracy*, as outlined in Chapter 20 of *The Doomsday Calculation* (Mohr, 2012c), rather than the highly oligarchical and antiquated Westminster system, and the highly hierarchical socialist systems that still govern most much of the world today, and only then, perhaps, might there be any real chance of avoiding increasing global catastrophes and perhaps extinction as a result of overpopulation etc., or nuclear and biochemical warfare (Mohr, 2012d).

I hope, therefore, that some of the ideas and information given in this book will help people deal with hierarchical problems they may have, whether they be in the workplace, in family hierarchies, schools, or other organizations such as religious ones.

The primary focus in dealing with hierarchy problems should be on getting on as well as possible with others, even if this is only involves superficial politeness and 'stroking' to 'butter up' people to get them to say or do what you want.

One should also make discreet use of 'propaganda' to promote one's own image positively and that of bad bosses negatively.

It also helps, of course, to improve one's health and lifestyle, so that one should then look and perform better in the workplace (Mohr, 2012b; Mohr, 2015).

It is also important to be able to get advice and help from family and friends, and also from at least one or two people in the workplace. If need be, however, it may often be worthwhile seeking professional help in dealing with workplace problems, or in trying to get a new job.

Professional help, including advice from lawyers and perhaps psychologists, might sometimes also be called for in dealing with bad bosses. If one, for example, got a few colleagues to rate a bad boss by filling out a questionnaire like the Hare checklist of Table 15.1, or a job performance questionnaire like that of Table 17.1, then the results might help make a case against the bad boss that can be discretely (and perhaps anonymously) presented to his or her superiors.

Finally, it should be noted that, having been made in jest, Murphy's Law is wrong, and according to Mohr's 10th Law (Mohr's Metrology), is should be more like:

Anything that can go wrong will **usually** *go wrong; and* **usually** *at an* **inconvenient** *time.*

That is, according to the Mohr Scale of 0-9, things can't **always** go wrong, and they will not go wrong at the **worst possible** time, but most people would agree that things go wrong at an inconvenient time, it being, of course, inconvenient when things go wrong, no matter when that is.

As for *that can go wrong* – machine parts that can wear out are, of course, an example of this.

Finally, yet another Mohr's Law, *Mohr's Law of Compatibility*, involving 'getting on' with people. This is that one should only expect to be able to get on reasonably well with approximately one person out of every two one meets.

The 1 out of 2 here is reminiscent of Mohr's Law of Politics, which was discussed in Chapter 11, where in the outdated and all-too-often farcical Westminster system of government there are usually two main parties and 90+% of people vote for these, the total votes for each main party usually being fairly close.

With compatibility with other people there are, of course, many factors involved, including age, sex, sexual orientation, appearance, educational history, income and wealth, political preferences etcetera.

Getting on with people, however, is one of the keys to success in life (Mohr, 2018a). A favourite example of how to 'get on' with people is given by John Dean, Attorney-General under Richard Nixon, in his book *Blind Ambition*. He tells that in the Nixon White House people used the term *stroking* for how they treated people they wanted establish good relations with and thence get them to do what they wanted them to do, help them, and give them useful information, etcetera.

Those readers who have ever had pet cats will, no doubt, understand this use of the word stroking!

Mohr's Law of Compatibility, however, reminds us that we can't expect to get on well with many people, and should concentrate our efforts on those with whom we can to improve our prospects of success in the hierarchical rat races that comprise almost every aspect of modern societies.

As for those bad bosses etc. that we can't get on with, despite our best efforts at 'stroking', it may help to get a few colleagues evaluate them using the Mohr Checklist for Psychopaths (MCLP) given in Appendix A.

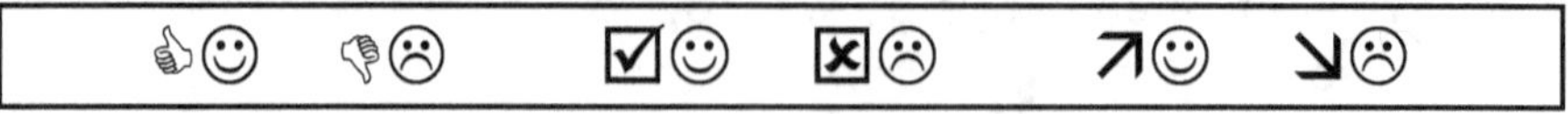

Appendix A

THE MOHR CHECKLIST FOR PSYCHOPATHS

> *Psychopathic personality: Madman, the maladjusted, psychopath, psycho, psychopathic personality, sociopath, unstable personality, aggressive personality, antisocial personality, dipsomaniac, drunkard - - drug addict,* Microsoft Bookshelf dictionary, 1994.
>
> *To treat a psychopath – at any time, in any place, or under any set of conditions – is the most onerous and unrewarding job a clinician can undertake.* Robert Lindner, *The Fifty-Minute Hour,* ch. 4 (1986).

Diagnosing psychopaths

As noted in Chapter 15, in 1980, Canadian clinical psychologist Dr Robert Hare, who worked in prisons, released the first version of the Hare checklist for identifying psychopaths, and several further versions followed.

As shown in Table A.1, it divides 20 personality traits into four groups: interpersonal, affective, lifestyle, and antisocial, these measuring traits including charm, propensity to lie, lack of remorse, and need for stimulation.

After an interview each trait is scored as 0 (not present), 1 (present but not dominant), or 2 (dominant), so that the maximum possible score is 40.

Average people score from 3 to 6, non-psychopathic criminals score from 16 to 22, whilst in the UK and US respectively, scores of >25 and >30 are taken as a positive diagnosis of psychopathy (Gillespie, 2017).

Table A.1. The Hare checklist for psychopaths.

	TRAIT	SCORE
	Facet 1: Interpersonal	
1	Glibness or superficial charm	1
2	Grandiose sense of self-worth	1
3	Pathological lying	2
4	Cunning or manipulative	1
	Facet 2: Affective	
5	Lack of remorse or guilt	2
6	Emotionally shallow	2
7	Callous or lack of empathy	2
8	Failure to accept responsibility for their own actions	2
	Facet 3: Lifestyle	
9	Need for stimulation (easily bored)	1
10	Parasitic lifestyle	1
11	Lack of realistic, long-term goals	0
12	Impulsivity	1
13	Irresponsibility	0
	Facet 4: Antisocial	
14	Poor behavioural controls	0
15	Early behavioural problems	0
16	Juvenile delinquency	0
17	History of conditional prison release being revoked	0
18	Criminal versatility	0
	Other traits:	
19	Many short-term marital relationships	0
20	Promiscuous sexual behaviour	0
TOTAL SCORE		**16**

In Table A.1 the author has scored a couple of bad bosses he once had, both of whom were too young and inexperienced for being HOD, and played a major role in destroying his promising University career when he was less than 40.

Their total score of 16 seemed too low, as both seemed at least somewhat psychopathic, suggesting that Table A.1 might apply more to hardened criminals for which item 17 relates to a form of 'treatment', namely continued imprisonment, presumably because of little or no sign of rehabilitation or remorse. Similarly, items 16 and 19 relate to past history.

Thus criteria for judging a bad boss should include:

➢ Bossiness.

➢ Assertiveness.

➢ Dishonesty and lying.

➢ Selfishness and greed.

➢ Vanity.

➢ Bullying.

Table A.2, therefore, shows the Mohr Checklist for Psychopaths (MCLP) in which a few items of the Hare checklist are replaced by new ones more relevant to 'bad bosses', and a few items are replaced by hopefully better alternatives.

After an interview or other assessment/judgment each trait is scored as 0 (not present), 1 (present but not dominant), or 2 (dominant), so that the maximum possible score is 40, but note that the MCLP also allows scores such as 1.5, as shown.

With the MCLP 'OK' people score from 1 to 10, 'borderline ' people circa 15+, whilst scores of 20+ indicate psychopathy, and 30+ serious psychopathy that can be classified as a serious mental illness.

I have re-scored the aforementioned two bad bosses as shown in Table A.2, the score of 26.5 giving a positive diagnosis of psychopathy, a diagnosis I wish had been made many years earlier before the two men in question ruined my career and life all too many years ago.

The MCLP

Table A.2. The Mohr Checklist for Psychopaths (MCLP).

	TRAIT	SCORE
	Facet 1: Interpersonal	
1	Glibness or superficiality of a salesman	1
2	Excessive sense of self-worth	2
3	Pathological lying	2
4	Cunning or manipulative	1.5
	Facet 2: Affective	
5	Lack of remorse or guilt	2
6	Emotionally shallow	1
7	Callous or lack of empathy	2
8	Won't accept responsibility for own actions	1.5
	Facet 3: Lifestyle	
9	Excessively ambitious	1
10	Excessively greedy	1
11	Parasitic life style	1
12	Extravagant life style	0.5
13	Irresponsibility	0.5
	Facet 4: Antisocial	
14	Bullying	1.5
15	Focuses only on own problems	1.5
16	Little care about others, such as subordinates in the workplace	1.5
17	Mixes only with other managers etc.	1.5
18	Stretches rules to make more money etc.	1.25
	Other traits:	
19	Vanity	1.25
20	History of sexual promiscuity	0
TOTAL SCORE		**25.5**

Conclusion

The main point of this appendix was to present Tables A.1 and A.2, scoring them for two bad bosses who played a major part in ruining my career as a university lecturer.

As for myself, I rate my score for anxiety between 1 and 2/10, much of that being the habit of liking to finish work fairly quickly/promptly.

On the depression scale, my score on that varied, of course, over the years, being >1 perhaps in 1965 and 1966, in 1966 having to repeat the whole of 2nd year Engineering being no fun at all. Likewise it might have been from 1 to 2 in 1971 working in my second full-time job which I called in retrospect "the sweatshop". In my 2 Cambridge PhD years there was great financial and thence time stress, finishing in record time (< 2 years) and flying home with only about $50 in the bank.

After my 'academic crucifixion' I had PTSD, of course, largely resulting in depression of varying from 3/10 to 4/10 for a couple of decades, and perhaps reducing to circa 2/10 a decade+ ago, and perhaps 1/10 now.

APPENDIX B

HIERARCHICAL STORAGE OF MEMORIES

Introduction

In Chapters 2 and 6 early learning by imprinting and imitative learning were discussed. Chapter 5 dealt with advertising, propaganda, and 'brainwashing'. As an appendix, therefore, it seems worthwhile to discuss how that all important organ, the brain, works, particularly as memories are often stored in a hierarchical fashion.

Memory structure

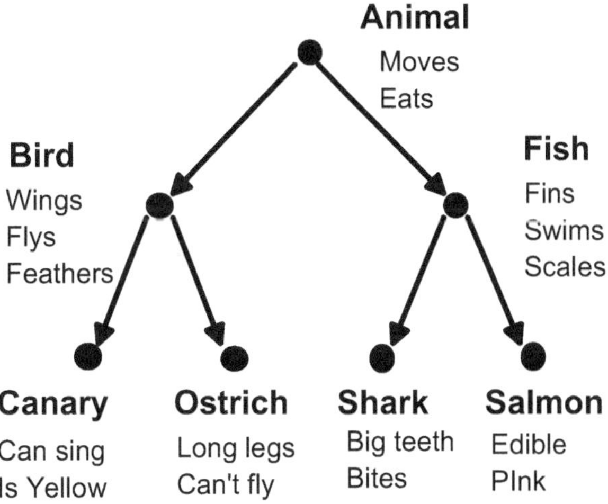

Figure B.1. Hierarchical organization of the mental lexicon.

Figure B.1 shows a proposed structure in which the brain stores information about animals, that is, as categories and sub-categories with properties attached to each 'node' in the structure (Collins et al., 1969).

Some experimental results do not fit this model, for example Ripps et al. (1973) found that people were quicker to agree to the truth of the statement: *A cat is an animal* than they were to the truth of the statement: *A cat is a mammal.*

They argued that MAMMAL should be closer to CAT than ANIMAL in the hierarchy.

More important, the word ANIMAL is more frequently used than the word MAMMAL, and frequency of reference to a memory certainly does enhance the speed of recall.

I would also argue that the brain almost certainly must store memories in a *precedence network* based on the order in which learning occurs. In such a network a memory search that succeeds in finding a 'connection' or *common* property shared by a 'new' item in short term memory and an item in long-term memory might then store the data on the new item in the same physical area.

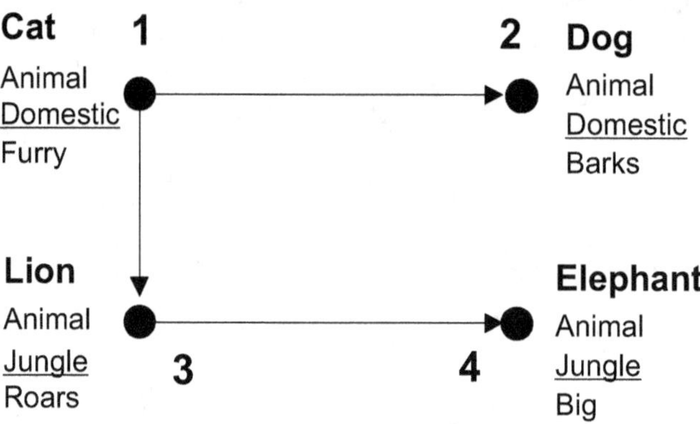

Figure B.2. Precedence memory network.

Then, for example, the first live animals that most children encounter might well be cats or dogs so that they will begin forming the memory structure shown in Figure B.2.

Here four memories have the *common property* 'animal' and cat is the first animal encountered by an infant and thence the first memory stored (at node 1, perhaps one or more brain cells). The second memory is dog, the third lion, and so on.

Then cat and dog are associated by the property *domestic* (in the child's language perhaps 'house' or 'nearby') whilst lion and elephant are associated by the common property *jungle.*

Such memories have a considerable visual 'content' and the ease of recall of a memory will depend its 'strength' which will depend on such factors as the degree of elaboration with which it was committed to long-term memory and the frequency and recency with which the memory has been revisited.

Network models of the brain

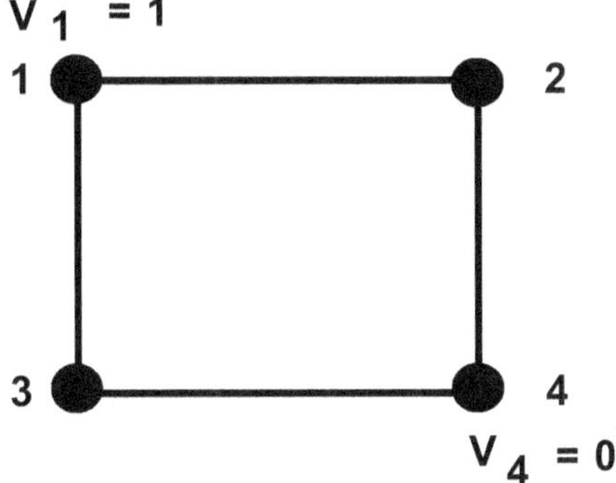

Figure B.3. FEM model of simple DC network.
Resistances 12, 13, 24, 34 all = 1.
Potential at node 1 = 1 and at node 4 = 0.

Long axons extend from neurons and their terminals connect to the short dendrites of other neurons in the brain.

Such networks can be modelled using the *Finite Element Method* (FEM). As a very simple example Figure B.3 shows a direct current (DC) network with four resistance *elements* connecting four *nodes* (corresponding to a group of neurons storing a memory item) an d this corresponds to the simple *precedence memory model* of Figure B.2.

The numerical FEM model for this 'structure' is obtained by summing matrices for each element formed by using Ohm's Law to write the current flow in each element ij as

$$Q_{ij} = (V_i - V_j)/R_{ij}$$

where V_i and V_j are the voltages at nodes i and j at each end, and R_{ij} is the *resistance* of the element.

Then writing the two equations for current flow at each end of the element as a matrix we obtain

$$\left\{ \begin{array}{c} Q_{ij} \\ -Q_{ij} \end{array} \right\} = (1/R_{ij}) \left[\begin{array}{cc} 1 & -1 \\ -1 & 1 \end{array} \right] \left\{ \begin{array}{c} V_i \\ V_j \end{array} \right\}$$

Doing this for each element and writing the entries from their *element matrices* in a *system matrix* in positions corresponding to the node numbers for each element we obtain the system equations:

$$\{Q\} = \left\{ \begin{array}{c} Q_1 \\ Q_2 \\ Q_3 \\ Q_4 \end{array} \right\} = \left[\begin{array}{cccc} G_{12} + G_{13} & -G_{12} & -G_{13} & 0 \\ -G_{12} & G_{12} + G_{24} & 0 & -G_{24} \\ -G_{13} & 0 & G_{13} + G_{34} & -G_{34} \\ 0 & -G_{24} & -G_{34} & G_{24} + G_{34} \end{array} \right] \left\{ \begin{array}{c} V_1 \\ V_2 \\ V_3 \\ V_4 \end{array} \right\}$$

where $G_{12} = 1/R_{12}$ is the reciprocal of the resistance or *conductance* of element 12.

This *assembly* process for the system matrix is easily done by a computer program and the matrix problem can be solved using the same short BASIC matrix solution program given below.

First, either input or output currents must be specified at some nodes to 'force' current flows. Alternatively, voltages are specified for at least two nodes, one of these being a 'datum' potential equal to zero.

This is done in the present example, in the program calculating equivalent current 'loads' by multiplying the columns in the system matrix for 'specified voltage nodes' by the voltage specified at them and adding the result to the load matrix $\{ Q \}$ or array V( ) in the program.

Then the problem is solved to determine the nodal voltages or potentials and the element currents are calculated using

$$Q_{ij} = (V_i - V_j)/R_{ij}$$

A short program that assembles and solves this problem is given below. Here key notation is

NN(,)	matrix storing the element node numbers
R( )	matrix storing the element resistances
C(,)	the system matrix
V( )	the nodal voltages
NP	number of nodes
NE	number of elements
NS	number of nodes with specified voltage
a$, b$	format specifier strings
X, S	temporary numbers

The program reads the data in lines 3, 5 and 9, 'deploying' the element matrices into the system matrix in lines 6 and 7 and modifying the RHS 'load' vector V( ) for the specified voltages in line 11.

Then only lines 14 to 20 are required to solve the problem using Gauss-Mohr reduction.

Here X is first used to store the *pivot* for 'row division' operations (line 14) and then used to store the 'row multiplier' (line 17) for the row subtraction operations (line 19) and doing these on the RHS vector V( ) (line 17) as well yields the solution.

```
DIM NN(20, 2), R(20), C(20, 20), V(20)                          1
a$ = "###": b$ = "######.###"                                   2
READ NP, NE, NS                                                 3
FOR K = 1 TO NE                                                 4
READ I, J, R: NN(K, 1) = I: NN(K, 2) = J: R(K) = R              5
C(I, I) = C(I, I) + 1 / R: C(I, J) = C(I, J) - 1 / R            6
C(J, I) = C(J, I) - 1 / R: C(J, J) = C(J, J) + 1 / R            7
NEXT                                                           8
FOR K = 1 TO NS: READ N, S                                     9
FOR I = 1 TO NP                                                10
C(N, I) = 0: V(I) = V(I) - S * C(I, N)                         11
C(I, N) = 0: NEXT I                                           12
V(N) = S: C(N, N) = 1: NEXT                                    13
FOR I = 1 TO NP: X = C(I, I): V(I) = V(I) / X                  14
FOR J = I + 1 TO NP: C(I, J) = C(I, J) / X: NEXT              15
FOR K = 1 TO NP: IF K = I THEN GOTO NEXK                      16
X = C(K, I): V(K) = V(K) - X * V(I)                            17
FOR J = I + 1 TO NP                                           18
C(K, J) = C(K, J) - X * C(I, J): NEXT J                        19
NEXK: NEXT K: NEXT I                                           20
PRINT " Node   Voltage"                                       21
FOR I = 1 TO NP                                               22
PRINT USING a$; I; : PRINT USING b$; V(I): NEXT I             23
PRINT " Element  Current"                                      24
FOR K = 1 TO NE: I = NN(K, 1): J = NN(K, 2)                    25
Q = -(V(J) - V(I)) / R                                         26
PRINT USING a$; I; J; : PRINT USING b$; Q: NEXT               27
DATA 4,4,2                                                     28
DATA 1,2,1, 1,3,1, 2,4,1, 3,4,1                                29
DATA 1,1, 4,0                                                  30
```

Note that the RHS line numbers are not part of the program.

The data appended to the program (lines 28 - 30) is for the problem of Figure B.3 for which the solution is $V_2 = V_3 = 0.5$ and currents = 0.5 for each element.

As a crude analogy the resistance of each element might be compared to the *frequency* of use of a path in the network of the brain and the voltage at each node might be compared to the *strength* of a memory 'image' or information 'bundle' stored in a neuron.

In practice a signal between two neurons is an electrical impulse passed along the axon of the first to the dendrites of the second via a synaptic junction. At this junction neurotransmitter chemicals pass the signal across a 'synaptic gap.'

Evidently these chemicals react with RNA or peptide macromolecules in the neurons that play a role in memory *coding*.

In the case of classical conditioning, therefore, with frequent 'dosing' in this way the storage of a memory is made more permanent.

Therefore a more realistic FEM model of a neural network might include a capacitance property for nodes so that the charge stored at these could model the strength and/or recency of a memory.

FEM network models lend themselves to 'structural' models of memory such as that of Figures B.1 and B.2.

That the resulting numerical model is a matrix suggests that some form of database model might also be used to model memory storage in the brain, not a particularly startling idea!

Another possibility is to combine the two model types so that each node in Figure B.3 is a database of some category like those in Figure B.1 and the links between the nodes are the *joins* between common *fields* in these databases.

As there are about 10^{12} neurons in the human brain, however, we can only hope to model its memory processes on a small scale.

Human learning and memory

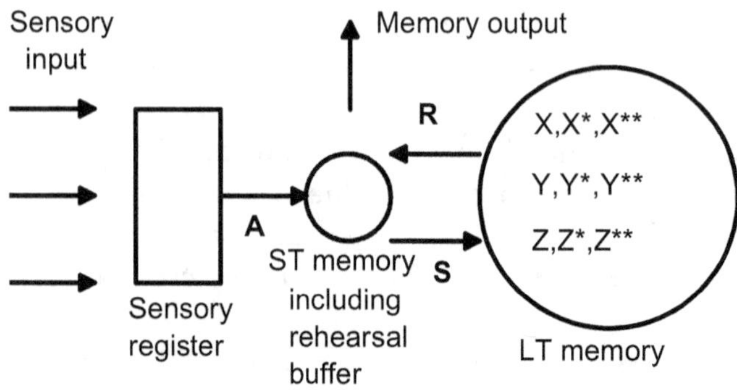

Figure B.4. Information processing model of memory.

Figure B.4 shows a simple information processing model of memory (Atkinson and Shiffrin, 1968). In this the *sensory register* processes information from sensory channels associated with vision, hearing and other senses.

The visual sensory register can hold 10 - 20 bits of information for only about 1 second, whereas the auditory sensory register can hold information for up to 4 - 5 seconds.

Of the up to 20 bits of information that the our visual registers can accommodate with a brief glance, for example an array of letters of the alphabet, we can only remember four or five of them, this number being called the *span of apprehension.*

As a consequence most information in the sensory registers is lost but that to which sufficient attention is paid is transferred to the *short-term-memory* (STM). Here it is held for about 20 - 30 seconds and some of it is processed by being rehearsed in the *rehearsal buffer*, the rest being lost.

This model fits everyday life fairly well. For example, when somebody tells you a phone number and you are interrupted while dialing it you are likely to forget it because it will be lost from STM. This is because the STM holds only about 5 - 9 items and, under certain conditions, as few as two or three.

Sternberg (1966) conducted an experiment that illustrates how memory, in this case STM, works. He showed a group of people sets of from 1 to 6 digits and seconds later asked them if the set contained a particular digit. Response times were closely proportional to the number of digits shown, demonstrating that the coding of the set in LTM was searched serially or one digit at a time.

In the rehearsal buffer such processes as repetition of the information link it to information already stored in memory and then pass it to *long-term-memory* (LTM) where it remains for periods of days up to a lifetime. In LTM information is *consolidated*, a process that may take from half an hour up to months. If consolidation is somehow interrupted some memory loss occurs.

Simple passive repetition of information, or *maintenance rehearsal,* is not sufficient to ensure that items are passed to LTM. The active process of *elaborative rehearsal,* involving reorganization of the material and attaching meaning to it is more likely to pass information to LTM.

There are four types of LTM:

[1] *Procedural memory* or implicit memory is 'knowing how' to perform some skill, often learnt by procedural or implicit learning. Procedural learning is discussed later in this chapter.

[2] *Declarative memory* is 'knowing that' or memory of data or facts and events.

[3] *Episodic memory* of prior life experiences is a type of declarative memory.

[4] *Semantic memory* such as words and language rules is another type of declarative memory which involves more 'preprocessing' in STM than episodic memory.

In such processing even inherently organized material is *subjectively organized* by the learner into categories. Up to a point, it is found that the more categories used the better the material can be recalled.

Semantic memory uses *constructive processes* to store information in an organized manner, often into a hierarchical structure of categories and sub-categories.

Recall of the information then occurs by *reconstructive processes.* With these speed of recall depends upon the hierarchical level at which information is recalled, more general 'heading' information being recalled more rapidly than specific information.

Thus when we have difficulty remembering a person's name, for example, we often can only remember one or more names similar in some respect such as their first letter and then finally remember the required name anything from seconds to days later.

Memory processing also makes much use of images and *concrete* images are easily formed for words like 'cat' whilst *abstract* images for words like 'mercy' are more difficult to form.

Australian aborigine elders, for example, remember centuries of tribal history by associating important events with environmental features and recall and pass on this history by 'walking through' these places.

Information stored in LTM is easier to recall if it is stored with *retrieval cues* which are associated with 'blocks' of information. Individual items within these blocks are then stored with 'tags'.

How easily information is recalled later depends much upon how well it has been associated with images, categorized and provided with cues.

An example of how images affect information recall from LTM occurs if witnesses who saw a speeding car crash are asked:

"How fast do you think the car was going when it _ _ _ _ _?"

with the final verb having such variations as *contacted, hit,* and *crashed.*

Speed estimates will increase in the order of these three verbs by as much as 25% because the new information in the wording of the question conflicts or *interferes* with the memory and associated images of the event in LTM.

Information that has been stored in a well-organized fashion can sometimes be recalled by *redintegration*, the process by which some event such as a 'leading question' unlocks a rapid sequence of memories that may be connected by a chain of associations.

This is the ideal situation when we read an exam question. One or more words in the question quickly trigger recall of a stream of relevant information. If the exam is the usual written answer one we tend to forget part of the answer before we can write it down.

Conclusion

Human memories, however, are often laid down in a split second and remembered permanently yet others, especially most of those laboriously lectured to us at school, are quickly forgotten.

Memories are often stored in the brain in a hierarchical fashion, as illustrated by Figure B.1, and a short BASIC program is used to analyse this very simple network.

Related to this somewhat, the information processing model of memory was discussed briefly, and this involves chemical 'long term potentiation' of memories when they are temporarily in the short term memory and rehearsal buffer.

An application of this is in advertising and propaganda, of course, where repetition is used to reinforce memory, and also in 'playing politics' to get elected, or on a personal basis, to get promoted in a workplace hierarchy.

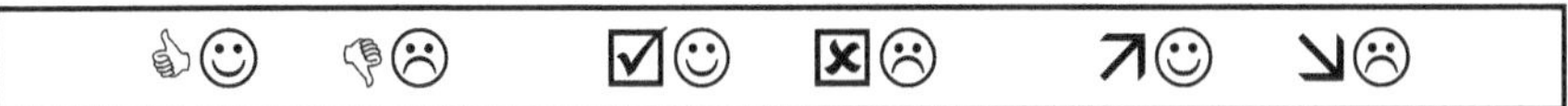

Appendix B

APPENDIX C

A HUMOROUS EXAMPLE OF A MEETING

Having stumbled across DVDs of a year of the Seinfeld TV series and the movie 'Meet The Fockers', I then went out of my way to get all 6 years of Seinfeld, the other 3 Focker movies, and all the episodes of 'Faulty Towers' also, inspiring me to plan a comedy series of my own entitled *Meet the In-Laws.* Here then is a rough idea of the pilot episode for this.

Scene: My lounge room & adjoining kitchen and meals area.
Situation: I have invited a few relatives to a joke engagement party one Saturday night.
The cast in order of appearance is thus:
Myself: Geoff Mohr

My fiancé: The stuffed ape shown above.

Her name is Sharmain, named after a woman to whom I rented my large, private spare room at the other end of my house in 1988. She had lost a managerial job at circa 35 and was actually looking to catch a husband, and thus got involved with me. She got pregnant but had a miscarriage just 3 days before a big church wedding.

A day or two later I absent-mindedly told her I was going to see the violent 'hair-pulling and strangling' ex-lady friend, Helena, mentioned in Chapter 2. Sharmain immediately left in fear, saving me from being 'caught' and made a 'man slave' by a woman driven by her hormones, like all forms of life, including bacteria, from which we evolved (Mohr, Sinclair & Fear, 2014), to breed/multiply.

A past lady friend: An attractive 'bird', as the picture above shows, the violent woman mentioned above who out of jealousy, and having got a bit drunk starts a fight with my fiancé similar to that in the 'hair pulling out' episode of ch. 2.

The in-laws to be: namely Sharmain's parents.

My extended family:
My eldest brother's widow and one of her children.
My two sons and their de facto wives.
The surviving parents (3) of these 2 wives.
The de facto wife of my other older brother F.

Recent lady friend: a 'fat lady' met at a club a few years ago with several psychiatric conditions including anxiety/OCD, schizophrenia, and depression.
A female escort: hired by me as a joke, she only stays for an hour (charging $200 to do so).
The bastard ex-boss in my CIT days.
The bastard ex-boss in my Auckland Uni. Days.

The proceedings are basically the successive arrival of the guests, who upon arrival are given several presents, including:

(a) Giving one pair of in-laws a dictionary because I have never been introduced to them previously, and because they were immigrants from Europe many years previously.

(b) Giving another in-law a book on management fraud because they work fairly comfortably up the hierarchy of a large organization.

(c) Giving the de facto wife of my brother F a book on hairdressing to remind her that she once said to my face that I had a *"bodgie hairdo"*, one of many acts of bullying I suffered early in my 'down-and-out' days playing psychiatric nurse for my defunct parents in "Ward 13" in 1985 and 1986 (my typically 'up himself' Cambridge clod father called the house a home for "down-and-outs").

(d) Giving the 'fat lady' friend a book on psychiatry.

(e) Giving the widow of my late 'Big Brother' a book on financial fraud and elder abuse (by way of financial fraud) to remind her of how BB cheated my parents, me and my other brother of a lot of family money on a few occasions.

(f) Giving the two bastard ex-bosses, who were 2 of the 4 villains that destroyed my very promising University career which I had worked so hard and made so many financial sacrifices to build, a bottle of 100 Seconal capsules asking them to use them by the expiry date, if not ASAP.

The evening progresses with everybody chatting profusely and drinking various amounts, and the fiancé, ex-lady friend, and female escort (who I introduced as "an old friend") jealously eyeing each other, and then later in the evening Sharmain and Helena coming to blows.

When I try to separate them, they both attack me, resulting in my looking worse for wear the next day, as shown above.

Finally, the disastrous evening could end with me and the fiancé 'making up' as she helps bandage my wounds, and with the 'fat lady' singing before, having had too much booze, throwing up over my fiancé, bringing an end to the relationship.

Well that's it folks, just the basic ideas for a farcical movie tentatively entitled *Meet the In-Laws*.

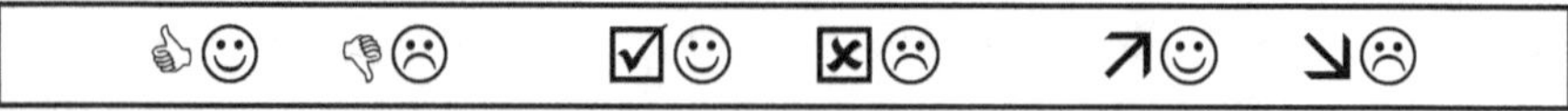

Appendix D

A Religion Based on Mohr's Laws

Mohronism

Mohronism is one of the newest religions. It was launched by the (limited) publication of the book *Mohr's Laws, What Went Wrong With You and the World and What To Do About It* (Mohr, 2002). Unfortunately few copies of this book are extant now. This book holds that the Real Truth is that Murphy was God's prophet, this being Mohr's 9th Law (Mohr, 2002; Mohr & Fear, 2015), explaining why, throughout history, mankind has lurched from one disaster to another and is now threatened with extinction, not salvation (Mohr, 2012c).

And who pray tell is Murphy? He was the celebrated Murphy of Murphy's law, credited to the eponymous Edward Murphy who in 1948, when strain gauges failed to work on a sled on rails carrying a chimpanzee to test the effect of 'g' forces on the body at the now named Edwards Air Force Base, blamed his assistant, saying something along the lines: *"If that guy has any way of making a mistake, he will."*

Team discussions then modified this to:

"Anything that can go wrong, will go wrong"

and named it for Murphy.

In charge of the tests was Dr John Stapp, who published a collection of aphorisms and adages in 1992. In his first press conference about the project he referred to Murphy's Law which soon spread widely.

Stapp is credited with Stapp's Law:

"The universal aptitude for ineptitude makes any human accomplishment an incredible miracle" (Wikipedia, 2013).

The first corollary to Murphy's Law is: *If anything can go wrong, it will, and at the worst possible time.*

There are countless other Murphy's Laws and a book on project scheduling called *The Pertatorium* had a list of 100 of them along the lines of:

➢ *The first 90% of the job takes 90% of the time, the last 10% takes the other 90%.*
➢ *When you throw out the instructions and warranty for an appliance, it is then that it will break down.*
➢ The law of selective gravity: *An object will fall so as to do the most damage.*

The bottom line, of course, is that in mankind's ongoing history of one disaster after another, everything does indeed go wrong usually. Occasionally, something good happens, for example the discovery of penicillin, but that too was an accident resulting from 'bugs' from a lab whose door had been mistakenly left open overnight invading a Petri dish in another lab. The next morning it was discovered that a mould in that dish had prevented multiplication of bacteria.

Murphy's God (MG), indeed, must have been the person who so many writers of religious fables and creeds had visions of, and who commanded them to write such drivel as is found in almost all religious texts.

They should be converted from insanity to Mohronism, and to believing that, indeed, Murphy was God's prophet. I can even give you his phone number but have forgotten it right now, just when I need it. Even when I do remember it, however, I only get his answering machine on the line with the message:

I can't get to the phone right now because I've lost it.

Note that anyone offended by anything I have said should not blame me. Why not pray tell? Because Murphy's God is to blame for anything that goes wrong, including anything that I've said that might be deemed by some to be wrong for, indeed, I was, of course, only trying to tell the truth and shine a light on the true path to righteousness and thence salvation. Furthermore, anyone so inclined should not have a fatwa issued about me, or place a curse on me. Even if you do, you see, in all probability Murphy's God will make sure it backfires and comes back to haunt you.

Table D.1. The 10 laws of Mohronism

Law #	Law name	Subject	Principle
1	Mohr's morphology	human personality	three basic personality types
2	Mohr's mentation	education etc.	brainwashing
3	Mohr's metamorphosis	home, work & pub	life in three boxes
4	Mohr's mirage	sex	myth of love
5	Mohr's malady	hierarchy & power	law of the 'rat race'
6	Mohr's mechanism	achievement	madness required
7	Mohr's motto	power	power corrupts
8	Mohr's misery	crime & war	human condition
9	Mohr's mantra	man's history	the prophet Murphy
10	Mohr's metrology	final judgment	?/9

Table D.1 shows the laws of Mohronism. These are the 10 Mohr's Laws also given in Chapter 1, having first been proposed in 2002 (Mohr, 2002), and then having been adopted by the new religion of Mohronism (Mohr & Fear 2015).

Briefly then, the laws are:

[1] The first law is that there are three human personality types: placid, neutral, and aggressive (Mohr et al., 2017).

[2] The second concerns itself with the brainwashing we are subjected to throughout life, whether by education, religion, political propaganda, or ubiquitous modern advertising.

[3] The third concerns the increasingly 'boxed in' nature of the lives of we troglodytes who spend most of our time cooped up in an often crowded house, at work slaving for greedy bosses (and being paid a pittance), and at the pub, supermarket, etc. (giving back that pittance to the bosses).

[4] The fourth law is that sex is God's joke on mankind, we being too stupid to realize this, the point being that 'breeding' is simply an animal activity, whilst mankind's lack of effective communication has been the major factor in his seemingly endless history of conflict.

5] The fifth is Mohr's Law of Hierarchies:
In hierarchical organizations the amount of real material-producing work people do is inversely proportional to their rank or level in the organization. The amount of compensation they receive, however, is proportional to their level, sometimes to an exponential degree.

[6] The sixth law is that 'madness' is required to achieve anything important. The 'mad scientist' is an example where a typical Murphy-type contradiction appears: the scientist who makes an important discovery is not really mad, but exceptionally sensible. The mad people are the rest of us suckers who think sex, some brand of soft drink or beer, or who wins some game or other, is important.

[7] The seventh law is that power corrupts, as all history shows, and this needs little elaboration. Indeed, there are aspects of Transactional Analysis (TA) here, as people made boss usually undergo a change of behaviour for the worse.

[8] The eighth law laments the misery of the pathetic human condition, and thus man's never-ending history of mistakes, including crime and war. Indeed, that we have bred like animals so that our survival is now threatened, like that of so many other species, is testimony to our stupidity (Mohr, 2012c).

[9] As already noted, the ninth law is that we are governed by the law of the Prophet Murphy. I thought I had better mention this again, however, in case you had forgotten.

[10] The final law is that 10, or perfection, is impossible, and 0 is impossibly bad, for example, in the case of health (or how much alive one is) zero would be dead. Thus there are only 9 possible scores by which to judge people. The really important point here, however, is that no issue of any complexity is 'simply black and white'. Generally, therefore, we should judge things on the Mohr Scale of one to nine (Mohr, 2002; Mohr & Fear, 2015).

Bearing in mind that Christianity was not accepted as the official religion in Rome until 380 AD, I will not guess how long the new religion that Murphy was God's prophet (Mohronism) will take to be accepted by the public.

When disciples of the prophet Murphy do get around to writing the Bible of Mohronism I hope it is filled with outlandish claims, dire predictions, and repetition and mistakes, just as other religious texts are, and in accordance with Murphy's Law which, of course, governs all religions.

I doubt that great churches like the 6th century Hagia Sophia in Constantinople will be built to celebrate Mohronism, however, and its worshippers might have to make do with natural places of worship or erected stones (menhirs) as the Celts and other peoples did.

In fact, those worshipping the prophet Murphy might do well to 'get stoned' in the current Australian colloquial sense, not in the sense that Matthias, the apostle chosen to replace Judas Iscariot did, that is, being stoned before being beheaded. If Murphy's disciples do get drunk, however, I should not like them to 'lose their head' as Matthias did, but only in the colloquial sense.

Mohronism should have, of course, some sort of 'power sign'. Bearing in mind Mohr's 9th Law, this cannot be Winston Churchill's famous 'V for victory' sign. Nor can it be raising the index and little fingers, which supporters of the Texas Longhorn football team understand as representing the horns of a bull, but which Italian men take to mean that you are going to bed with their wife (Pease, 2004).

I hope that the sign I propose for Mohronism as an alternative to crossing one's chest, as Christian priests do during services, does not cause offence. This is a representation of Mohr's Circle, much used in Structural Mechanics to represent the equations that express how stresses and strains change when measured in different directions. Thus the sign is made by touching one's thumb and forefinger together to form an 'O', thus representing a circle, an object to which traditional North American religions attach much importance (Mohr & Fear, 2015).

Indeed, the *natural strains* much used by Argyris et al. are based on the equations of Mohr's Circle (Mohr, 1992). Argyris said to me late one night (Melbourne time):

You are the hope of the future.

As I discuss in my recent book *The Doomsday Calculation, The End of the Human Race* (Mohr, 2012c), we humans, thanks to the prophet Murphy's great law, do not have much of a future unless we wise up a bit, and that is a big ask.

I hope the Mohron Church will not give scientists a bad time, as the Christian Church did Copernicus and Galileo, Martin Luther calling the former "a fool who went against the Holy Writ", whilst we all know at least a little of the trial of Galileo and his being sentenced by the Catholic Church to life imprisonment (in fact he served time under house arrest because of his being 70 at the time).

Better that than going to a Catholic School and being abused, however, by a priest!

Catholicism is, of course, the strictest Christian sect (of many), and therefore, it follows, also the most hypocritical.

The same applies to the strictest, most rabid, Muslim sect, the Wahhabi sect that Osama Bin Laden belonged to.

Finally, remember that Murphy's God is a benevolent God, not an evil one like most others who repeatedly promise dire vengeance on countless people, as one reads in so many parts of the Bible.

When things always go wrong, you see, it is always our fault, and Murphy's Law is based on our behaviour, not his. If, indeed, we followed Mohr's laws, we would be much better off. For example:

> Aware of the 9th law, we might be more careful and not rush into things.
> If we followed the 10th law, we would not be so prejudiced and inclined to fight over minor differences between people such as hogwash religions, and instead we would make more measured judgments. We should not merely have friends or enemies, for example, but rate people on the Mohr scale of 0 to 9.
> The other 8 laws should give us a better understanding of the human condition and how to cope with it.

Finally, is there to be some end of world scenario according to Mohronism? This I discuss in the recent book *The Doomsday Calculation* (Mohr, 20121c), the quotation which opens Chapter One being:

In 1956 Professor W.A. Lewis calculated that if the world population were to double every 25 years (a rate of increase currently observable in some parts of Africa and Asia), it would reach 173,500 thousand million by the year 2330, at which time there would be standing room only, since this is the number of square yards on the land surface of the earth.
John Carey, *The Faber Book of Science* (1995),
'The Menace of Population.'

Finally, note that, according to Mohr's 10th law, your overall score on anything can never be more than 9/10, so that, in fact, things only go wrong 9 times out of ten.

This is certainly more rational than, for example, the Jews claiming to be the chosen people amongst all others.

Indeed, at a time when most religions are on the wane, it is hoped that the new religion Mohronism will gain millions of followers and be followed with the same fervour that, for example, fans of British Premier League teams show.

For example, the Australian Football League star Gary Ablett was often referred to as 'God' or 'The Pontiff' by fans, with good reason according to another former AFL star, Doug Hawkins (Hawkins, 1995).

Conclusions

Mohronism has no son of God such as JC, so there can be no great schism in the Mohron Church such as occurred over the *filioque*, that is, whether the Holy Spirit proceeds from the Father, or both the Father and the Son.

Note too that Murphy's God (MG) arises out of ontological, not cosmological thinking. The Universe always existed in some form or other (Mohr, Sinclair & Fear, 2014), it is simply Mohr's 9th Law that mankind has usually followed the prophet Murphy's Law throughout his disastrous history.

Mohronism does not require baptism, but, in cases of advancing age, a brain transplant, this new 'awakening' being accompanied by substantial Mohronist brainwashing.

O'Toole's commentary on Murphy's Law, namely: *Murphy was an optimist,* should also be noted. Indeed, Mohrons are optimists as they always hope that, eventually, something will go right, not wrong.

Finally, it is left to disciples, of whom it is hoped there will be many, to spread the word of the prophets Murphy and Mohr (Mohr & Fear, 2015).

One appropriate way of doing this would be in the manner of the stylites, of whom there were many in the century following the death of St Simeon Stylites in 459AD (they hung themselves on high for long periods).

Myself, having been dragged to see a performance by the late Billy Graham at Adelaide Oval by my mother's childless sister, I hope that a preacher of his calibre can be found to spread the word on Mohronism.

Then, at major public preachings of the new religion Mohronism, followers would be urged to bring something broken as a votive sacrifice, broken pottery, for example, as did ancient Egyptian worshippers if they were poor. The prophet Murphy would be pleased, of course, to see something else had gone wrong.

Having been a choir boy myself for a couple of pre-pubescent years, I would recommend, of course, that weekly 'services' be held to honour Murphy's God.

As an alternative to Christmas Day on the 25th of December, Mohrons can celebrate with Murphy Day on the 13th of December, a practice which the author began in 2020.

For special occasions the most rabid supporters of Mohronism could be exhibited in like fashion to the regular Sunday exhibitions of lunatics at the Bethlehem madhouse in England which continued until 1815. These are immortalized in the English language by the word 'Bedlam' which is a contraction of Bethlehem (Youngson & Schott, 1996).

At the 'madhouse-type' shows for Mohronism, of course, Mohrons would be encouraged to wear ridiculous clothing (as do Muslims, for example only), sing as loudly as possible, wave their arms about wildly, and thus behave as much as possible like raving lunatics.

Indeed, instead of heaven, Mohronism could promise its adherents to spend their afterlife in a lunatic asylum, rather than heaven.

Finally, if reading this book convinces a few people of the folly of religion, then that would be a good thing.

If, on the other hand, this book convinces people that they should become Mohrons, then I would ask them not to resort to conflict and violence on account of their new faith.

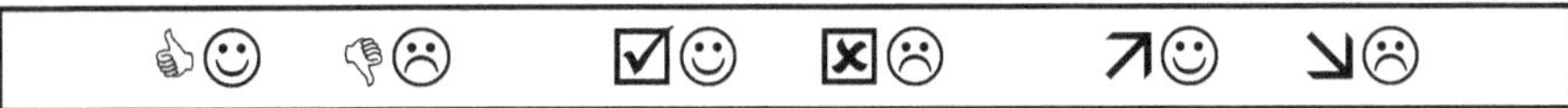

REFERENCES

Atkinson RC, Shiffrin RM, Human memory: A proposed system and its control processes. RW Spence, JT Spence (eds), *The Psychology of Learning and Motivation, Vol. 2,* Academic Press, New York (1968).

Atrens D, Curthoys I, *The Neurosciences and Behaviour: An Introduction,* 2nd edn, Academic Press, Sydney (1982).

Ben-Menashe A, *Profits of War, The Sensational Story of the World-Wide Arms Conspiracy,* Allen & Unwin, Sydney (1992).

Black E, *IBM and the Holocaust,* Little Brown, London (2001).

Blondel J, *Voters, Parties, and Leaders,* Penguin, Harmondsworth (1963).

Broom L, Jones FL, McDonnell P, Williams T, *The Inheritance of Inequality,* Routledge & Kegan Paul, London (1980).

Brook-Shepherd G, *Iron Maze, The Western Secret Services and the Bolsheviks,* Pan, London (1998).

Butler-Bowden, Tom, *50 Psychology Classics,* 2nd edition, Nicholas Brealey Publishing, London (2017).

Carter P, *IQ and Psychometric Tests* 2nd edn, Kogan Page, London (2007).

Cateora, PR, *International Marketing,* 9th edn, Irwin, Chicago (1996).

Cattell HE, Schuerger JM, *Essentials of the 16PF,* John Wiley & Sons, New York (2003).

Clark JL, *Mind Magic & Mentalism for Dummies,* Wiley, Chichester UK (2012).

Collins AM, Quillian MR, Retrieval time from semantic memory, *Journal of Verbal Learning and Verbal Behaviour* 8 (1969) 240-247.

Cooke T, ed., *Concise History of World Religions,* National Geographic, Washington DC (2011).

Cozolino L, *The Neuroscience of Psychotherapy, Building and Rebuilding the Human Brain,* W.W. Norton & Co., NY (2002).

Crough G, Wheelwright T, Wilshire T (eds), *Australia and World Capitalism,* Penguin (1980).

Davies, D, *An Introduction to Clinical Psychiatry,* Melbourne University Press, Melbourne (1971).

Dawkins R, *The God Delusion,* Mariner/Houghton Mifflin, Boston (2008).

Dawood NF (translator), *The Koran,* 50th anniversary edition, Penguin, London (2006).

Dean, John, *Blind Ambition* (circa 1985).

Eagly AH, Chaiken S, *The Psychology of Attitudes,* Harcourt Brace Jovanovich, Orlando FL (1993).

Egerton Eastwick RW (ed.), *The Oracle Encyclopaedia,* George Newnes, London (1896).

Elkington J, *Cannibals with Forks: The Triple Bottom Line of 21st Century Business,* Capstone, Oxford (1999).

Encarta Encyclopedia 1999, Microsoft Corporation, 1998.

Emerick Y, *The Complete Idiot's Guide to Islam,* 3rd edn, Alpha/Penguin, New York (2011).

Forbes HD, *Ethnic Conflict: Commerce, Culture, and the Contact Hypothesis,* Yale University Press, New Haven (1997).

Galton D, *In Our Own Image, Eugenics and the Genetic Modification of People*, Little Brown & Co, London (2001).

Gillespie, David, *Taming Toxic People, The science of identifying & dealing with psychopaths at work & at home,* Pan MacMillan Australia, Sydney (2017).

Gosling SD, Rentfrow PJ, Swann BJ, A Very Brief Measure of The Big Five, *Journal of Research in Personality,* 37, 504-528 (2003).

Govoni N, Eng R, Morton G, *Promotional Management: Issues and Perspectives,* Prentice-Hall, Englewood Cliffs NJ (1988).

Hall, T, *White Collar Crime in Australia,* Harper & Row, Sydney (1979).

Hawkins Doug, *Hawk Manure, Funny Footy Yarns, etc.,* Celebrity Books, Melbourne (1995).

Jay P, *The Crisis of Western Political Economy,* The Australian Broadcasting Commission, Sydney (1981).

Jencks C, Smith M, Acland H, Bane MJ, Cohen D, Gintis H, Heyns B, Michelson S, *Inequality: A Reassessment of the Effect of Family and Schooling in America,* Penguin, Harmondsworth (1975).

Krueger RF, Derringer J, Markon KE, Watson D, Skodol AE, Initial construction of a maladaptive personality trait model and inventory for DSM-5, *Psychological Medicine* 42, 1879-1890 (2012).

Kaufman, Josh, *The Personal MBA, A World Class Business Education in a Single Volume,* Portfolio-Penguin, London (2012).

Larsen RJ, Buss DM, *Personality Psychology, Domains of Knowledge About Human Nature,* McGraw-Hill, NY (2002).

Lieberman JA, *Shrinks, The Untold Story of Psychiatry,* Little Brown & Co, NY (2015).

Lifton RJ, *Destroying the World to Save It: Aum Shinrikyo, Apocalyptic Violence, and the New Global Terrorism,* Metropolitan Books, New York (1999).

Likert R, *New Patterns of Management,* McGraw-Hill, New York (1961).

Linton DK, Power J, The personality traits of workplace bullies are often shared by their victims: Is there a dark side to victims?, *Personality and Individual Differences* 54(6),738-743 (2013).

Lindzey G, Hall CS, Thompson RF, *Psychology,* 2nd edn, Worth, New York (1978).

Lopez. Shane J., *Making Hope Happen, Create The Future You Want for Yourself and Others,* Atria, New York (2013).

Lynne R, Vanhanen T, *IQ and The Wealth of Nations,* Praeger, Westport CT (2002).

Marta, Suzy Yehl, *Healing the Hurt, Restoring the Hope,* Rodale, London (2004).

Maxwell N, Yahuda M, Wheelwright T, Jayawardena C, The Chinese model: politics in command, in *Political Economy of Development,* Australian Broadcasting Commission, Sydney (1977).

McCormack MH, *What They Don't Teach You at Harvard Business School,* Fontana/Collins, London (1986).

McGuire WJ, A syllogistic analysis of cognitive relationships, in *Attitude Organization And Change,* CI Hovland and MJ Rosenberg (eds.), Yale University Press, New Haven (1960).

Mohr GA, Milner HR, *A Microcomputer Introduction to The Finite Element Method,* Pitman, Melbourne (1986), Heinemann, London (1987).

Mohr GA, *Finite Elements for Solids, Fluids, and Optimization,* Oxford University Press, OUP Oxford (1992).

Mohr GA, *Mohr's Laws, What Went Wrong With You and the World and What To Do About It,* Independent Publishers Limited, Mohr (2002).

Mohr GA, *The Pretentious Persuaders, A Brief History & Science of Mass Persuasion,* Horizon Publishing Group, Sydney (2012a).

Mohr GA, *Curing Cancer & Heart Disease, Proven Ways to Combat Aging, Atherosclerosis & Cancer,* Xlibris, Sydney (2012b).

Mohr GA, *The Doomsday Calculation: The End of the Human Race,* Xlibris, Sydney (2012c).

Mohr GA, *The Variant Virus: Introducing Secret Agent Simon Sinclair,* Xlibris, Sydney (2012d).

Mohr GA, *Heart Disease Cancer & Ageing: Proven Neutraceutical & Lifestyle Solutions,* Horizon Publishing Group, Sydney (2013a).

Mohr GA, *The War of the Sexes: Women Are Getting On Top,* Xlibris, Sydney (2013b).

Mohr GA, *The History & Psychology of Human Conflict,* Horizon Publishing Group, Sydney (2014a).

Mohr GA, *Elementary Thinking For The 21st Century,* Xlibris, Sydney (2014b).

Mohr GA, *The Pretentious Persuaders, A Brief History & Science of Mass Persuasion,* 2nd edition, Horizon Publishing Group, Sydney (2014c).

Mohr GA, Sinclair R, Fear E, *The Evolving Universe, Relativity, Redshift, and Life From Space,* Xlibris, Sydney (2014).

Mohr GA, *The 8-Week+ Program to Reverse Cardiovascular Disease,* Book Venture, Ishpeming MI (2015).

Mohr GA, Fear E, *World Religions, The History, Issues, & Truth,* Xlibris, Sydney (2015).

Mohr GA, Fear E, Sinclair R, *World War 3: When & How Will It End?,* Inspiring Publishers, Canberra (2015).

Mohr GA, Fear E, *The Brainwashed: From Consumer Zombies to Islamism & Jihad,* Inspiring Publishers, Canberra (2016).

Mohr GA, Sinclair R, Fear E, *Human Intelligence, Learning & Behaviour,* Inspiring Publishers, Canberra (2017).

Mohr GA, *The Scientific MBA,* Balboa Press, Bloomington IN (2017).

Mohr GA, Mohr RS, Mohr PE, *The Psychology of Hope,* Balboa Press, Bloomington IN (2018).

Mohr GA, *The Psychology of Life: A practical introduction to psychology,* Amazon-Kindle (2018).

Mohr GA, Mohr PE, Mohr RS, *The Psychology of Success: Keys to a successful and happier life,* Amazon-Kindle (2018a).

Mohr GA, *The Psychology of Depression: Developmental, attitudinal & lifestyle factors,* Amazon-Kindle (2018b).

Mohr GA, Mohr PE, Mohr RS, *Brainwashed Zombies: Religious, Political & Consumer Persuasion,* Amazon-Kindle (2018).

Mohr GA, Mohr PE, Mohr RS, *World Religions: From Animism, to Mohronism,* Amazon-Kindle (2018).

Mohr GA, Mohr PE, Mohr RS, *World War 3: Global Islamic Jihad,* Amazon-Kindle (2018).

Mohr GA, *Economics: A Concise Introduction,* Amazon-Kindle (2019a).

Mohr GA, *The Education System: Improvements at all levels,* Amazon-Kindle (2019b).

Mohr GA, *The Bullying Epidemic: The Psychology, Incidence & Prevention,* Amazon-Kindle (2019c).

Mohr GA, Mohr PE, Mohr RS, *DIY Psychology & Psychotherapy: A practical introduction,* Amazon-Kindle (2019).

Mohr GA, *Finite Elements & Optimization for Modern Management,* Amazon-Kindle (2019).

Mohr GA, *Finite Elements Using Natural Strains & Basis Transformation ,* Amazon-Kindle (2019).

Mohr GA, *An Introduction to Developmental Psychology*, Amazon-Kindle (2021).

Mohr GA, *Combating Ageing, Heart Disease & Cancer: Proven Neutraceutical & Lifestyle Solutions,* Amazon-Kindle (2021).

Mohr GA, Mohr PE, Mohr RS, *The Doomsday Calculation: Exponentiating population, conflict, pollution, disease & global warming,* 2nd edn, Amazon-Kindle (2021).

Mohr GA, Mohr PE, Mohr RS, *The Doomsday Calculation: & Covid-19,* 3nd edn, Amazon-Kindle (2021).

Mohr GA, Mohr RS, Mohr PE, *The Big Bang Debunked, Life from Space & Relativity Revised,* Amazon-Kindle (2021).

Mohr GA, Mohr AV, Mohr TS, *The Psychology of Anxiety: and how to cope with it,* Amazon-Kindle (2022).

Mohr GA, Mohr AV, Mohr TS, *The Psychology of Solitude: and how to cope with it,* Amazon-Kindle (2022).

Morgan CT, King RA, Robinson NM, *Introduction to Psychology,* 6th edn, McGraw-Hill, Tokyo (1979).

Newcomb TM, Persistence and regression of changed attitudes, *Journal of Sociological Issues* 19 (1963) 3-14.

Nojumi N, *The Rise of the Taliban in Afghanistan,* Palgrave, New York (2002).

O'Guinn TC, Allen CT, Semenik RJ, *Advertising and Integrated Brand Promotion,* Thomson South-Western, Mason OH (2006).

Ostrander S, Schroeder L, *Superlearning,* Delacorte Press/Confucian Press, New York (1979).

Packard V, *The Pyramid Climbers,* McGraw-Hill, New York (1962).

Packard V, *The Waste Makers,* Pelican, Harmondsworth, London (1963).

Packard V, *The People Shapers,* Nelson, Melbourne (1978).

REFERENCES

Parkins IS, Fishbein HD, Ritchey PN, The Influence of Personality on Workplace Bullying and Discrimination, *Journal of Applied Psychology,* 30(10) 2554-2577 (2006).

Parkinson, Cyril Northcote, *Parkinson's Law: the Pursuit of Progress* (1958), ch. 1.

Parkinson, Cyril Northcote, *The Law and the Profits,* ch. 1 (1960).

Parkinson Cyril Northcote, *The Law,* Schwartz, Melbourne (1980).

Pease A, Pease B, *The Definitive Book of Body Language, How To Read Other's Thoughts By Their Gestures*, Pease International, Buderim QLD (2004).

Penn, *Microtrends, The Small Forces Behind Today's Big Changes*, Allen Lane, London (2007).

Peter LJ, Hull R, *The Peter Principle,* Souvenir Press, London (1969).

Pringle P, Spigelman J, *The Nuclear Barons*, Holt, Rinehart and Winston, New York (1981).

Ripps LJ, Schoben EJ, Smith EE, Semantic distance and the verification of semantic relations, *Journal of Verbal Learning and Verbal Behaviour* 12 (1973) 203-210.

Robertson I, *Sociology*, 2nd edn, Worth, New York (1981).

Sampson A, *The Arms Bazaar,* Coronet Books, London (1977).

Seigne E, Coyne I, Randall P, Parker J, Personality traits of bullies as a contributory factor in workplace bullying: an exploratory study, *Int. J. of Organization Theory and Behaviour,* 10(1), 118-132 (2007).

Self P, *Administrative Theories and Policies,* 2nd edn, George Allen & Unwin, London (1977).

Smith CM, Davies ET, *Anthropology for Dummies,* Wiley, New Jersey (2008).

Solomon MR, *Consumer Behaviour: Buying, Having and Being*, Allyn and Bacon, Boston (1992).

Sternberg S, High speed scanning in human memory, *Science* 153 (1966) 652-654.

Sweeney MS, *Brain, The Complete Mind, How it Develops, How it Works, and How to Keep it Sharp,* National Geographic, Washington D.C. (2009).

Sweezy PM, *The Theory of Capitalist Development*, Dennis Dobson, London (1946).

Sykes CJ, *Dumbing Down Our Kids: Why American Children Feel Good About Themselves But Can't Read, Write or Add,* St Martin's Griffin, New York (1995).

Thomas M, *As Used on the Famous Nelson Mandela, Underground Adventures in the Arms and Torture Trade,* Ebury Press, London (2006).

Thomas J, Hughes T, *You Don't Have to be Famous to Have Manic Depression: The Insider's Guide to Mental Health,* Michael Joseph, London (2006).

Tong RP, *Feminist Thought, A More Comprehensive Introduction,* 2nd edn, Allen & Unwin, Sydney (1998).

Vander AJ, Sherman JH, Luciano DS, *Human Physiology,* 6th edn, McGraw-Hill, New York (1994).

Vernon PE, *Intelligence and Attainment Tests,* University of London Press, London (1960).

Weiss ML, Mann AE, *Human Biology and Behaviour, An Anthropological Perspective*, 2nd edn, Little Brown, Boston MA (1978).

Wolfe L, Brainwashing: How the British Use The Media For Mass Psychological Warfare Brainwashing. Posted on the Internet and originally printed in *The American Almanac,* May 5, 1997.

Wolfe L, Americans Target Of Largest Media Brainwashing Campaign In History. Posted on the Internet and originally in *Executive Intelligence Review*, 16/10/2001.

Wonnacott, P, Wonnacott, R. *Economics.* McGraw-Hill, New York, 1979

Youngson RM, Schott I, *Medical Blunders,* Robinson, London (1996).

Zajonc RB, Attitudinal effects of mere exposure, *Journal of Personality and Social Psychology,* 9 (2, Pt. 2), 1-17 (1968).

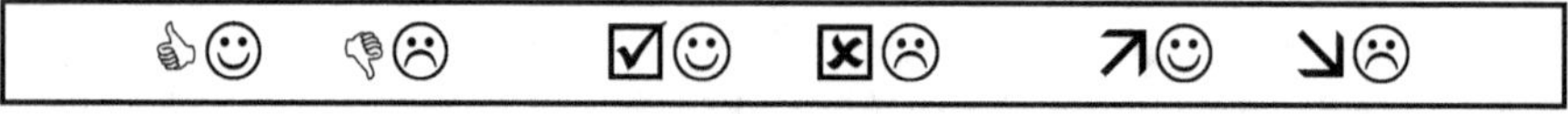

The book discusses some key laws re. hierarchies, in particular the Peter Principle: *In a hierarchy every employee tends to rise to his own level of incompetence, and then stays there* (L Peter & R Hull, 1969).

Other important laws discussed in the book include:

➤ Mohr's Law of Hierarchies.

➤ 10 Laws of the new religion Mohronism.

➤ Mohr's Law of Capitalism and Mohr's Power Law.

➤ Mohr's Law of Bullshit: $E = BS^2$, and Mohr's Laws of War.

➤ Mohr's Law of Politics and Mohr's Laws of Decisions (10).

The book discusses the problems encountered in hierarchies:

➤ In family life, education and training, and the workplace

➤ In religions, politics and the criminal world.

The psychology of attitudes and conflict also discussed, and how to deal with and rise in hierarchies.

G. A. Mohr did his PhD at Churchill College, Cambridge.
He published circa 60 journal papers and 40+ books, including:
A Microcomputer Introduction to the Finite Element Method
Finite Elements for Solids, Fluids, and Optimization
The Pretentious Persuaders; Elementary Thinking for the 21st Century
The Doomsday Calculation: The End of The Human Race
2045: A Remote Town Survives Global Holocaust
 The War of the Sexes; The Variant Virus;   The Scientific MBA
The History & Psychology of Human Conflict;   Mohr's Law of Hierarchies
The 8-Week+ Program to Reverse Cardiovascular Disease
New Ideas for the 21st Century ; Economics: A Concise Introduction
The DIY Cardiovascular Cure;   Combating Cancer
Finite Elements & Optimization for Modern Management
A Half Life: The memoirs of Geoff Mohr
Finite Elements Using Natural Strains & Basis Transformation

Also with R.S. Mohr/Richard Sinclair & P.E. Mohr/Edwin Fear:
The Evolving Universe: Relativity, Redshift and Life from Space
World Religions: The History, Psychology, Issues & Truth
World War 3, When & How Will It End?
The Brainwashed, From Consumer Zombies to Islamic Jihad
Human Intelligence, Learning & Behaviour
New Theories of The Universe, Evolution, and Relativity
The Psychology of Hope;   The Population Explosion
Brainwashed Zombies: Religious, Political & Consumer Persuasion
Human Conflict: An Attitudinal Psychology Model

Also with A.V. & T.S. Mohr:
The Psychology of Anxiety;   The Psychology of Solitude